# MAY'S
# BOY

# MAY'S BOY

## An Incredible Story of Love

by
## Shirlee Monty

**THOMAS NELSON PUBLISHERS**
Nashville • Camden • New York

Published in Nashville, Tennessee, by Thomas Nelson, Inc.
and distributed in Canada by Lawson Falle, Ltd., Cambridge, Ontario.

Printed in the United States of America.

Cover design by American Motivate.
Cover black-and-white photo *The Milwaukee Journal* by Dale
Guldan.

**Library of Congress Cataloging in Publication Data**

Monty, Shirlee.
  May's boy.

  1.  Lemke, Leslie.  2.  Mentally handicapped—
United States—Biography.  I.  Title.
RC570.M54      362.3'092'4  [B]      81-14160
ISBN 0-8407-5784-0                   AACR2

This book is lovingly dedicated
to
Leslie Lemke
my nephew Mark Turcin
and
retarded people everywhere.
To their potential, their growth,
and our understanding.

# Contents

# Acknowledgments

Few books are written alone. Standing in the shadows are those people who give so freely of themselves—offering advice, encouragement, and support when needed.

With these people I wish to share the credit, and to them express my gratitude.

To my husband, Lee, who urged me to write this book and offered valuable suggestions, emotional support, and in so many ways helped make the path easier.

To my four children, Lynn, Joe, Jane, and Anne, whose lively presence and enthusiasm for their own lives so often distracted and refreshed me from the long, lonely hours of writing.

To the editors at Thomas Nelson Publishers, Peter Gillquist, Larry Stone, Bruce Nygren, and Lisa Hemby, who so patiently guided me through this project, and with tact and encouragement helped develop my journalistic approach into a more narrative style.

To Stance Bergelin, Dr. Darold Treffert, Paul Baumgartener, and John Wilberding, for giving so willingly of their time, insight, and expertise.

To May and Joseph Lemke, who shared so much of their lives, so that ours might be enriched.

And most of all, my gratitude to Jesus Christ, who made it all possible.

# MAY'S
# BOY

# Chapter 1

## *Who Are the Lemkes?*

---

I don't know why certain people etch themselves in our minds forever, while others slip out of our thoughts without ever leaving a mark.

The first time I met the Lemkes, I knew I would not forget them. They were there to stay, forever in my memories.

I first heard of May, Joe, and Leslie Lemke in July, 1980, when I was in the final stages of a book on the life of Terry Meeuwsen, former Miss America and Milwaukee television personality.

Almost a year earlier, when we had started the book, I had suggested taping at my home in the suburbs rather than at her office in the studio. I thought Terry might like to get away from her desk and enjoy the informality of a home, where we could both curl up on a chair or sofa.

Usually Terry drove across town and I fixed a light lunch, which gave us a chance to share a little of our personal lives before the grueling afternoons of taping.

So what if the phone sometimes rang or one of my girls dashed in with, "I'm sorry, Mom, but I've just *got* to ask you a question!" Often, it was a nice break from the intensive questioning, and we'd both laugh at the breathless urgency of teenaged daughters.

On this particular day, however, Terry didn't breeze in with her usual, "Hi, how's everybody?" Obviously, she had something else on her mind. Before I could say a word, she was halfway through the doorway and had blurted out, "Shirlee, did you see the show this morning?"

"No, I didn't," I confessed. I had been rushing around, fixing lunch, organizing questions, setting up the tape recorder, making sure everything was in order.

Terry continued excitedly, her words tumbling over each other. "I had a guest this morning who was *incredible*. In fact, there were three guests: May, Joseph, and Leslie Lemke. The Lemkes took Leslie in when he was six months old. He was totally helpless—severely handicapped—and May literally devoted the next twenty-eight years of her life to that boy—every minute of the day. She was determined to make something out of him—'to find God's gift for him,' as she put it.

"She told about all the years she had worked and waited for some sign, all the heartbreak she had suffered, and finally, what she called 'the miracle.' That was the night he first played the piano.

"Anyway, we were all crying—the audience, the staff, the cameramen, and me—right on camera! The phones started ringing before the show was even over. The whole thing was just unbelievable!"

I was intrigued. But since I hadn't seen the show and we had other things to talk about, the subject was dropped.

My phone rang the next day. A close friend was calling. Had I seen Terry's show on Friday? Well, there was this incredible lady, May Lemke, and she had this retarded son, Leslie. . . .

Two days later, I received another call. "Shirlee, if you're ever looking for another book project, you ought to contact the Lemkes. Did you see them on Terry's show?"

After a half-dozen more phone calls, I called Terry. "Do you have the Lemkes' phone number? I've got to meet this family. They seem to have created quite a stir!"

I called May, and she said she'd be delighted to see me. Her voice was lively, with a heavy British accent. We set a date for the following Wednesday afternoon.

On Wednesday, I drove twenty miles out to a small town west of Milwaukee, then circled Pewaukee Lake until I spotted a mailbox with JOE LEMKE inscribed in large, black letters. Leaning against the fence, watching for me, was Joe.

He was much older than I had expected, possibly in his late seventies. I began calculating mentally how old he must have been when they took in Leslie. Could he have been fifty? And he took in an infant—a helpless, handicapped baby, at that. Wow! The thought was mind boggling!

I took a good look at his face. He had a gentle expression; his skin was softly lined, crinkles around the eyes, a warm, merry smile. He was dressed like a working man in old worn jeans, a faded flannel shirt, and shoes that were showing the wear. As we walked through the gate, I noticed that he was a trifle stooped, his gait that of a man beginning to feel the years. He looked like a good man—honest, no airs. I liked him at once.

A small yellow cottage sat at the bottom of the hill; beyond, I could see the lake, placid and green. Only a sailboat and a few fishing boats had ventured out on this languid afternoon.

I saw that the Lemkes were not isolated. There were homes on either side of their property and many more scattered around the lake. The lake probably came alive on weekends, but today it was quiet.

"That's where I keep all my tools and chop my wood," Joe said as he pointed to an old basement on our way down the hill. He spoke softly, a bit muffled, and I had to listen carefully in order not to miss a word. He was showing me his tomato plants and flower beds when something flew out the back door, captured me in a bear hug, and abruptly finished whatever Joe was telling me.

Was it a leprechaun? For a moment, I wasn't sure. It turned out to be May Lemke, all four and a half feet and ninety pounds of her.

A trifle reserved myself, I was nearly overcome by this dynamic little Englishwoman, with her blond, curly hair and bright red lipstick, who darted around the yard like an animated teenager.

"We planted all these trees, everything out here. I have lots of pineys in the spring . . ." I saw they were peonies. I had to adjust to the British accent. "And we have a pear tree," she went on, "here, try one. Why, we get two or three bushels, I share them with the neighbors, we share everything, you know. . . ."

My frenetic tour included grapevines, raspberry bushes, some friendly chipmunks (she pointed to the little sign, *Chipmunk Crossing*, and said they always let the chipmunks pass first), more fruit trees, blue spruce, dozens of friendly birds hovering around, maybe waiting for an introduction.

All of a sudden, she stopped in front of a slightly misshapen evergreen tree. "This is Joe Perry," she said. I wondered if some sort of greeting was expected. But she went on.

"You see, Joe Perry used to sell bushes and trees. He was a lovely man, but he's dead now. Anyway, I went in looking for trees, and I found this one in a corner, looking kind of wobbly and out of shape. Joe saw me looking at it pitifully and he said, 'May, I've been telling that tree that someone who really loves trees will come in some day and take care of it,' and I said, 'Well, that's me.'

"So I brought it home and I call it Joe Perry and I talk to it every day. 'Joe Perry,' I say, 'you are really looking lovely today,' and just look at it. It was nothing but a little cripple when I got it, and now it's getting tall and strong and that little hole is filling up real good."

Finally, the tour over, May pulled me into the house to meet Leslie. In the tiny kitchen, I was able to take a closer look at May.

Her face was well lined, dominated by pale green, deepset, rather heavy-lidded eyes. In the months ahead, I discovered that those eyes were a barometer of her feelings. They could flash with anger or sparkle with laughter. They would harden when she talked of the pain and terror of war and then suddenly soften as she spoke of her love of Jesus Christ.

Like Joe, she looked to be in her late seventies, but that's where the similarities between them ended. She was as lively and irrepressible as he was calm and soft-spoken.

"Would you like something to eat? Now, just make yourself at home. Act like you live here. And where are your people from?" My answers couldn't keep pace with her questions.

I looked at my surroundings and saw that beyond the small living room was a narrow, closed-in porch, much of it taken up with an upright piano. Surrounded by other rooms, the living room was rather dimly lit, and I was halfway through before I realized that someone was sitting in a chair.

I turned and there was Leslie, with his head down, hands folded, very still. Had he heard me come in? I reached out to take his hand. When I touched him, his whole body trembled. "Speak to him first," May said, right at my shoulder. "You have to let him know you're there. Then you can touch him or take his hand. But you must do it softly, gently—never abruptly."

"Hello, Leslie," I said. "I'm Shirlee Monty, and I've come to hear you play the piano." (What else would I do wrong? I wasn't sure if he could understand me. I didn't know much about retardation. I had been told that Leslie was severely retarded. What did that mean? Could he understand me? Could he talk?)

I felt a bit uncomfortable, uneasy. Leslie was

obviously very handicapped. When May asked him to go to the porch to play for me, I wondered if I ought to help him. She must have read my thoughts, because she motioned me out of the way.

"Let Leslie go first," she said. "We don't help him. We want him to learn to do things for himself."

So, by holding onto a ledge, a doorknob, the arm of a chair, Leslie managed to feel his way to the piano, his limbs trembling, and with a little more effort, he positioned himself on the bench.

When he first stood up, I had been surprised at how tall he was. I noticed he was several inches taller than Joe—about six feet. I had expected him to be heavy, which so often happens to people who are sedentary. But Leslie was not overweight. He looked as if he weighed about a hundred and fifty pounds.

His eye sockets were a bit sunken, his forehead somewhat prominent, but even though his eyelids were always closed, there was nothing unsightly or unattractive about him. He had a strong, square face and reddish-blond hair, and if anything, looked younger than his twenty-eight years.

"Now, what would you like to hear?" May asked.

"What would I like to hear?" I repeated. "What can he play?"

"He can play anything," May said. "Just ask him."

*This must be some kind of a joke,* I thought to myself, but May persisted.

"Does he play classical, modern, religious music, or what?" I asked. I noticed that Leslie was not even attempting to talk. "I mean, what is his area?"

"Anything," she repeated.

I decided to go along with it. Funny, I could hardly

think of a song. "Okay," I said, "play 'Everything Is Beautiful.' "

"Yes, yes," Leslie said in a flat, guttural tone. From a slumped position, he straightened his body, lifted his head, and positioned his hands. Suddenly, those spastic fingers flew up and down the keyboard, striking rich, strong chords, interspersed with delicate, running notes—loud, then soft, with perfect timing, never missing a note. A deep, baritone voice filled the room, sending the lyrics resounding throughout the entire house. "Everything is beautiful," he sang, "in its own way."

"Doesn't he have a powerful voice?" May was saying, but I was too preoccupied with Leslie to answer. Thoughts were tumbling all around in my mind in a jumble of confusion. *Where did he learn that song? He can't read music if he can't even see the piano keys. How does he know the keyboard? If he can hardly speak, then how can he sing like that? If he's spastic, how can his fingers find the keys, never missing a note?*

I suddenly felt challenged by this young man. " 'Rhapsody in Blue,' " I offered. The rendition was magnificent. " 'The Entertainer' from *The Sting*." He never missed a note. *Something faster. Let's see, what's really fast?* "Elvis Presley's 'Jail House Rock'." I couldn't even see his fingers on that one. *Something really tough.* "Rachmaninoff's Concerto No. 2 in E Minor." I closed my eyes and mentally drifted off to Carnegie Hall.

The hours flew by as I tested him on more classics, ragtime, rock, ballads, show tunes, old war songs—everything I could think of. Leslie kept flipping them out of some inexhaustible storehouse, some never-ending repertoire.

When I ran out of titles, *he* kept going. I was treated to German waltzes, French cabaret songs, and beautiful Italian arias.

He finally capped his performance that lovely afternoon with two powerful hymns: "How Great Thou Art" and "The Lord's Prayer." That was when my cautious, questioning mind dissolved in a flood of tears. *Who cares where this strange phenomenon comes from?* I said to myself. *Whatever the explanation, it's beautiful!*

I left that afternoon feeling that I had overstayed my welcome, but the Lemkes couldn't have been more gracious. Leslie was obviously a tireless performer.

I told them they would hear from me soon. I needed time to think about what I had seen and heard. I knew I wanted to write about Leslie, but did I have the time immediately to do another book?

Why not start out with the *Milwaukee Journal?* A feature article would be a good test run. I called Jim Cattey, metro editor. I had done assignments for Jim before. He liked the idea and told me to go ahead. I returned to the Lemkes, and the *Journal* sent out a photographer. He came back with one good shot, but he didn't feel it was enough. "We really ought to do an entire layout on this one," he said. "Those people are something else!"

Two weeks later, the Lemkes landed on the front page of the *Journal* with close to a full page spread inside. The story was picked up by the Associated Press and used in newspapers all over the country.

In less than a week, every local television station around Milwaukee presented a segment on the Lemkes and their story of hope and love and faith.

National radio and television shows followed. In less than two months, the Lemkes were featured on "Paul Harvey News," "Walter Cronkite Evening News," "That's Incredible!" and a few months later, "The 700 Club."

The Lemkes had touched a troubled and cynical world, restoring to awareness the fact that love is powerful, perseverance prevails, and Jesus Christ still lives.

Yet viewers were far from satisfied. They wanted to know more about the Lemkes. Who were they? Where did they come from? How had May and Joe persisted in their love for Leslie?

I set out to answer those questions, and I found myself retracing May's steps until we reached the point where it all began: a little village in northern England, almost eighty years ago.

# Chapter 2

## *Beginnings*

Dusk in the little fishing village of Monkwear-mouth, England, at the turn of the century . . . The smell of fish and chips permeates the night air as villagers slowly make their way to the open-air stalls, where vendors are cooking the day's catch, fresh cod, dipped in batter and fried in oil. Another community pot of oil is sizzling with thickly sliced potatoes.

"Middle or tail?" the vendors call out. Some customers like the thick, fleshy part of the fish while others prefer the crunchiness of the tail. The steaming pieces of cod and potatoes are wrapped in news-paper and exchanged for threepence.

Meanwhile, children hustle to the pub on the corner with empty jugs, to bring back robust ale for their fathers. Finally, everything is ready at home: salt and vinegar for the fish, hot tea for the women and children.

Such was the nightly ritual of the sturdy Englishmen of Monkwearmouth, who worked from sunup to twilight on the boats or in the mines. Fish and chips, plenty of ale, and the family crowded close to the fire.

Later in the evening, the men drifted to the pubs for a quiet draught of ale, silently puffing their pipes until closing time.

On one of those typical nights, Samuel Hansen came running out of his house, calling for a midwife. "She's started! She's started!" he shouted. Everyone knew that Maria Hansen was expecting her seventh child. Mr. Hansen ran to the home of one of the women who knew how to deliver babies and pulled her out of her house, down the narrow street, and through his own door.

He was back outside in less than an hour. There was a bit of a swagger in his walk now. Pride had replaced concern. "Another girl," he announced to his neighbors who had gathered outside. "We're callin' her May."

The peculiar name *Monkwearmouth* is derived from the location of the village. It is situated near a centuries-old monastery on the northern mouth of the Wear River.

At the southern mouth of the river lies Sunderland, a shipping port as well as a shipbuilding and coal-mining center. The Wear empties into the North Sea, a body of water about the size of Texas with a shore line of four thousand miles. To this day, much of the eastern seaboard of England and Scotland is devoted to the fishing industry.

Fog moves in almost daily in this region, and the sea keeps the weather moderately cool year-round.

Icebergs loom to the north, giving the massive black waters an eerie, desolate look. Sometimes you can almost hear the cries of the people who have gone down in that sea.

Monkwearmouth is a very, very old village, reputed to have been built by the Romans. Stone houses line the cobblestone streets, and after a rain, everything is clean and glistening, the white stones sparkling in the sunlight. But when the fog rolls in, the village takes on an almost opaque look, gray and hazy in the mist.

In the early 1900s, almost everything in the village was built from stone—the steps to the houses, the huge fireplaces, the long cooking tables, the floors. There were even scouring stones to clean and polish the tables and steps to a bright, translucent finish. Only the inside stairs and second floor were made of wood.

The daily life of the people was as routine and predictable as their evening fish and chips. The village began to come alive at three or four in the morning, when the "knocker-uppers" arrived with their long poles. For a few pennies a week, they awakened the villagers by tapping on their bedroom windows. The tap-tap-tapping sounds could be heard faintly throughout the village as the knocker-uppers moved from house to house, alerting the drowsy occupants that morning was nigh.

Soon less gentle sounds echoed through the streets. Coal miners' heavy boots made loud clanking sounds on the cobblestones as they trudged off to their underground caves. Later came the hurried footsteps of fishermen, shipbuilders, and butchers, off to begin their day's work. Shortly afterwards, the children skipped off to another day at school, then housewives came bustling or sent their small children scurrying at the first sign of the milk carts jolting awkwardly over the cobblestones.

"How much milk today?" the vendor asked at each house. "A pint or a quart?" Then he carefully ladled one portion as the child or mother held out an empty jug. "Any eggs? Butter? Cheese?" The subtle fragrance of fresh cheeses and creamy butter drifted through the air.

More wagons clattered over the cobblestones—some loaded with cod, others heaped with produce. Women hurried out of their kitchens with the day's order. "Heads on today, dearie, to make soup. Nay, not that one, yer silly bloke. G'wan. I want a middle to it!" Later, in the market, the wives rummaged through the vegetables for the largest cabbage, the longest carrots, the freshest brussels sprouts.

At the end of the week, they walked to the butcher's to buy beef, lamb, kidneys, or rabbit. Although fish and chips were the weekly staple, the Sunday dinner might be steak and kidney pie, boiled rabbit, shepherd's pie, or roast beef with Yorkshire pudding.

Most of the work at home centered around the fireplace, with its large iron ovens on either side. The first tantalizing odors of the day came from these ovens as breads were baked to perfection. On Sundays, the aroma of rabbit or the day's stew permeated the kitchen as dinner was set to simmer in the large iron kettle that hung from a bar directly over the coals. Another huge pot sat on the fire for boiling clothes. Next to the oven was a small basin for washing up. On days the floor had to be swilled, the hot soapy water that had been used for clothes was poured on the floor and the stones scrubbed with stiff brushes.

Life was hard work; the simple chores of survival—cooking, cleaning, and gathering food into the house—were enough to keep a household busy from dawn to dusk.

Samuel Hansen was a big man, a shipbuilder by trade, and he wasn't home much to see his ten children grow up. The royal service sent him all over the world, often for months at a time.

But when he was home, he always found his curious little daughter May waiting with plenty of questions. He loved this lively child with the curly, golden hair and the wide, greenish-brown eyes. She wasn't a chatterbox like the three younger girls, but she was inquisitive, fascinated with everything around her.

"Daddy," she began on one of his rare trips home, "everybody in our family is big except me. Why am I so small?"

Samuel put his hand on his daughter's head and said gently, "May, dear, don't you ever worry about being small. You have a quick brain and a good sense of humor, so wherever you go, you'll get along fine."

Maria Hansen was a serious woman, very kind and gentle. A nurse and midwife, she often was called away from home to deliver a baby. Sometimes her patient would be only down the street, and the children would listen for the first cries of the new arrival. "Mama will be home soon," May would say. "I can hear the baby crying!" Mrs. Hansen must have brought a hundred babies into the world; not once did she ask a fee.

Like many of her neighbors, Mrs. Hansen was an expert on herbs and home remedies. She gave her children a dose of sweet spirits of niter when they were sick and applied a paste of slippery elm bark for rashes, sores, and wounds. Eating parsley was supposed to break up kidney stones.

Whiskey or brandy was poured over wounds as an antiseptic. Sweet oil was a staple in every medicine cabinet, for it was rubbed liberally on arms, legs, shoulders, and chests anytime there were aches and pains or fevers. Children received cod liver oil or a mixture of cod liver oil and malt from the time they were babies.

But if they were very ill, they were taken to the infirmary for medication or injections. Infirmaries, as well as hospitals, were financed by the government, so that all examinations, operations, medications, and services were free.

Bedtime at the Hansen home began with stories, most often about Jesus, and ended with music: hymns, English folk songs, and the children's favorite, "Ten Little Indians."

May's prized possession for many years was the rag doll her mother had made for her when she was just two. She carried the doll everywhere, including to meals, where she kept up a constant conversation with her "child." "Now, mind your manners. Stay clean and neat whilst you eat!" When one of her brothers accidentally sat on the doll one morning, May spent the rest of the day nursing it back to health.

Beggars frequently knocked on the door of the Hansen home, knowing that the kindly Mrs. Hansen always would offer them a sandwich and a cup of hot tea. How often her children heard her say, "If someone knocks on your door, don't turn him away. You never know who it's going to be!"

Music was the home entertainment in those days, and in the evenings music often came through the windows of the Hansen home. Maria might be cradling a new baby in her arms, singing a soft lullaby. Sometimes the family played the gramophone that Samuel Hansen had brought home to his wife. Maria played Caruso records until they wore out.

When May was older, she played the piano, singing at the top of her voice, "I'll Take You Home Again, Kathleen" (her father's favorite). Whoever the performer, one thing was certain: Those Hansens loved music!

Young men and women left home early to marry, the custom in England in the early 1900s. They were frequently "traded off," which meant their parents selected a husband or wife for them. Somewhere around the age of twelve, children were expected either to marry or to support themselves with a trade. By the time a girl had a menstrual cycle, she was deemed old enough for wedlock. One of May's sisters was married at twelve, and all the Hansen boys left at that age to go out and earn a living—all except one.

When May was not quite two years old, her oldest brother, not yet twelve, was already out learning a trade. He came home early one day, looking pale and strange around the mouth.

"Are you all right, Snowball?" Mrs. Hansen asked. The family called him Snowball because of his beautiful, golden hair. May ran to her mother and held onto her mother's skirts, which she always did when Maria looked worried.

Snowball said he didn't feel well.

"I just made a rabbit pie, dear," Mrs. Hansen said. "Come and eat. Then you can go to bed."

"I don't feel like eating, Mama. I'm so tired."

"All right. If you don't feel well, I'll help you up to bed."

*He really seems quite ill*, Maria thought to herself. *I'll take him to my own room, where he can rest on the big bed.* Still clinging to her skirts, May followed her mother into the big bedroom with the large oak bed and the beautiful valance that her father had made. She loved this room with her mama's patchwork quilt and the frills all around the bottom of the bed. When one of the children was very ill, Maria Hansen always brought him into her bedroom.

But now May was distracted. "Why is Snowball so tired? Is he sick?" she kept asking again and again. Too preoccupied to answer, Maria carefully turned down the covers, plumped up the pillows, and gently helped her son into the bed.

In a very faint voice Snowball asked, "Mother, would you put your arm around my neck? Pull me up a little bit."

As she lifted her son, blood flowed out of his mouth in a gush and ran all over the bed. Mrs. Hansen screamed, then called out, "Oh, William! Oh, William!" He died in her arms.

Coming home from work that day, Snowball had

stopped to help a friend move a sewing machine up a long, narrow flight of stairs. When they nearly reached the top, Snowball slipped. The heavy machine struck him, and machine and boy fell all the way down the steps.

May's sunny disposition was a comfort after William died and soon made her a favorite with her mother—as well as with everyone who knew her. She seemed to sense when to be funny and when to be serious, an unusual trait in a child so young. Maria Hansen called her "my little ray of gold."

Because of her curiosity, May became an explorer almost as soon as she could walk. The first time she disappeared, she was just three years old. Mrs. Hansen knocked on every door, looking for her little girl. She was searching the streets when at last she found her, walking along with a blind man.

Sensing that Mrs. Hansen was upset, the man asked how old her daughter was. "She's only three," Mrs. Hansen answered.

"Only three?" he remarked. "Well, she's quite a little girl. She's taken me to every house and sold all my laces for me!"

"God must be with that child," Maria Hansen often said. "She goes investigating everywhere, but He always brings her home."

May was four when she wandered into the Jewish colony on one of her journeys. In Monkwearmouth, the Jewish people lived in a segregated area that the Gentiles normally didn't visit. She was intrigued by this new territory, so she walked the lanes and looked around. The Jewish mothers were outside nursing their babies, and May sat down to watch for a while. They told her how the first milk from the mother's breasts was used to wash out the baby's eyes.

"Did they do that to my eyes?" May asked.

"I think they did, but you'll have to ask your Mama," she was told.

After a while, May walked on. She climbed some steps, looked through a window, and saw a man with a black hat standing at the head of a long table full of children. The group looked as if they were praying. May knocked on the door, and the man invited her to eat with them.

All the children were very friendly, and they chatted amiably during the delicious dinner. Some of the dishes tasted strange to May, but she was too polite not to eat everything. When they had finished their meal, the man kindly suggested that May go home— her mother most likely would be worried. But before May left, he gave her what looked like a stack of large cookies to take home to her mother. She thanked the man, said good-bye to the children, and started home.

When May walked in the door, she saw at once that her mother was worried. "May, I've been looking all over for you," she scolded. "I've been up and down the street knocking on every door. Where have you been this time?"

"But, Mama," May said excitedly, "see what I brought you. Some beautiful cookies!" She handed the parcel to her mother.

Mrs. Hansen's face softened, and then she smiled. "Now I know where you were, my little wanderer.

You were in the Jewish colony. Those aren't cookies, May. They're Passover cakes. Come. We'll spread butter on them, and they'll be delicious!"

May earned her nickname "The Searcher" from a priest, when she ended up in his church on one of her excursions. She had gone into the church by herself and was kneeling in one of the pews when he saw her. He walked over and put his hand on her head.

"Hello, there. It looks like you came to pay us a visit," he said, smiling down at her. "Did you know I have a name for little visitors like you? I call them 'the searchers.' "

Then he took her by the hand and led her to the street. "And where do you live, my little friend?" May pointed in the direction of her house.

"I'll take you there," he said. With all the courtesy of a gentleman, he escorted the little girl home. "Remember now," he remarked as he left her at the door. "You are called a searcher!"

Another time when May was out walking, this time with her mother, she saw a horse with a broken leg lying in the street. Immediately she ran over, slid to her knees, and lifted the horse's head into her lap. People were already gathering around. Bobbies had arrived to keep order until someone could come to put the animal to sleep.

One of the bobbies asked Mrs. Hansen to take her daughter away. "She will never leave that horse," May's mother replied. "May will try to make him stand if she can. Perhaps you can explain the situation to her."

Nodding his head, the bobby walked over to May

and spoke from his lofty height. "It's very sad, child, but this horse has broken his leg and can never walk again. We'd like to help him, but there's nothing we can do. We'll have to put him to sleep. The horse won't suffer that way. Now, perhaps you'd better run along with your Mum."

May listened very thoughtfully. Then resolutely she stood up, said good-bye to the horse, and mother and daughter walked silently home.

Children in Monkwearmouth didn't decorate Christmas trees or enjoy visits from Santa Claus, but they did get "goodies" on Christmas Eve. Their mothers made aprons, large and roomy, and on Christmas Eve the children could go out begging. Custom mandated that the children be five years of age or younger to beg, and they were allowed to go to only one house.

They knocked on the door, and when it opened, they sang:

> *I wish you a Merry Christmas*
> *And a Happy New Year.*
> *We are teetotalers*
> *And we don't drink beer.*
> *A little bit of spice cake,*
> *A little bit of cheese.*
> *A glass of cold water or*
> *A penny if you please.*
> *And if you haven't a penny,*
> *A farthing will do.*
> *And if you haven't a farthing,*
> *Well, God bless you.*

Then they held out their aprons to be filled with apples, oranges, pears, nuts, candy, pieces of cake, and sometimes, even a farthing (a quarter of a penny).

Monks from the nearby monastery walked through the village streets on holidays and holy days, carrying lighted candles. May was fascinated by their long, flowing robes, and it was not at all unusual to see the tiny girl walking alongside them, asking if she could carry a candle, too.

School began early for these English youngsters. They started in at the age of three and usually were finished with their formal education by age twelve. Discipline was severe. May was only three years old when she was punished for jumping up and crying out to go to the water closet. For this unruly behavior, she was rapped on the hand with a ruler so hard that a small bone was broken. Her father went to school to express his anger, but his remarks carried little weight.

Besides learning reading, writing, and arithmetic, the boys were introduced to trades, while the girls were taught the rudiments of housekeeping: mending, cooking, cleaning, and needlework.

May was six or seven when her teacher announced that they would take up baking. Mrs. Hansen made May some white elasticized sleeves to cover her arms and a little white apron and cap. And May's teacher soon sent the child home with two small loaves of bread, one white and one brown. "Take these to your mother, May, and show her what fine work you've done for y'self."

When the boys and girls were twelve, they were given certificates, their entry card into the working world. The certificates confirmed that they had passed their examinations and were of good character and of sound health.

Most children began their working lives as servants in rich households. From there, they advanced in the areas to which they were suited. Boys became footmen, chauffeurs, bootblacks, gardeners, and butlers, while the girls learned to be maids, cooks, and nurse-governesses.

But many of May's generation would never find their way to their appointed trade. Ominous warnings had been in the air for months. Almost certainly, England would go to war.

# Chapter 3
## *The Cruel, Cruel War*

Beginning in the late nineteenth century, tensions among the European powers led to increased militarism, the buildup of arms, and the development of new weapons. By 1907, the six great European powers had squared off into two armed camps: the triple Alliance of Germany, Italy, and Austria-Hungary and the Triple Entente of Great Britain, France, and Russia. The international situation was so volatile by 1914 that Wilhelm von Schön, German ambassador to France, remarked, "Peace remains at the mercy of an accident."

The accident occurred on June 28 of that year, when Archduke Francis Ferdinand, heir to the throne of Austria-Hungary, was assassinated by a Serbian nationalist. As a result, Germany, the greatest military power in Europe, declared war on Serbia, then Russia, and finally France. The most bloody and costly war in modern history to that time had begun.

England entered the war on August 4, 1914, after

Belgian neutrality was violated. It was 1915 before enough men could be recruited to wage an all-out battle.

Much of World War I involved trench warfare and hand-to-hand combat between the largest armies ever seen up to that time. Eventually, six hundred miles of trenches stretched across France and Belgium. Huge underground caverns served as first-aid stations, supply centers, and living quarters for the troops.

The Germans developed dirigibles, or blimps, as part of their Air Force and used them to bomb London in 1915. In 1916, the British army first used the tank. Other new, mechanized vehicles—trucks, automobiles, and motorcycles—accelerated the war on land. For the first time, airplanes and airships bombed soldiers and civilians. Submarines torpedoed merchant ships without warning.

On April 22, 1915, Germany unleashed a new weapon in its drive to the French coast: chlorine gas. French troops fled as the poisonous, greenish-white mist drifted toward them and stung their eyes and throats. Into this massacre, England sent her finest men.

May Hansen lost her father, her four brothers, and most of her uncles, male cousins and friends in the war. One by one, they all were killed.

Maria Hansen cried many times in those four years. Whenever she raised her white apron to her face, May always knew what was wrong. Even though she was older now (almost twelve) she still reverted to her old habit. Quietly, she went to her mother and held onto her dress.

Boys fourteen and fifteen years old, who had never held a gun before, went off to war. Their mothers, using what little food they had—usually biscuits and tea—gave farewell parties for them.

Mrs. Hansen always put a dash of rum in the tea to give the boys courage for where they were going. Then she said, "Go on now, children. Enjoy each other. Sing, dance, and be happy." She knew this might be their last chance to be together. "They'll be gun fodder when they get to France," she told May. She was right. Not one of them ever came back.

When May's Uncle Bill had to leave, he took her in his arms and said, "May, dear, this is good-bye. Your Uncle Billy has to go." He was killed two weeks later.

Maria tried to explain his death to the children. "It's horrible," she said. "They use mustard gas. It rolls on the ground and goes right into the trenches. The gas burns the men all over, and they come out looking like a roasted piece of meat. Oh, it's terrible!" And she began to sob all over again.

Shortly afterwards Maria received news of her husband's death. This time she could hardly speak about what had happened. "Children," she said between sobs, "your father died today. He died a horrible death. They said he'd been in the sea for days and days, and he was just dead rotten. They're bringing him home to be buried in a closed coffin, so none of you can look at him. That's all I can tell you."

May noticed that with all the sorrow, her mother was beginning to waste away. But Maria still tried to comfort her friends, who arrived almost daily, distraught over another death. "Oh, Maria, do you have a little drop of rum?" they asked, and although Maria was no drinker, she always put a few drops of rum in their tea. Her children, too, often came to her upset and crying about the war. Maria always stopped whatever she was doing and said, "Come, love, let's have a cup of tea and talk about what's bothering ya'."

One day when May and her friends were kissing the young boy soldiers good-bye, one lad, crying, said to May, "I have to go to France, but I don't want to leave England." And he clung to her.

May had never seen him before, but she hugged him anyway and said, "Maybe you'll be all right. Remember, you're fighting for England, like we all are."

"But I don't even have a mother to say good-bye to," he protested.

May thought for a moment. "Then why not say good-bye to my mother? She'll cuddle you."

Mrs. Hansen took the boy in her arms, and he sobbed. "Good-bye, son," she said gently. "Of course, you'll come back."

Before England entered the war, Maria Hansen, anticipating the worst, began to put a bit of strawberry jam in a large stone jar every day. She covered and sealed it with rice paper so it wouldn't spoil. The children always wondered what it was for.

Later, when supply ships were being sunk and no food was coming in, she lined up May and her three younger sisters and said, "You were always wondering why I did this. I knew things were going to be bad. There's no food for us now, so this teaspoon of jam will be your meal for today. It will get you by."

Mrs. Hansen had another method for warding off hunger. She told her children to pick up a fresh piece of tar in the street and to chew on it. She said it would keep their teeth nice and lessen the pain of hunger.

So the children chewed tar, and it helped—some.

Everyone was always hungry in the early days of the war. In fact, when the Americans arrived in England in 1917, people were literally starving to death. They could not even take advantage of the ocean's fare because of the bombing and the burning debris on the water. Children were going through garbage, eating anything.

Today May still remembers one poignant time when her prayers for food were answered. If she ever writes a book, she says, it will be called *My Loaf of Bread*.

At one point during the war, word had circulated that a large supply of flour had come in. The bakers went straight to work again, and the people were instructed to line up the following morning. Each family was allotted one loaf.

Mrs. Hansen was helping with the wounded every day, so she told May to pick up their ration. "But go early," she said. "Then you won't have to wait so long."

When May arrived at the distribution center at a little past five the next morning, a long line had already formed. She finally reached the counter late that morning. May received not only a big, beautiful loaf of bread, but an egg and a quarter pound of butter as well.

She couldn't wait to get home to show her mother. As she left, the lady behind the counter cautioned her, "Remember, this is for you to take home. Don't eat any of it on the way, for it must last your family at least a week."

May could hardly keep her promise to get home without eating that loaf of bread. "It smelled so delicious," she told her mother later. "The aroma tormented me every step of the way. I kept saying to myself that I mustn't touch it, but I was craving to get at it." When she finally arrived home, she nearly collapsed from hunger.

May laid the bread on the table, and her mother said, "Well, you've certainly earned something, standing there all that time."

Mrs. Hansen put some butter on a dish, while May prayed silently that she would get the crust. Her mother must have heard, because she cut off a big piece of crust, covered it with butter, and handed it to May. Then she cut herself a thick slice and wrapped the rest for when the other children came in from playing. By then the tea was ready and she poured two big cups of hot tea. The two of them sat together and ate their slices of bread very, very slowly, relishing each bite. Tasting that bread was to become one of the most precious moments of May's childhood.

The war raged on. There was a shortage of everything. Along with food, wood and coal became more and more scarce. May watched in shock as her mother chopped up some of their furniture to build a fire to keep them warm.

Stories came home regularly about the war and the atrocities committed by the Germans. But life on the home front was violent, too. Dirigibles flew overhead, dropping bombs and toppling buildings. Sometimes the crafts would drop low to the ground, and the pilot would shoot tracer bullets through the people below. No matter how fast the victims ran, there was no way of escaping.

Once May and her mother saw a zeppelin explode in the air, scattering German soldiers in all directions. "Oh, Mama, this is terrible!" May cried.

"We must weep for them, too," Mrs. Hansen said. "We all suffer, even the enemy."

Air raid sirens constantly sent people fleeing to their basements or to shelters, where they waited, sometimes all night, for the "all clear" signal.

The people of Monkwearmouth watched ships sink right in front of their eyes. Often they said good-bye to their loved ones as they boarded a vessel in the morning, and by day's end, they were weeping as they watched the ship go down.

Sometimes they looked out over the beach to see hands and feet that had drifted in with the tide; sometimes whole bodies were washed ashore.

On August 6, 1917, the United States declared war on Germany. The British people wept for joy as the Yanks arrived and marched through the streets singing, ". . . and we won't be back till it's over, over there."

The Americans also brought food. One of the first shipments to reach Monkwearmouth was American cheese. The four Hansen girls ate and ate, but they could not get their fill. Finally, Mrs. Hansen cried, "If you children don't stop eating cheese, you're all going to turn yellow!"

The Hansen home, like many English homes, became a gathering place for American soldiers. May's mother nursed the wounded, shared the little food they had, and tried to add a bit of fun to these soldiers' lives before they crossed to the Continent.

One young man who often came to the Hansen

home was a gunrunner from northern Wisconsin named James Pollard. He was a big man, six feet tall and weighing two hundred and forty pounds. Mrs. Hansen loved to hear him describe America and his way of life on a dairy farm. She had a special, motherly feeling for this serious and intense young American.

She learned to love all these Yanks, who were so lonely and far from home. They came to the Hansen home to dance and sing around the piano, trying to forget the war for a few hours. But nobody forgot it for long. The next morning, when Maria Hansen saw a group of soldiers on the beach, looking cold and miserable, she'd say, "Well, I can at least make a pot of tea for those poor fellows. A drink of hot tea is better than nothing."

One of the most heart-wrenching aspects of the war for Maria Hansen was watching lovely, innocent children suffer and die. As the war raged on, more and more English children were orphaned and had nowhere to go. They became beggars and scavengers, wandering the streets.

Often the heads of these precious children were crawling with lice and their clothes were torn and dirty. Whenever Mrs. Hansen saw such neglected youngsters, she gathered them up, brought them in the house, boiled some kind of liquid that killed lice, and cleaned them all up.

As bad as things were, Mrs. Hansen always was able to cheer up her family with a funny story. One such story took place on a morning when she had to go thirty miles away to help with the wounded. While she was in this strange place, the area was bombed and everyone had to go underground. The closest place for safety was an open cellar, so Mrs. Hansen and another lady ran down to wait for the all clear signal.

They kept watch silently through the dark, cold night. Finally, the next morning, the siren sounded. All of a sudden, something ran past the two women like a streak of lightning. They both glimpsed enough to see that it was a naked man. "Just think," Mrs. Hansen told her children, laughing, "we spent the whole night in a cellar with a naked man and didn't even know it!"

As the war progressed, England lost more and more men. Soon everyone was called into the effort, even the children. May was about fourteen when she began working in one of the munitions buildings, first assembling bags of TNT and later filling shells with explosives. Then, a year later, she was assigned to the task of pushing a small trolley loaded with sixty-pound shells to the loading dock. There they were transferred to large trucks.

Food was still very scarce at that time, but the munitions workers were given something each day, usually a sandwich and lemon water to drink. May often wrapped part of her sandwich and took it home to her mother, that sense of kindness and love for others continuing to grow in her.

The ritual was the same every day. May asked, handing her mother the sandwich, "Mama, do you have any tea to drink?"

"No, not today, dear."

Then May took some tea leaves out of her shoe and said, "Well, I sneaked some for you, Mama!"

Mrs. Hansen always smiled and brushed off the leaves, then together they sat and drank their tea,

May watching her mother enjoy her only nourishment of the day. May's mother used the same tea leaves for a week, scalding them over and over again.

An atmosphere of melancholy prevailed at the munitions factory, for most of the girls were older than May and had boyfriends or husbands fighting in France. May was always trying to cheer them up by laughing, singing, and dancing. On one of those days when she had everybody laughing and singing, May's bright little world collapsed.

The girls had finished loading a trolley, and May was starting to push it away. They were singing: "There's a long, long trail a-winding, into the land of my dreams." On the word *dreams*, there was a deafening roar. The trolley blew up, throwing fiery fragments of explosives in every direction.

Suddenly the whole area was engulfed in flames and screams. People were thrown against walls and machinery. Buildings exploded. The bursting and crackling of fire and explosives were everywhere. Then at last the destruction was done, and new sounds began: the wails of survivors.

May Hansen was a survivor. She had been thrown thirty feet against the corner of a building. When they found her, she was unconscious and badly burned. The one hundred fifty girls who had been working outside the building were badly injured or maimed. The girls inside, all one hundred fifty of them, were killed.

The entire area was a shambles after the explosion. Nothing was recognizable. Bodies were found in fields as far as a quarter mile away. The area had been hidden and thought to be safe. The trucks were camouflaged, and the buildings situated very low, partially underground. Authorities later concluded a spy had tampered with the fuses on the trolley, causing the explosion.

In the hospital May drifted in and out of consciousness for many months. Her mother came to visit, but May rarely recognized her. She only stared at the pretty bouquets of violets and wild flowers that her mother brought, with little understanding of what was happening.

She experienced shooting, searing pain—agony beyond anything she had ever known. Bandages covered almost all of her small frame, with tiny slits to expose her eyes. Tubes ran in and out of her body, and every tooth was missing. Her mother told May later that when she was found after the explosion her mouth was full of TNT.

All of her hair was burned off. One foot was badly burned; it never did resume its normal shape. Her jawbone was broken. An enormous amount of surgery was needed to restore her disfigured face. Her thyroid gland was damaged, and she never grew again after the accident.

May was terrified whenever the nurses came to change her bandages. She began screaming as soon as she heard the sound of their footsteps coming down the hall. The bandages stuck to her burns, and some of the tired, overworked nurses just ripped them off, leaving the little girl bleeding and sobbing helplessly. Somehow, instead of becoming embittered, May grew even more patient, more compassionate, from these harsh experiences.

Finally the burns began to heal, and the pain subsided. May Hansen knew she would make it.

The day arrived when May began the long process

of learning to walk again, this time on crippled feet and legs. She joined with other girls in the hospital who were missing legs and arms. Together they tried to find the courage and strength to overcome their losses and to get on with their lives.

As soon as she was able, May shuffled daily to the infirmary, which was located outside the hospital. There she received two injections daily for pain, one in each arm. Her stoic attitude and cheerful disposition soon made her a favorite with the nuns.

"To think she walks all the way down here, lifts up her little arms, and never cries," one of the sisters said one day. Then she handed May a coin. "Here is a nice golden penny for being such a darling." May limped back to the hospital, clutching the penny and feeling very, very rich.

People at the hospital were kind to little May, knowing she was fighting a huge battle with herself. They knew she was terrified at the thought of facing the world crippled and disfigured.

Often they saw her praying by herself, talking to Jesus. They did what they could to give her courage for her life ahead, wondering if she would ever ask, "Why?"

When her bandages came off, May quickly took up the habit of covering her face with her hands. Her doctor, noticing this, sat down with her one day. "May, dear," he said, "I don't want you ever to cover your face again. Let people see what you look like. You aren't to blame for what happened. You must go out and face the world. Don't ever hide from it. Always look out at the world."

Not long after that talk, May was ready to leave the

hospital. Her doctor hugged her when she left and repeated his admonition. "Now remember, May, don't be afraid. You have courage. You're going to be all right."

When people stared at her or when children teased her and called her "Scarface," May remembered what her doctor had said. She would not hide her face. She would look out at the world. His words gave her the courage to go on.

Maria Hansen was a great comfort to her daughter. She cradled her in her arms and sang to her and tried to encourage her. "No one on earth can protect you, my dear. And there is nothing more that anybody can do for you. Now, it's up to you. May, you are cheerful and clever, and you have such a funny sense of humor. People will always love you."

After four long years the battering of England was over. On November 11, 1918, the fighting was ordered stopped on all battlefronts. The armistice was signed.

The war had been costly in terms of human lives— 8,300,000—and in terms of dollars—337 billion. England alone lost nearly a million men.

But for May Hansen the battle was just beginning. The time had come to go out and face her world.

# Chapter 4

## *Nurse May*

---

Although May's education was interrupted by the war years and her stay in the hospital, she had begun training as a nurse-governess when she was twelve years old. "Now you must go to work," her mother had said. "It's up to you."

A nurse-governess differed from a "nanny" in that she was trained in nursing as well as child care. However, both occupations were held in high esteem, and women in those positions often left a lasting impression on the mind and character of their young charges. Winston Churchill wrote of his nanny: "Mrs. Everest it was who looked after me and tended all my wants. It was to her I poured out my many troubles." A high-ranking British naval officer once confided that, faced with an unexpected crisis, he usually asked himself, "What would Nanny do?"

The training was extensive and took several years before completion. The young ladies learned all about childbirth and child care by working under an experienced nurse. They first watched, then assisted at an actual birth, and learned to make formula and to care for babies.

May's initial on-the-job experience was at the home of a lady who was about to deliver her first child. The training nurse already had told May about labor, the process of birth, and exactly how to help during delivery. Since the expectant mother was not to deliver for several days, the nurse decided to take an afternoon off, leaving May alone with her.

As might be expected, a few hours later the woman began labor. Her husband rushed out to get an experienced midwife, and twelve-year-old May was suddenly in charge. May tried to remember what the nurse had taught her. *Let's see*, she thought to herself. *Oh, yes—get two big towels and tie them to the foot rail.* She looked around, found two towels, tied them to the posts, and gave the other ends to the lady.

"Now, pull on the towels when the pains come," May instructed somberly. "Don't cry, milady. It will soon be over. You hang on to your towels, now, and pull very hard. Pull! *Pull!*"

May stood at the foot of the bed, trying to act very experienced, but inside she was terrified. What if the midwife didn't get there in time? What would she do?

Just then she saw the baby's head, and simultaneously she heard voices. The door opened. "It's coming! *It's coming!*" May screamed. The midwife hurried over to guide the baby's head.

After the birth the midwife washed the baby in oil and laid him beside his mother. "Now then," she said to May. "You did a fine job, child. You'll make a splendid nurse-governess. You think very quickly!"

The lady's husband handed May a one-pound note. May could not believe her eyes! A pound note was worth twenty shillings, and a nurse-governess only earned about seven shillings (two dollars) a week. It was like getting a three-week salary!

Nurse-governesses are trained to be creative and are encouraged to use their own ideas. New situations come up all the time. Sharp thinking and immediate solutions are required. During their training, they often are asked how they would handle a particular problem.

May was still young and in training when she recognized such a problem and quickly used her head. A shoe vender came to visit her employer. He brought along some samples and warned his customer at length about how bootblacks often stain shoes and ruin them. Bootblacks were in the employ of most wealthy English homes at that time. Their primary function was to polish shoes and make sure they were in good condition.

"Where may I put these samples so your bootblack won't disturb them?" the vendor asked.

"Nurse May," her employer called. "Take these shoes to your room. They'll be safe there." Obediently May took them away, but as she was turning to leave her room, she looked at the shoes once more.

*They certainly do need a polishing,* she thought to herself. *What will make them shine without staining them?* An idea popped into her head. *Why not face cream?*

She tiptoed into the lady of the house's boudoir and found some face cream. Safe in her quarters again, she put just a bit of the cream on one of the shoes, then rubbed it off. The shoe looked beautiful, bright and shiny. So she covered all the shoes with cream and buffed them with a sock. The result was a gleaming finish.

When Milady came after the shoes, she asked, "Nurse, who cleaned the gentleman's shoes?"

"I did," May answered.

"Well, I hope he's not cross with you," the Lady said. In a few minutes she returned to tell May that the shoe vendor wished to speak with her.

A bit frightened, May went downstairs. *He doesn't look too angry,* she thought to herself.

"What did you put on those shoes?" he asked.

"You won't laugh at me, will you, sir?"

"No, I won't laugh at you." He smiled down at her. "They're lovely."

She held her breath. *He'll certainly think I'm crazy,* she thought. Then as fast as she could she said, "I used face cream."

His head flew back in gales of laughter. "Face cream? I never would've guessed it! Face cream! Well, yer a pretty clever nurse, after all. 'Ere's a pound note for yer secret. But ye've got to keep it to yer'self."

Eventually May's training was complete, and she went out on her own as a nurse-governess. Wherever she was employed, she was given total responsibility for the children for the first three years of their life. After that they were placed with a tutor to begin their formal education.

Often May began her employ when her charge was an infant; sometimes even before the child was born. The basic needs and training of the child were up to May. For instance, the British practice was to begin toilet training children from infancy. After the baby was fed each time, May spread a large towel on her lap, took up a tiny pot, and put the baby on it. This was also done at regular intervals during the day, until the baby was completely trained.

Manners had to be impeccable. Thus, another important responsibility was to teach the child to eat properly and to behave quietly and politely at the table. Children from families of the upper social classes were also taught the art of side-feeding, which meant learning to take food from the butler or maid and transfer it to their own plate.

May used example, humor, and praise to motivate her young charges. "Why, Mary, how beautifully you hold your fork."

"Charles, your mother will be proud of you."

"What a lovely party we're having today."

Her work was not always easy. The children could be challenging and unpredictable. One such time came during an evening meal. A new employee had been hired, a black butler, and three-year-old Mary kept staring at him quizzically. When he began to serve her pudding, she looked up at him and asked, "Sir, is the pudding black, too?"

"No, no, dear," said May. "It's only him that's black. It's like we say in our prayers, 'Black, white, bond, free, we're all God's children.' He's one of God's children."

Another duty of the nurse-governess was to accompany the children at social events or when the family traveled. May always appeared in the standard accepted attire—blue uniform, blue cape, and white collar and cap. The children were expected to be well-disciplined and to behave properly. The nurse-governess was to see that they did so.

Children were taught to address their mothers as "Mother, dear"; their fathers as "Sir." May was called "Nurse" or "Nurse May." "Please," "thank you," "yes, m'um" and "no, sir" were all obligatory.

May had a natural gift when it came to working with children. She soon earned the respect and admiration of her employers.

She seemed to sense quickly the emotional needs of her children. Once she was called into a home where the three-year-old was a hopelessly undisciplined tyrant. Nobody knew what to do with young Jenny. A new baby girl had arrived in the family, and May saw at once that the child resented her younger sibling.

"Hello, Jenny," May said as she took the child on her lap. "What a pretty girl you are. And how old might you be?"

"I'm three years old," Jenny said as she held up three fingers.

"My goodness." May looked amazed. "Then maybe you can help with the baby. I'll need lots of help if I'm to look after both of you."

Jenny looked interested. "May I help feed it and bathe it?"

"Of course you may," May said. "You're a big girl now. I'm to teach you to do many things for yourself."

Wherever she went, May stressed the importance of helping and learning, so that the children might feel an important part of the family. She also tried to teach them to think for themselves and to develop their natural curiosity.

At bedtime she told Bible stories and talked about God and Jesus Christ. And May taught this song:

> *Jesus bids me shine, with a clear, pure light,*
> *Like a little candle, burning in the night.*
> *Jesus says He loves me. Jesus says He'll come.*
> *You in your small corner, and I in mine.*

May became impatient with employers who paid too little attention to their children. "Children need parents who do more than poke their heads in the nursery a couple of times a day!" she was known to say indignantly.

One evening after dinner May took her current charge, Wendy, to the drawing room to recite a short poem for her father. The gentleman was reading a newspaper and acted as if he couldn't be bothered. May exploded. "You're the father of this child," she scolded, fists on hips. "You must play a part in your child's life. If she accomplishes something, who's going to tell her 'well done'? Listen to her! Encourage her so she'll wish to learn more!"

Wendy's father harrumped, put down the newspaper, and asked Wendy to recite the poem. "Wendy, that was splendid," he remarked when she was finished. "A fine job. Perhaps Nurse will be good enough to teach you another one for me."

A competent nurse-governess was given a great deal of authority, and May was never shy about using hers.

Once her employer was having a party, and during the evening, a young couple arrived at the nursery. May opened the door and saw at once that they were tipsy.

"We've come to see the baby," the woman announced.

"You are not coming into my nursery," May said.

"But the lady said we could."

May straightened to her full four feet, six inches. "You two have been drinking, and I don't allow anyone who smells of liquor to see this baby. You must come another time!"

"Well! What a nasty little nurse!" the man retorted as the two stomped back down the hall.

Although May was gentle and patient with children, she could be volatile with her employer, particularly if she felt herself to be the victim of an injustice.

One of these eruptions took place during her second assignment. May had the afternoon off and had made plans to meet her mother to attend a concert.

Just as May was leaving, the lady of the house walked into the nursery. "Nurse, take that rug and shake it!" she said, pointing to the floor.

May was furious. "My nursery was swept early this morning and it's been kept nice and clean. There is not a speck on that rug. This is my nursery, and I'm leaving to meet my mother now!"

Her employer repeated the order. "I want you to pick up that rug and clean it!"

Impulsively, May picked up the rug and threw it at the woman. "Now, you step out and shake it! My mother's not to be left standing in the rain!"

May left that home and never went back.

May's responsibilities occasionally included repetitious, time-consuming tasks, and when it came to those, May was ever on the alert for the more efficient way.

Early on, in one of her positions as a maid, the task she hated most was polishing the brass. Houses were filled with brass in those days—doorknobs, fireplace equipment, lamps, stands. Even the gates had brass-work on them. It took a full morning for May to clean the brass.

Exasperated, she went to a shop and asked if there was anything to put on brass so she wouldn't have to polish it every week. The shopkeeper sold her some clear varnish, assuring her she would never have to polish again.

She hurried home, and the first time the lady was out, May varnished every bit of the newly-polished brass, inside and out. From then on, all she had to do was wipe it clean every week. When she told the maids on the street what she had done, they all went out and bought varnish and did the very same thing!

Customarily, May had one afternoon off every week. Most often, she and her mother went to a concert or planned an outing together. After several years of working, May suddenly noticed that for several weeks her mother had seemed preoccupied— like she was thinking of something else.

Not long afterwards Maria said, "May, dear, on your next day off, I must talk with you. Come home, love. We'll have a cup of tea, and I'll tell you what's on my mind."

# Chapter 5

## *Off to America*

---

May's day off arrived, and dutifully she made the familiar trip to her mother's home. After a warm greeting, Maria poured two cups of hot tea and sat down with her daughter.

"May, dear, do you remember James Pollard, the American Yank who used to come to our house so much during the war? You were only a little girl, and he always called you his 'little sweetheart.' He'd come in, look around, and say, 'Where's the little one, the one who's always so full of zip and pep?' "

May replied that she wasn't certain which one James Pollard was. There had been so many Americans coming and going in those days. And that was so long ago.

"Well dear," Mrs. Hansen went on, "he felt so terrible about your accident. He even went to see you once in the hospital. But you wouldn't remember. When he left, he gave me his address and promised that if I ever wanted to send you to America, he'd marry you."

For once May was speechless. "I've written him,

and he's still willing," her mother said. "He's a fine man, May, and he'd make a good home for you. You've suffered enough in England. You deserve to live someplace else."

Leave England, her work, her mother? May had never thought of such a thing. Marry a stranger? Of course, lots of English parents chose husbands and wives for their children. But to leave *forever?*

Deep inside, May knew that her mother was ill. *Possibly she suspects she is dying*, May reasoned. *She wants to make certain I'm cared for.* All kinds of thoughts raced through May's head.

"I'll write to him," she told her mother.

Soon May began getting letters from her Yank. He described the animals, the fields, the garden, how he made his own butter, all about life on his 200-acre farm. He wrote that he had been raised on this farm. His parents, who were both close to ninety, had turned it over to him when they were unable to work any longer. But they continued to live there. May told him that she was a good cook, and although she had never been on a farm, she had a quick mind and could learn anything. A diamond ring arrived, and finally, money for her passage over.

Shortly before she was to leave, May was living with her mother when there was a knock on the door. May answered but didn't recognize the man standing there. He was in terrible shape. "Mama!" she called.

For a moment her mother did not recognize the man either. Then suddenly she embraced him and sobbed, "Oh, my son, my son!"

May had not recognized her second oldest brother, Charlie, nor did he know her. Early in the war, his letters had stopped coming. Mrs. Hansen never heard whether he had been killed or captured. May had ceased talking about Charlie, trying to spare Maria the pain.

As they sat down and recounted the years, Charlie told them he'd been captured in Italy and put in a German concentration camp. He had been badly burned by chlorine gas. "The skin rolled off me," he said slowly and painfully. "It got in ma' throat and it 'erts ta eat 'er talk."

May began to realize the struggle that Charlie faced daily simply to live. He told them that the only way he could eat was to take a teaspoon of kerosene first to numb his throat. When Maria started to pour him a cup of hot tea, he stopped her. "No, Mama, I c'nt drink anything 'ot. It burns ma' throat. I'll 'ave to drink ale." His eyes, too, were affected. He slowly was losing his sight.

"Look at me, Mother," he said with tears in his eyes. "Home to stay. But nothin' to look at. No good at all."

Charlie's homecoming made May even sadder about leaving for America. "I won't last long," he told her, and he urged her to go. "There's nothing left for you here, May. Just a broken-down house and not much family. We'll all be gone soon."

The day before May was to leave, Mrs. Hansen again wrote to James Pollard. "I know you'll make a good husband for my daughter, and she'll not disappoint you," she said. "But I want you to know how much I'll miss her. When May goes, so will the last little bit of sunshine out of my house. She has always been a darling to us all."

At last the bags were packed. May and her mother took the train to Liverpool, where she was to board her ship. That day was the first time that May had ever been out of Monkwearmouth. The city, the people, the hustle and bustle all were strange to her.

In all the confusion of getting on ship, the gangplank went up before May could say good-bye to her mother. The captain was already giving orders to move out. Glancing anxiously at the dock, May ran to the bridge.

"Oh, please, Captain," she begged. "I didn't say good-bye to my mama."

"Lower the gangplanks," the captain called out. "This little one hasn't said good-bye to her mother!"

The sailors lowered the gangplank. May ran halfway down, her mother ran halfway up, and they hugged and kissed one another. "Good-bye, dear. This is the last time we will ever meet," Maria said in a whisper.

May did not want to let go of her mother. Finally the captain himself took her gently by the hand. "Come, dear," he said. "It's time for us to leave." But he waited patiently while May stood on the gangplank and waved until her mother was back on the pier.

The trip to America lasted two weeks. May wasn't long, of course, in getting acquainted with the other passengers. Soon they were laughing, singing, dancing, and telling each other stories.

If loneliness threatened to take over at times, May thought of the verse her mother had taught her when she was a little girl.

*When you're alone and have no one to love you,*
*When you're alone and have no one to care,*

*You'll never find one half so kind,*
*Or so willing your troubles to share—Jesus.*

One lady on board said to May, "You are too sweet, child, to ever go on a farm. Just wait! You'll be out looking for a job as a nurse-governess before you know it."

Although many of the other passengers were miserable with seasickness, May never suffered a moment. Her father had given her his secret remedy once when she was small—*dog biscuits!* She took along enough to last all the way to America, and she never did get sick.

As the long journey was coming to an end, May's thoughts turned more and more to her future, and her new husband. The ship was to land on the east coast of Canada, in Ottawa. The visas and immigration papers for May could take weeks—even months—to fill out. She could not enter America until all the papers had been processed. When would he come for her?

What would James look like? *He sent me a picture, to be sure,* she thought, *but what can you tell from a picture?* Would he like her? Her scars were hardly noticeable now, and everybody admired her long, golden hair. People even told her she was beautiful.

When would they be married? And what would the farm look like? May had never been on a farm before. Bulls, pigs, roosters, ducks—she had never seen most of the animals Jim wrote of. But they would like her. She had never been afraid of anything.

A government official was waiting for her the day the ship finally landed. He took her to the home of a family named Stewart, where she was to live until the paperwork could be settled. She had her own room and was to help out until James came for her.

On the way to the Stewarts' the official said to May, "Miss Hansen, are you aware that your future husband suffers from shell shock? Sometimes people with that condition can be very irritable. They can even be dangerous."

"I don't know what shell shock is, but I want to marry James," May answered. "He was always very good to my mother."

He went on to explain that when a person has shell shock, he constantly relives the terrible events of the war. Victims may be very sad and cry, or be depressed, or have trouble concentrating. Often they have recurrent nightmares, and the condition seems to stay with them all their lives.

"I can cope with anything," May said matter-of-factly. "After all, I'm a war baby, too. I've seen horrible things all my life. I'll understand what he's going through."

They finally reached their destination, a small town near Ottawa, and Emma Stewart came running out to greet May. They carried in her bags, and soon May was settled with the Stewarts. A month passed before she had a message from James.

May was dusting the floor in her bedroom when Emma came running up the stairs and burst through the door. She handed May a letter. "May, it's from Jim! Hurry! Open it! He must be coming!"

May's hands trembled as she ripped open the letter:

> May, dear,
>     I'll be there on Friday, October 23. We'll be married on Saturday. I'll only have a few days before I have to

be back. I can't leave the farm for long. I'll have to return alone. Your papers are still not in order.

Love, Jim

May was happy, then disappointed—all at once. But she had little time to think about her feelings, there was so much to do. They cleaned the house, started the baking, washed and dried and ironed May's clothes. Her wedding dress had been hanging in the closet for a month, and May had to freshen it up, too.

The day for Jim's arrival drew closer and closer. May wondered what she would say to him. She was not really nervous. Long ago, she had learned to accept whatever happened. She was not afraid; simply curious. And very, very excited.

Friday came. May awoke early, full of anticipation. She could not concentrate on anything; instead she was forever looking out the window.

"Why don't you go sit on the front steps?" laughed Emma.

"Oh, I couldn't do that!" May laughed. "He might think I'm crazy!"

Finally they heard Jim's car, a Model T, coming to a stop in front of the house. May sneaked a look out the window. "Oh, he's so big," she said. "And little me! We'll make quite a couple."

When they opened the door, Jim walked straight over to May and said, "Well, here I am, May. I hope you're not disappointed." He leaned over and gently kissed her.

*Mother was right*, May thought to herself. *He is a nice man. And really, quite handsome.*

On Saturday, October 24, 1920, Emma and Robert Stewart and another couple who were friends of the

Stewarts went to the church with May and Jim. When the priest pronounced them man and wife, Jim promptly turned around and kissed the wrong woman—the lady friend of Emma's. "Oh, my goodness! She's over there!" she said as she pointed toward May. At the same time Emma was calling out, "That's not her! She's over here by me!" May laughed at all the confusion. "He must have forgotten how small I was," she said gleefully. "He couldn't even find me!"

Since Jim had to return to the farm in a few days, the newlyweds were unable to have a honeymoon. Instead they remained at the Stewart home, taking drives through the lovely Canadian countryside where so many of the trees were still in their glorious fall colors.

"This is so beautiful and quiet," May said over and over again. Most of all, she loved the clean, fresh smells around her. "For the first time, I can't smell the gas and the awful smells of war—houses burning and smoldering all around."

All too soon Jim had to leave. "I'll send for you," he promised, "as soon as I have the papers."

A month passed. Then two. A third had begun when the letter came.

> May, dear,
>    Everything taken care of. Your papers are enclosed. Take a train to Port Huron on January 2. A government official will meet you and put you on a train to Chicago. I will be there to meet you.
>
> Love, Jim

He was waiting in the station when the train rumbled into Chicago a week later. America! She was really in America! And with her husband!

All the confusion was finally over. May would have a home of her own at last. The ride back to the farm was long, and the sun dipped out of sight before they arrived on the second day of travelling. May breathed in deeply the cold, fresh air. It felt good to be alive!

As they drove onto the property, May heard all kinds of noises: banging, ringing, clanging. "What is that?" she asked her husband. "Where is it coming from?"

"That's a shivaree," Jim laughed. "A shivaree is when you get married and all your friends serenade you."

Sure enough, the yard was full of Jim's neighbors, all wanting to meet the new bride. They had brought food and gifts to welcome May to America.

May soon found life on a farm in northern Wisconsin had little in common with life in Monkwearmouth, England. But she loved America at once and said it took away all the misery and torture she'd been through in England. She loved the friendliness of the people. "Everyone smiles here," she said to Jim one day, "whether they know you or not. One lady told me she loved my accent so much she'd like to sit and listen to me all day!"

She also loved the children. "Such beautiful, handsome children you have in America!" she said so often. Inside, she wept for those crippled, orphaned English youngsters who had suffered so much during the war.

She never did learn to like lettuce. "We never had salads in England," she said, "and I can't eat that kind of food. I'll leave mine for the rabbits!"

Almost every day May discovered something she had never seen before. One day it was the warrior ant. She was out in the fields with her husband when she spotted a large, black ant moving slowly across the ground. She got down on her knees to watch it more closely and saw that it was dragging a worm six or eight inches long. Pretty soon the ant nipped off a piece of the worm, made a little hole, and buried it. Then it went a little further, nipped off another piece, and buried that one. May followed along on her hands and knees until the ant had buried the last of the worm.

"May, what are you doing?" Jim called.

"I know you're going to think me odd, but I'm watching a little ant storing up food for the winter," she shouted back. "Isn't it fascinating?"

May met another unfamiliar creature in the middle of the night, the time a bat flew into her hair. She put her hand to her head and screamed, "Jim, there's something in my hair!"

"That's a bat! Hold still! I'll kill it!" her husband yelled, instantly awake.

"Oh, don't kill it," May wailed. "It didn't mean anything. It was just so scared that it wanted to sit in my hair!"

Jim went after the bat anyway, with May screaming, "Oh, please, let it go!" But this time May didn't have her way.

Even without the bat May managed to find plenty of pets. Any creature that needed a little special attention came under May's doting care: a crippled rooster, an orphaned duck, a pig that was the runt of the litter.

She bottle-fed the tiny piglet from the moment it was born and for the first few months kept it in a box in the kitchen. At about two each morning it ran under the bed and squealed. Jim said, "May, your baby's under the bed. I think she's hungry!" And May always got up to feed her pig.

She later taught the animal to lie on its back and hold the bottle with its legs. Next, it was taught to sit up and roll over. And May gave it a bath every day.

When the pig weighed as much as Jim, he decided they had to do something. He finally gave it to a friend. He didn't have the heart to butcher it himself.

One of May's most memorable achievements was when she helped bring a calf into the world. Her husband showed her how to kneel behind the cow and ease the calf out. But as usual, May did it her way.

She lay down on the barn floor, covered herself with a sack, and braced both feet against the cow. When she saw the head and two feet coming out, she gently pulled, like her husband had told her to do. But alas, it came out suddenly—and landed with a thud right on top of May, feet sprawling in every direction. Jim had to lead the startled calf to its mother while May recovered from her first experience as a veterinarian.

Another time May proved her mettle when Peggy, their black horse, was gored by one of the bulls. "It's a terrible rip," Jim said. "I'm afraid I'm going to have to destroy it."

"You're not going to touch that horse," May warned. "I'll take care of her."

She found some iodine, boric acid, vaseline, string, and a darning needle, and set to work. She used the boric acid, mixed with water, and iodine to clean and sterilize the wound. Then she took the inner skin, sewed it with heavy string, and rubbed vaseline on it. Next she brought the heavy coat together, cleaned it out, and sewed it shut.

All the time she was working, she kept talking. "You better behave yourself, Peggy. I've got to make you well, you know. You had an awful slash!"

Jim watched incredulously and said the stitching would never hold.

"It'll hold," May said. "You just watch and see!"

Peggy was put out to pasture by herself, and May was right. The stitches held. In fact, Peggy delivered her first foal the following year, a healthy colt they named Pollyanna.

May's life on the farm was never lonely, even though they were too isolated to go to town, attend church, or visit friends. Along with the animals, the Pollards soon had children running around the farm—three in eighteen months. First there was a girl, Mary, who was followed by twin boys, Douglas and James. Later they had another girl, Patricia, and one more boy, Charles.

Jim's parents lived to see the first three children, but they died just a few weeks apart, soon after the twins were born.

Jim's father was from England, his mother from Ireland. "Just think," he said again and again, "a tiny little girl came all the way from England where I was born, and she brought me a pair of grandsons. I didn't have any grandchildren so it took a little four-foot lady to have twins for me." He'd hold both boys in his arms and say, "May, which one looks like me?"

May always looked them over very carefully and

then she said, "This one looks like my husband and that one looks like you, Grandpa."

May learned to live with death those first few years of her married life. After Jim's parents died, she received word that her brother, Charlie, was also gone. Soon after that word came that her other brother had died.

She sat down at the table, tears streaming down her cheeks. Little Jimmy came to her. "Mama, you're crying, aren't you?"

By then Douglas and Mary had joined their brother. "Yes, children, there's been another death in my family—this time, my last brother. You know, it's not very good when they go one by one like that. Only my mother and one sister are left."

Mary reached up and wiped the tears off her mother's face. "Don't cry, Mama. Everything will be all right." A few months later there came an airmail letter from May's sister in England. "Mother has died," it said. "We are the only ones left."

But May had to get on with her life. After all, she had five young children, a husband, and plenty of work on the farm to keep her busy.

As the children grew older, May told them how she had baptized them as babies. Each time, she had filled a bowl with warm water, holding the new infant in her arms, and had made the sign of the Cross on the little forehead with water. Then she had sprinkled the child and had said solemnly, "I baptize you in the name of the Father, the Son, and the Holy Ghost."

Although they rarely could go to church, May taught her children about Jesus Christ. Someday, she said, they would find their own churches and worship the Lord in a congregation. Her Christianity went beyond Sundays-only. One of her boys was having trouble with schoolwork one day, and he came to his mother, very discouraged. "I can't do it. I just can't do it," he said.

"Why don't you go to your room and talk with God about what you can't do?" May asked.

He went to his room and was back in a half hour. "I did it!" he said. "I asked God, and I did it!"

"You see," May said, "you can't live without Him. He's there to help you whenever you need Him."

May was a natural storyteller. At night, she gathered the children around her feet and told them stories: fairy tales, adventures, mysteries, and stories about Jesus. The children hung on every word, for May always left them wondering what would happen in the next episode.

At Christmas and Easter she read from the Bible, and the children asked questions about Jesus. "Isn't it awful how Jesus suffered so much for us and for our sins?" Douglas asked one night. "And He never did anything wrong."

May also had a beautiful voice, and the children often heard her playing the piano and singing hymns, including her favorite, "The Old Rugged Cross," long after they had gone to bed.

Sometimes, Jim came in the house to find his wife scurrying under tables and chairs, playing tag and hide-and-seek with the children. "There are some advantages to being small," he told her, laughing. "You can hide in the tiniest places, and nobody will ever find you!"

Along with the stories and games, May was a strict disciplinarian. She insisted on good manners and respect for authority. She was also a hard worker and expected as much from her children.

Besides the personal talks with God that were at the hub of her daily life, May lived according to strict biblical dictates, which she passed on to her children.

She was very fussy, for example, about honesty and the importance of never taking anything that did not belong to them. She had no tolerance for any kind of prejudice and warned her children never to judge people by their color, clothes, or education. "There is only one place God judges a person," she said, "and that is where the heart is."

"Always be your own person," she said over and over again. "Don't try to imitate someone else. You were given your own personality and your own talents, so use them. Be natural. Be yourself."

May's children were as fearless and loving toward animals as their mother was. On their way home from school one day, Mary and Pat saw a family of baby skunks, which they mistook for kittens. The two girls sat in the field playing with them for a while, then hurried home.

When they burst through the kitchen door they were talking at once. "Oh, Mama, we saw the most beautiful black kittens on the way home. They had beautiful white stripes. . . ."

"What you saw are skunks and you smell terrible!" May interrupted. "Take off all your clothes. I'll have to bury everything!"

As the years passed, Jim had more and more bouts with shell shock. Sometimes May saw him standing in the field trembling and crying. Those times she would call one of the children to help bring him back into the house. "Come on, love," she said tenderly, "come into the house. You must be cold out there." She took him in and held him close, cuddling him like a baby.

She explained to the children that their father was ill and might always have that sickness. "Oh, it must have been awful for him in the war," she said, wiping away a tear. Sometimes Jim went to the hospital for two or three weeks, but May never went to visit. The hospital was too far away, and her husband insisted it was better for her to care for the farm and the children.

The children were well taught and were able to do many chores on the farm. Douglas was milking a cow when he was five years old. "Why, just look at all the farmers I have running around," May often said, laughing.

Between Jim's hospital visits, the Pollards enjoyed long periods of tranquility when it seemed that nothing could disturb the contentment of their lives.

On one of these lovely days, a glorious summer afternoon, Jim was harvesting the summer wheat, and May was tending the children. Then disaster struck.

Several nearby farmers came running through the fields shouting, "Fire! Forest fire! It's headed this way! Houses are burning down! We need every man we can get!"

"We'll put your wife and kids down the well!" one of them shouted to Jim. "They'll be safe there! Get some boards! Mrs. Pollard, get some blankets and milk for the babies. Hurry!"

The men lowered several wide boards down the thirty-foot well, and by then May was back with a basket for the twins, plenty of blankets, and milk. They told May not to worry. If the fire did come, it would pass over the well. She and the children would be safe.

The night was long for May. The children were restless and making them comfortable wasn't easy in those close, damp quarters. But she sang to them, told them stories, and reassured them that Daddy would come soon.

By morning May could smell smoke, and she knew that the fire was raging toward them. She heard the roar of flames as the fire reached the farm and the crackling of timber as buildings came crashing down. May wept as she thought about her husband, his failing health, and the heartache of having to start all over again. What would the farm look like when they lifted her out of the well? Would anything be left?

She soon found out. The men returned, and May was lifted up into a strange black world of charred earth, heaps of smoldering ashes, and grotesque, smoky shapes where the buildings had stood only a few hours earlier. Everything was gone: animals, furniture, clothing, letters from Jim, pictures of the children, every evidence of their life together. Nothing was left.

The Pollards moved in with a distant neighbor until a second house was built. But Jim was never the same. His war injuries were returning to plague him, and less than a year after they moved into their new home, Jim began a long hospitalization. May and the children ran the farm as best they could.

A second tragedy occurred when the children were

older. Although the twins were only ten, they were doing men's work. The girls were cooking, baking, canning, and looking after May's chickens. Jim was still hospitalized. The family faced obstacles and adversity every day, but they were managing to keep their lives together. Each day the world looked a little brighter.

A devastating tornado knocked them to the ground again. When the storm had gone, once more the house was gone. There was no one to turn to. The Pollards had no car, no telephone, no close neighbors. The season was late fall, and the weather was cold. There was no food.

The only building left standing was the small chicken shack on one side of the farm. May took the children there. There were holes in the walls, so they had little protection from the wind. May began wishing she could at least start a fire. Her hands were blue from cold.

She fell on her knees in the tiny shack and prayed, "Oh, Jesus. I need help and I need it badly. You gave me these beautiful children. Please save us now from destruction." She felt better after praying, like a heavy burden had been lifted from her shoulders. She could almost sense Someone in the room saying, *Have no fear, May. You're going to be all right.*

Minutes later there was a knock on the door. The visitor was a young boy, and he said, "We thought you might have been hit. Don't worry. I'll get some help for you."

A group of men soon arrived, and one of them took May and the children to stay with a neighboring family. Then they began to rebuild the shack for the Pollards. They put in new walls, new flooring, and installed a ceiling, making it livable. Next they put in a stove, chopped wood, and stacked a supply of logs around the building. They collected beds, a table, chairs, blankets, clothing, dishes, food—all the necessities. In less than two weeks the little house was ready for the Pollards to move in.

May was ecstatic. "Oh, thank You, Jesus," she prayed. "You have performed a miracle for us. You brought us all these things from people we don't even know. And they came as soon as I asked for Your help. This is truly a miracle!"

Jim returned to live with his family, but he was never well again. However, he had been a good father while he was able. He had taught his boys well, and they could work almost as hard as he had. May bought more and more chickens and managed to sell enough eggs to buy the groceries.

In 1943 Jim Pollard died. May sold the farm and took the two girls to Milwaukee to finish their education while she found a job. The boys all joined the armed services.

In Milwaukee she found a minister to care for the girls, and an employment agency found her a position at once as a nurse-governess. "We don't have many authentic nurse-governesses in Milwaukee," she was told. "You'll always have a job."

So May was at work in her trade once again, and she still knew her business. In her first position three-year-old Billy was scheduled to have an operation. He was terrified, so May went along and took his favorite toy car.

On the way to the hospital she told Billy that she

was going to buy some gasoline for his car, and it would smell "real bad." When the doctor was ready to operate, she said, "Well, Billy, it's time to put the gasoline in your car. But before it will go, you have to sniff some of that gasoline. So you take a real good sniff and, boy, will that car make a rumble!"

By that time the ether was turned on and Billy was out. "The story was a kind deed," May told the doctor, "so the boy would go peacefully."

"I've never met a nurse-governess before," the doctor said, laughing, "but you sure know some tricks. I'll have to try that one sometime!"

For the first time in her life May had a chance to travel with the families who employed her. She spent six weeks in New York, six months in Pennsylvania, and many summers in Naples, Florida—all places she had never been before.

"It's nice to see those places," she said, "but I'm working, just like I'd be doing in Milwaukee. When you're a nurse-governess, you stick to your work." She was always glad to get home and be close to her girls again.

May's work as a nurse-governess in England had been cut short when her mother sent her to America. After a few years in Milwaukee her work was interrupted once again—this time by a man named Joe Lemke.

# Chapter 6

## *May, Meet Joe Lemke*

---

Joe Lemke was born in Manitowoc, Wisconsin, a city located about eighty miles north of Milwaukee on Lake Michigan. With thirteen children in the family, every member had to learn to fend for himself early. Joe was fifth in line. He quit high school when his mother died and went out to earn a living.

He chose construction work and began working his way south to Milwaukee, where he knew he could find jobs. Always close with his money, he even managed to save during the Depression. In 1932 he was able to pick up the lien on a one-room shack on Pewaukee Lake, twenty miles west of Milwaukee, and have a place of his own. He had just turned twenty-eight years old.

Although jobs were scarce during the Depression, Joe had a lot of pride, and when his construction boss lowered his hourly wage from sixty-five to forty cents, Joe quit. "If I'm going to starve, I might as well starve at home!" he told his boss.

He didn't work for over a year, but he had some savings. The bank where he kept his money folded, but another bank bought it out and paid fifty cents on the dollar. Joe got half his money back: five hundred dollars. The windfall was like five thousand dollars today. It got Joe by.

Joe's needs and wants were basic, and they never included an automobile. Streetcars, buses, and friends' cars carried him everywhere he wanted to go. "I've never been behind the wheel of a car," he maintained steadfastly, "and I never care to."

When World War II broke out Joe was thirty-seven. He was inducted into the Army in June of 1942 and sent to Africa to work in a station hospital unit. When the war was over he returned to Milwaukee and construction work.

Six years passed, and Joe's life changed little. He worked during the day and came home to his little shack at night. At forty-four he was still a bachelor. "Haven't found the right girl yet" is how he put it.

But at a dance on a lovely summer night in 1948, Joe Lemke found the right girl. She was a pretty little thing, less than five feet tall with golden-blond hair. She was wearing a beautiful red gown with a hoop skirt that she said had come all the way from Switzerland.

Her name was May—May Pollard—and she had come all the way from a place called Monkwearmouth on the northern coast of England. She told Joe that she was a nurse-governess in a home in Milwaukee. "A nurse-governess?" Joe looked puzzled. "What is that supposed to be?"

May laughed and told him about her training in England and her succession of positions in Milwaukee. He was fascinated with this little English lady. He found her clipped British accent as charming as her quick sense of humor.

A few days later Joe proposed. "I'm not perfect, May, but will you marry me?"

"Well," May answered, "I don't care to know all your shortcomings, but you are a bachelor and you're getting older. I'll soon be that way, too." So they agreed to be married.

"Say, on your next day off," Joe said, "I'll show you the place I'd like to buy for us. My little shack suited me fine, but it's no place for a lady. I could sell it and maybe buy this one." Accordingly, the following week Joe took May to see a little cottage that was for sale on Pewaukee Lake. May said it was fine.

Of course the cottage needed work. The wood floors were old and worn. Wallpaper was peeling off the walls. There were neither closets nor kitchen cupboards. The yard was littered with rocks, branches, and other debris. But May and Joe were clever and industrious, and they knew they could fix the place up.

They figured out how much money they would have if they pooled their resources. There was enough to cover the asking price, so they decided to complete the transaction on May's next day off. Afterwards there would still be time to get married.

The ceremony was brief, and May and Joe promptly moved in and went to work. They added paneling, new flooring, a large closet, and kitchen cupboards. They papered, painted, scrubbed, and varnished until their cottage was just the way they wanted it to be.

Next they tackled the yard. Joe began tearing down

an old building that was deteriorating at the back of the property. He hired someone to help him lay a concrete roof on top of the basement and covered it with gravel. "Now I have a place to chop my wood and keep my tools," he told May. "And if we ever need a bomb shelter, we've got it!"

In the meantime May hauled away branches, rocks, and leaves, often on her days off when Joe was at work. She planted trees, bushes, flowers, plants, and vegetables, and she hung bird feeders, filling them to the brim with sunflower seeds.

May had to continue her work in Milwaukee to make ends meet, coming home weekends to be with Joe. Sometimes she found odd jobs for him where she was working, as a gardener or handyman.

They were always busy, always working at something. For four years, life for the Lemkes was routine, predictable, and tranquil. They had much to be thankful for.

Then, in 1952, on one of those lovely Wisconsin summer afternoons, the Lemkes' life changed, drastically and permanently. They had been puttering in their yard, occasionally watching a few fishing boats drifting lazily on the lake. Warm sunlight filtered through the trees, and a soft breeze was moving in quietly from the south.

They were jarred from their tranquility by the sudden appearance of one of their neighbors, a dentist, who lived down the road. People usually kept to themselves on Pewaukee Lake, and the Lemkes knew only a few of their neighbors. They had never met the dentist, so May was a bit uneasy.

"Are you Mrs. Lemke?" the intruder inquired.

"Why, yes," May answered. "Why do you ask?"

"Someone called my house and left a message for you. They said you don't have a phone."

May hurried away with him. Who would be calling her? One of the children? Was someone hurt? She dialed the number. "This is May Lemke," she said. "What did you wish?"

"I'm calling from a hospital in Milwaukee," the voice at the other end of the line said. "We heard that you had married and moved out to Pewaukee. We've been looking for you. You may be the one to help us out."

"What is it?" May asked

"We have a six-month-old baby here who's had his eyes taken out. He also has cerebral palsy and is retarded. He won't live long. We thought maybe with your background and all, you'd take him and look after him. The parents don't want him. There's nobody to take him—no family, no nothing. Would you think about it, Mrs. Lemke?"

"I don't need to think about it," May said. "I'm moved in, and I can take him. I have a little vacation right now, so bring him out."

"But don't you want to discuss it with your husband, Mrs. Lemke? He might need time to think about it," the woman inquired.

"I know my husband," May said flatly. "If I choose to do something, he won't object. He's a good man, and he has a soft spot in him."

May's work as a nurse-governess had earned her a reputation around Milwaukee for being excellent with children. Several of the nurses at the hospital had heard stories of May's expertise with her young charges, but nobody seemed to know who she had married or where she lived. When they finally tracked her down that summer afternoon, she was between jobs.

A nurse brought the baby to the Lemkes the day after the phone call. His name was Leslie. Joe took the tiny infant, wrapped in a blanket and wearing a blue knitted cap, and held him carefully in his arms. Joe had not been around children much since he left home as a teenager, and now he was nearly fifty years old. But there was a tenderness in his eyes as he looked down at the baby, and a sadness on his face as he saw the terrible disabilities of the child.

It took only a glance to see that something was wrong. Born prematurely and weighing only three pounds at birth, Leslie still looked like a newborn infant—long and very thin. The sunken sockets where his eyes had been made his other features seem out of proportion. His hair was reddish-brown, his skin pale and wan. Saddest of all was the way he lay in Joe's arms: like a flimsy doll without movement or response.

May took the baby from Joe, tears streaming down her cheeks. "Oh, Joe, he looks terrible! So forlorn, so long and thin and helpless. But God loves all children, even this little creature. We'll just see what we can do."

They took the baby inside and talked about where to start. "We need a good formula," May said, "one that will begin to put some weight on him. Mama always used slippery elm paste for the sick babies in England. Joe, you stay with Leslie, and I'll take a bus to that health store in Pewaukee. They might have something."

May soon returned, carrying a small parcel. "They had it, Joe. It's a slippery elm powder. I'll just mix a teaspoonful with a pint of milk and water and add a bit of sugar. I want it sweet, but not too sweet." May mixed the formula and held the bottle to Leslie's mouth. "Try a little, love. You'll like this," she said softly. Leslie didn't seem to understand. He lay motionless, his tongue pushing out the nipple. "Suck, baby, you must suck it in," May encouraged. Still, he lay motionless.

May put her mouth against his cheek, making loud sucking sounds. Then she put the bottle in his mouth, hoping he might catch on. She kept up the procedure most of the afternoon, sucking on the baby's cheek and putting the bottle in his mouth, over and over again. At last, he began to suck a little, tentatively at first. As the warm milk trickled down his throat, he grew bolder. Pretty soon he was sucking with the zest of a normal, healthy infant. May danced with him around the room. "Baby," she cried out, "you're going to live!"

Besides the formula, May had to do something about the sockets where Leslie's eyes had been. They were still red, and mucous was seeping through the tissue.

The nurse had told May that Leslie's eyes were cloudy at birth, and as the weeks passed, he had not opened them as normal infants do. Doctors were unable to dilate the pupils, and both corneas continued to be cloudy and scarred. Later there was a discharge from the eyes and they became swollen. There was apparently no sight in either eye.

The nurse was not clear as to what had caused the inflammation of Leslie's eyes. "It's hard to pinpoint these things," she had said. "It could be any number of diseases or circumstances—we don't always know." When Leslie was four months old, the symptoms were worsening, and doctors removed Leslie's left eye. Six weeks later they removed his right eye as well.

May made a boric acid solution and dropped it into the empty sockets several times a day to keep them clean. When the sockets were healed, the eyelids closed by themselves. They always stayed shut after that.

Leslie continued to suck well and swallow his formula when May fed him. He seemed to be thriving on the concoction, but he wasn't doing anything else. He hardly moved at all, and his arms and legs were limp. May often lifted them hopefully, but they always dropped back down again.

He rarely cried or whimpered like babies do when they're hungry. He hardly made a sound. May couldn't tell if he was asleep or awake, because his eyes were always shut. Finally she decided to treat him like a normal baby and feed him every four hours. He always ate, and the food stayed down.

Months passed. May got down on her knees every night, praying for Jesus to "do something with Leslie." But still he remained silent and helpless.

Leslie was about a year old when May started him on solid food. She began with small portions of oatmeal and hard-boiled eggs, mashed up with butter. She didn't give him much, only a bit at a time. At first, Leslie spat the food out. He didn't seem to know what to do with it.

But slowly he began to swallow a little, and it

wasn't long before he seemed to enjoy eating. But progress was slow. Meals were very small until he was several years old.

As soon as Leslie was eating fairly well, May decided to teach him to drink from a cup. The first time she tried, she put a little bit of water in a tiny cup and held it to his mouth. No response. May finally had to pour the water into his mouth and let it drain down his throat. Weeks went by before Leslie made any effort at all to try to drink by himself.

By this time May's daughters, who had remained in close contact with their mother, were getting concerned. After all, May was close to fifty. Although she *seemed* to have an inexhaustible supply of energy . . . well, she couldn't go on forever. They knew that the longer she kept Leslie, the harder it would be for her to give him up. Both girls lived in Wisconsin and wrote their mother frequently. Occasionally they came to visit.

On one of her trips to Pewaukee daughter Pat realized fully how hard her mother was working. "Mother," she said, "what are you doing? Are you giving up your work as a nurse-governess?"

"Yes, I've earned enough money," May answered. "I've got my husband now. I can't go back to work, not with a baby like this. I have a job to do for Jesus now, and I'm going to do it. I could never leave this boy."

When Leslie was still physically inactive at almost three years of age, May decided to take him to a doctor. Maybe he could tell her some way to get Leslie crawling and walking. Even though he had cerebral palsy, May thought that Leslie ought to be making attempts to move around. The doctor shook his head. "I really don't know what to tell you, May," he said. "It's hard to tell how long it will take. But you've got a lot of faith. Maybe something will happen."

"I know that God can do things," May said. "If He can do them for others, then He can do them for me!" *But I do think I've waited long enough,* she thought to herself. She decided to go home and wait a little longer.

May cuddled Leslie in her arms every day, rocking him and singing softly to him. "I want him to know that he's loved," she said over and over again to Joe, "to know he has a mother and a father who love him just like other children."

Despite May's gentleness, Leslie always tensed, startled, as if he were frightened whenever she picked him up. He never relaxed his body against her like a normal baby. He was more like a plastic baby, rigid, with rarely a cry, never a smile.

But May refused to give up. "Children respond to love," she told Joe. "They can feel it in your body when you hold them close. I know he'll feel it eventually. It just takes more time with a child like this."

When the neighborhood children heard that there was a baby at the Lemke home, they began streaming over to play with him. But when they saw that he couldn't respond to them, they soon stopped coming. One of the neighbors brought over a teddy bear for Leslie. "That's kind of you," May said, "but he won't know what it is."

"Give it to him anyway," the woman said. "Maybe someday he'll be able to play with it."

When Leslie was almost five years old, he began to

relax a little and lay his head against May's body when she rocked him. But he never lifted a hand to touch her.

Undaunted, May tried to think of some way to get more movement in Leslie's arms and legs. A ritual emerged. She laid him on his bed and massaged his legs, arms, and back with sweet oil—twice a day, morning and evening. Then she exercised his legs, moving them up and down against his body. Finally she went through a routine with his arms.

Yet even this therapy did not seem to help. When May tried to sit Leslie up, his body still collapsed. His bones seemed to be made of spaghetti.

Joe brought home an infant chair for Leslie. The child was six years old, thin and frail. "Maybe we can sit him outside to get some sun and fresh air," he said to May. Leslie slumped forward in the chair, so they had to tie him securely with a cord.

In the summers May laid him naked on a soft rug in the sunshine almost every day. She hoped that the warmth and lack of restraint might encourage him to move around a little. But he never did. He was a distressing sight, a long, thin, pitiful little creature.

When May worked around the house, she always made sure that Leslie was close to her, so he could hear her and know that she was around. She propped him up with pillows on the sofa or laid him flat on his bed. Winters, when Joe made a fire in the fireplace, he laid Leslie on the rug in front of it where he'd be warm.

May chattered to the boy constantly. If she wasn't talking, she was singing.

"I'm making an apple pie for you today, love."

"That's a fire that you smell. But you can't touch it. It is hot and it burns."

"That's Daddy coming home, love. Can you hear him? He's going to pick you up and cuddle you."

Still no response, never a sound. May never knew if Leslie was hurt or needed anything. She had to do everything for him.

Again and again concerned friends and neighbors told May to put Leslie in an institution. "He'll never do anything or learn anything. Look what you're doing to yourselves," they said. "You and Joe are giving up your whole lives for that boy."

Leslie's doctor began to suggest that the time was coming when institutional care would be necessary. He applauded May's patience and devotion but warned her that when Leslie was older, she might not be able to keep up the responsibility. After all, she was in her mid-fifties, and Leslie was a seven-year-old boy.

But May wouldn't listen. She only prayed more. "Oh, Jesus, help me reach this little boy. Please, show me what to do. Help me to turn this little creature into a more normal human being."

She cried enough for both of them. She held Leslie so close that her tears ran down his cheeks as well as her own. Sometimes she put his little hands on her face so he could feel her tears.

Every facet of May's life continued to involve Leslie. If she needed to go shopping, Leslie went along, even though she had to carry him. Although he was still a thin, frail child, it was becoming harder for May—so tiny herself—to lift and carry him.

Since the Lemkes didn't own a car, May always

called a cab to take her to the grocery store. Once inside the store she handed her list to a checkout girl or simply told her what she needed. The girl then shopped for May, bagged her groceries, called another cab, and carried the groceries out. If May had to make another stop in her shopping expedition, she went through the routine all over again.

May and Leslie were well-known all over Pewaukee. Policemen were constantly on the alert for the tiny little Englishwoman carrying the retarded boy. When she crossed the street, they were there beside her, fearful that her pint-sized frame might give out or not be seen by motorists.

As going places with Leslie became more and more difficult, May decided it was time to teach him how to walk. Although he was small for a seven-year-old, he weighed nearly fifty pounds, and she knew the boy could not be carried around forever. She certainly didn't want Leslie spending the rest of his life lying around doing nothing.

May had an idea. She took a three-inch-wide leather belt and strapped Leslie to herself around the waist, with Leslie standing directly behind her. Since Leslie couldn't hold on by himself, Joe made a little leather loop for his hands on each side of the belt. This way May could grasp Leslie's hands and walk, dragging him along behind.

May called the operation "trailing." The idea was to let Leslie feel how she walked in the hope that he would imitate her. May walked with him almost every day for three years, until he was nearly ten years old, but Leslie never took a single step.

Neighbors often saw the tiny Mrs. Lemke walking

slowly up and down the road, young Leslie trailing behind. "Some of the neighbors think you're being cruel, May, but most of us understand that you're trying to help him," encouraged Agnes Myers, a longtime friend.

One summer afternoon when Leslie was nearly nine years old, May was sitting by the lake, looking out at the water and wondering what to do next. The trailing wasn't producing any noticeable results. What else could she try?

As she stared at the water, a new idea came to her. *The lake! Why not the lake?* she thought. *Water ought to be good for a child like Leslie. Joe is a good swimmer. He can take him in!*

As soon as Joe came home from work that night, May laid out her plan. "You can swim, Joe. Take Leslie in the water, swim around with him, and bump him up and down. Then maybe he'll start to move."

After dinner Joe carefully eased Leslie into the cool water. He swam with him, bounced him up and down, played with him—but nothing happened. Finally Joe lay on his back in the water, letting the little boy rest on him. Patches of orange sunlight left traces in the sky where the sun had retreated a few minutes before. The water was still except for a few muffled ripples from flying fish. Joe silently wondered if Leslie felt as peaceful as Joe did. Neither his body nor his face showed any signs of content—or discontent. There was no way to know how Leslie felt.

From then on Joe took Leslie into the lake regularly, at night after work and on weekends. He splashed him around, held him to his chest while he swam on his back, and bounced him up and down. He talked to him often, trying to make him laugh, hoping to stir some emotion, some response. They usually stayed in the water so long that May said Leslie looked like a withered old carcass when Joe brought him ashore.

Late one Sunday afternoon in the middle of summer, Joe was floating lazily on his back, holding the boy. Joe was close to sixty now, and he was weary after the sessions in the water. He closed his eyes, drifting a little in the gently rolling waves.

A scream from May brought him abruptly to his feet. "What's wrong? What happened?" he called out.

"Did you see it? Did you see it, Joe?"

"Did I see what?" he shouted.

"Leslie! He moved his hands! He did it himself! I saw it, Joe! Thank God! Thank God! Leslie's moving!"

# Chapter 7
## *The Miracle*

---

That first sign of activity in Leslie wasn't much—only a tiny, almost imperceptible movement of the hand.

But May hadn't missed it. She had been with Leslie too long not to notice a change, no matter how small.

Freshly inspired, May and Joe tried a new routine. It started with Joe taking Leslie down to the lake and exercising him in the lapping water, moving him back and forth. Joe tenderly glided the frail, limp boy through the water for at least thirty minutes, sometimes an hour. At the end of the session he carried Leslie, dripping and wrinkled, up on the shore.

Then May took over. She toweled him off, chattering and singing as she briskly rubbed him dry. After dressing him she carried him to a wire fence that bordered the lot. She wrapped Leslie's elastic fingers around the netting, hoping he'd try to hang on by himself and hold his body erect. Time after time, May stood him up, attached his hands, and then watched disappointedly as Leslie's body buckled and dropped to the ground.

May kept up the trailing, too, every day, around and around the yard, up and down, back and forth, hoping and praying for some sign of movement, some indication that her untiring efforts were getting through to him.

Neighbors watched the diminutive Mrs. Lemke carrying and trailing the sixty-pound boy who was almost as tall as she was, and they were appalled. "Why don't you put him someplace?" one of them asked. "It's been nearly ten years, and he's still not doing much of anything. May, you're wasting your life away."

"I'm not wasting my life," May retorted. "I'm doing something for an innocent boy who will be something someday. You wait and see. I believe in God, and He's going to do it!"

Even her daughter, Mary, approached her gently. "You might have to give him up, Mother. It's going to break your heart, I know."

But May persisted and, if anything, became more stubborn and determined. "I'm not going to give him up for you or for anybody else. It might take me all my life, but I'm going to do something with this boy. If God says He can do things, then He can do them for me. If He doesn't, then I'm just going to pester Him to death!"

So May went back to work: trailing, lifting, carrying, in the water, out of the water, standing, holding, massaging—everything she could think of. Leslie still could not hold on to the fence.

Feeling a little discouraged, May walked down to

the lake one afternoon. She sat at the edge of the water, near the spot where Joe was playing with Leslie and watched them impassively, half-concentrating on what steps to take next. Nothing she was doing seemed to work.

Suddenly her eyes raced to Leslie. *Am I dreaming?* she thought. *Or is someone playing tricks on me?* But she wasn't dreaming. She could see it. It was true! "Joe!!!" He could have heard her halfway across the lake.

"Joe! He's moving! His legs are moving! His arms are moving! His whole body is moving! He's splashing! Joe, it worked! It worked! That boy is going to walk!"

Excitedly they took Leslie out of the water. May's hands trembled as she wrapped him in a towel. She was laughing and crying all at once. "Help me, Joe. Help me get him dressed. I can't do anything right. Joe, do you think he can stand now?" Joe pulled Leslie's shirt over his head and slipped on his shoes. They both helped him to the fence.

Joe stood Leslie up, then fastened his fingers securely on the netting of the fence. May began as she had a hundred times before. "Come on, love. Try to hang on, just for a few seconds. Hold on tight. Come on, baby, you can do it! You can . . ." May caught her breath. "Joe! Joe! He did it! He stood alone! Leslie stood alone!"

Leslie wavered in the air for only a few seconds, and then he fell in a heap, but May was ecstatic. "See, God is listening," she said. "He does things for other people, and He does them for me, too. I just have to keep after Him!"

An early venture into Pewaukee Lake for Joe and Leslie.

May on her wedding day. She was barely 18 when she married James Pollard.

Leslie, almost 10, stands alone.

The morning of "The Miracle." Soon after, Leslie's frail body began to fill out.

An early practice session with May and Joe.

Leslie's first concert. As ever, May is an irrepressible emcee.

Joe and May at a recent concert, waltzing while Leslie performs.

Leslie plays a favorite — "I Was Nobody's Baby But I'm Somebody's Baby Now."

The Lemkes at home. May coaches Leslie with praise and humor.

The Milwaukee Journal by Dale Guldan

May's boy —
an incredible
story of love.

As before, May brought Leslie to the fence daily to stand. The seconds began stretching into minutes, and after several weeks, Leslie could stand for several minutes, holding onto the fence. Then May or Joe carried him into the house, exhausted.

They kept the ritual up for months. Still Leslie did not walk. May refused to be discouraged. "I can wait forever," she said. "At least he's standing by himself."

One cool fall evening Joe made a crackling fire in the fireplace and propped Leslie up on several large pillows on the sofa. May was sitting with him, staring at the fire and trying to think of some way to get Leslie to walk.

"Maybe if I took him to a clinic of some kind . . ." she mused to Joe aloud. "Don't they have places where they teach children to walk?" Joe nodded that he was sure they did.

She called her doctor the next day, and he told her of a clinic in Milwaukee where they specialized in physical therapy. "Perhaps they can help Leslie," he said encouragingly.

She got up the next morning and called her neighbor Agnes to see if she would drive her to Milwaukee. Otherwise she would have to take the bus, most likely changing several times, and Leslie was getting too heavy for that. A cab to Milwaukee would be far too expensive. Agnes often drove May places and never took money (so May always bought her something over her protestations).

"Of course I'll take you," Agnes said, without a moment's hesitation. "When do you want me to come?" May wondered sometimes what she would do without Agnes Meyer, her closest friend on the lake. Agnes lived in the second cottage south of the Lemkes and had been there almost as long as May and Joe—nearly sixteen years. Agnes was as soft-spoken as May was effervescent. The two had formed a strong bond over the years. Agnes could always be depended on.

May washed and dressed Leslie, dressed herself, and by 9:30, Agnes was already at the door. Agnes drove the twenty miles to Milwaukee, and after asking for directions several times, finally found the clinic.

Agnes helped carry Leslie inside. After a half-hour wait a therapist called them in. He tried a few tests with Leslie to see if the boy would respond. He lifted his arms and legs and massaged his body, then began asking May questions.

"How long has he been this way?"

"What have you tried with him?"

"What changes have you seen?"

"I'm sorry, Mrs. Lemke," he finally said, almost apologetically, "but I don't think we can do anything for this boy. I don't know what to tell you. Working with him will take a long time and a lot of effort, and you still might not get him walking. You can keep doing what you're doing and maybe someday you'll get him moving around. But I can't promise anything."

"I *will* get him walking someday," May said as she carried her helpless son toward the door. "I surely *will* get him walking!"

May returned to the old routine: trailing, water exercise, propping Leslie by the fence—hour after hour and day after day. As they turned the corner of winter and Leslie passed his tenth birthday, she began to notice a change in him.

At first it was hard to put her finger on. Did he seem to cock his head—just a bit—when she was talking? Did his body tighten—just a speck—when she was near? The change was miniscule, but she was sure he was beginning to *listen*.

She noticed the difference again when he was standing by the fence a few days later. He seemed as if he was paying attention to her. His body, instead of being limp and sluggish, was poised and alert.

She moved close to him and held out her arms. "Come to me, love, turn around." Leslie *moved!* She called out again. "Come to me, love! You're a boy already! Walk to Mama! Over here!" Leslie moved his foot slightly.

May called out again. "Come to me, love! Walk to me!" He fell in her arms. May was jubilant. Leslie had taken his first step. He would walk someday! It would only take time.

With renewed vigor May took Leslie out several times a day and watched him move his feet, little by little, inch by inch, until he could slowly move his body along the fence. The pace was very, very slow at first, but *he was walking*.

Sometimes May watched him from a window, moving so haltingly, agonizing over every step. And she wept all the tears that had been filling up in her. She cried because he still could not get out of bed, could not hold anything to his mouth properly, could not drink by himself, could not do much of anything by himself.

When Leslie was twelve years old, May began to pray a new prayer for her son. She prayed that he might have a gift, something to give his life meaning. Several times a day, she implored, "Dear Lord, the Bible says that you gave each of us a talent. Please help me find the talent in this poor boy who lies there most of the day and does nothing."

Soon after May began praying this way for Leslie, asking for a talent, she noticed another difference in him. Whenever he felt a taut piece of string or cord, he plucked it with his fingers. He seemed to respond to the activity and draw satisfaction from it. May was puzzled by this strange, new behavior. She watched him day after day, searching for some meaning. Could Leslie be making music? Was he trying to strum to some mysterious tempo?

What else could they do? Leslie's birthday was coming up in January. He would be thirteen years old. Why not buy him a piano? The idea seemed silly, to be sure, but May could play a little by ear. She could play some simple tunes and show him how the keys make different sounds. If he liked to strum a chord, why wouldn't he enjoy hitting the keys of a piano? At least a piano could produce sounds. A piece of string could not do that.

She and Joe began searching through the newspaper ads for a used piano. They couldn't afford much, but surely they could find something within their budget. "I found one!" Joe said one evening as he was scanning the columns. "It's two hundred fifty dollars. What do you think, May?"

"Let's call them," May said. "If it sounds good, we'll go and look at it." It sounded fine, so Joe and

May got Leslie ready, called a cab, and went to see the piano. They talked it over. "Can you deliver?" Joe asked.

The man said he had a trailer, and if Joe and May would take it, he would deliver it the following day.

"Do you think we did the right thing?" May asked on the way home.

"What's the difference?" Joe answered. "You like to play the piano. If Leslie isn't interested, you can enjoy it yourself."

When the man came with the piano the next day, May asked him to put it in Leslie's bedroom, close to his bed. "Are you sure you want it there, ma'am?" he asked in disbelief. "That's an awfully small room. Wouldn't you rather have it in the living room or on that porch?"

"No, it's his piano." May had made up her mind. "Someday the boy might play it, you know."

He looked at her incredulously. "Well, if that's where you want it. . . ." He and his husky young son moved the piano into Leslie's bedroom. They could hardly get it through the narrow door, and there was barely space left to move around. "Thanks a lot, lady," he said as he left. "I hope he likes his piano."

May began to play simple little tunes for Leslie. Then she ran his hands over the keyboard again and again, so he could hear the different sounds. "You see, love, that's music," she said. "That's part of God's language."

Leslie seemed to enjoy music more and more. He often sat listening to records or radio for hours, head down, serious, intense, a study in concentration.

Sometimes his foot or hand even moved methodically with the beat.

Then, in his sixteenth year, something May calls "The Miracle" occurred.

The family had been in bed for hours. About 3:00 A.M. May awoke and thought she heard music. Assuming that Joe had left the television on, she got up to turn it off. But when she walked into the living room, the television was dark and silent. The music was coming from Leslie's bedroom.

She opened the door and saw her son sitting at the piano, playing Tchaikovsky's Piano Concerto No. 1. The music was Liberace's theme song, and he had heard it numerous times on television.

Leslie had never played a note of music in his life, but now he was playing like a professional, racing up and down the keys, never missing a note, as if he'd been practicing for years.

May fell down on her knees and cried. And laughed. And cried again. She ran for Joe. They were both on their knees for most of the night, praising God and thanking Him for giving their boy the gift of music. At last, God had given him a talent. And what a wonderful talent!

Amazingly, Leslie still could not walk alone. He had never gotten out of bed by himself before. Yet somehow he had slid out of his bed and pulled himself up on the piano bench and begun to play.

The next morning May called friends, neighbors, Leslie's doctor—everybody she could think of—to tell them about Leslie's amazing talent. They all came to listen and found the impromptu concerts both magnificent and incredible. Impulsively May taped Leslie at the keyboard and played the tapes outdoors so that all the world could hear what "my helpless, spastic son" had become.

Leslie began to play everything he heard: classics, hymns, marches, ragtime, ballads. He amazed his mother by playing many of the old English songs that she had sung earlier to him. From then on everything that Leslie heard, he could repeat. May began to be more selective about what he listened to. She bought good records by accomplished artists, so that her son would hear nothing but the best music.

Although Leslie's palsied hands could not yet hold a cup or pick up a piece of food, they were relaxed and controlled when he played the piano. They moved decisively, the long fingers gliding gracefully. His timing was good; his interpretation powerful. Playing the piano, Leslie Lemke was in his own special world—a world he loved, a world where all of his senses came alive.

He obviously enjoyed performing and disliked having to stop. He never seemed to tire and never ran out of the endless selections that he was storing up every day. The dozens of songs in his repertoire grew to hundreds, then thousands, until nobody knew how many pieces he could play at will.

Joe and May had to have the piano moved out of Leslie's bedroom and onto the porch to make room for all the people who were coming to hear him.

The neighborhood children, who had stopped visiting when Leslie showed no response as a baby, began to come again, asking Leslie to play all their favorite songs. Sometimes as many as ten or twelve youngsters crowded around him, each interrupting the other with requests.

Visitors came and played some little-known piece,

then reacted with disbelief when Leslie played it right back to them, often in a different key. There seemed to be no music that Leslie could not repeat and remember. He needed only to hear it once.

Word spread all over Pewaukee that Leslie had received his gift and May her miracle. And May's prayers changed from prayers of supplication to expressions of thanksgiving. Instead of asking God for help, she was thanking him for a miracle.

"Oh, thank You, thank You, dear God," she praised. "I asked for a gift, but I didn't expect anything so big! You really brought me to my knees! Thank You for the wonderful thing you have done for Leslie!"

The miracle was only the beginning. After that night of Tchaikovsky, all kinds of things began to happen.

# Chapter 8

*Growing*

---

May noticed that Leslie's thin, frail body was changing. Instead of looking like a withered child, he was filling out, looking less like a boy and more like a man. He was nearly seventeen, and he was growing so fast that he would soon be as tall as Joe. Although he was thin, he weighed well over a hundred pounds. His hands, his body, his senses all seemed to be coming alive, suddenly springing out of their lethargy.

He was not walking alone, but May noticed that each day he walked a little faster, a little steadier along the fence. His hands grew raw and blistered from gripping the fence too hard, so she bought him a pair of gloves.

In the next few years she bought Leslie *dozens* of pairs of gloves. He gripped the fence so intensely that in no time at all, the gloves were in shreds. Leslie spent more and more time walking up and down the fence, enjoying the outdoors, listening to the neighbor children play. He became stronger and stronger until he was nearly running as he held on to the fence.

One hot July afternoon Leslie was going up and down the fence when a boy of about fourteen called to him from the road that passed the house. He stood by the fence and began to tease Leslie.

"How fast can you travel up that fence?"

"What's your name, or can't you talk?"

May came flying out the back door in a rage. (Leslie was never out of her sight for long.) "What do you think you're doing, mister?" she screamed. "You're annoying the child, and he can't even defend himself! You should be out doing something for these kinds of people, not teasing or making fun of them. You might have one of your own someday. These children need to be loved and protected, not tormented!"

Concern for Leslie was always foremost in May's mind. Later that summer she looked down at the lake one morning and said to Joe, "I think we ought to have a fence built between the house and lake. One of these days that boy is going to end up in the water."

So they had another fence built to enclose the back yard, giving Leslie plenty of walking space.

May reasoned that if Leslie was able to hold onto the fence and walk outdoors, couldn't he hang onto her and walk indoors? They tried it, and it worked. Leslie learned to put both hands on May's shoulders and shuffle along behind. Soon, instead of carrying him or trailing him with a belt, May walked her son to his bedroom, to the piano, to his chair.

Joe retired the year Leslie was seventeen, so May

had more help with the boy. If one of them had to shop or run errands, the other could stay home with Leslie.

With Joe home, May also thought the time had come to teach Leslie to go to the bathroom by himself. "After all, he can walk with us now, Joe," she said. "So maybe you can teach him." All the years that Leslie couldn't walk, May had relied on a bedpan for her son. "What a wonderful thing it would be, Joe, if he could be like other boys."

Joe took over the bathroom training and proved he was every bit as patient as May. There were several months of constant observation and surveillance, but eventually, Leslie began to catch on. And May happily threw out the bedpan.

Next May tried to teach Leslie to walk by hanging onto the furniture. But he seemed frightened and unsure of himself if May or Joe were not right there with him. Patiently May decided to let him walk along with her for a while longer until he felt secure. Eventually she taught him to feel his way around the house.

Meanwhile the Lemkes' life fell into a comfortable routine again. No more having to carry Leslie to the store, no more dragging him down to the lake for water exercises, no more standing him by the fence to watch him fall in a heap, no more bedpans to clean.

After breakfast Leslie went to the bathroom and May dressed him. Then she took him to the piano, where he played for an hour or so. Next she or Joe helped him to the fence for some exercise and fresh air.

After lunch May walked him to his favorite chair in

the living room and played records for him while he rested. Sometimes he took a nap. After resting he played the piano again. Then May or Joe took him back outside for more exercise until dinner.

With Leslie responding, May sensed an even greater challenge to discover new things for him to do. One day she bought a large ball and took Leslie out in the backyard, sitting him on a chair. She let him feel the ball, then she bounced it up and down, letting him hear the sound of it.

"I'm going to throw the ball to you, love," she explained. "It will make a sound like a swishing noise when it goes through the air. Now, you try to catch it."

May was astounded. Leslie caught the ball every time. He clearly was enjoying the activity and apparently could hear the ball coming through the air. "His ears must be magnificent!" she said to Joe that evening.

May had another idea. As Leslie continued to play the piano his fingers were becoming stronger and more agile. His eighteenth birthday came and went. "Why can't he learn to eat and drink by himself?" she asked Joe one evening. "Even with the palsy, I bet he could learn to hold a cup or pick up a piece of meat."

She began this new series of lessons with a tiny bit of milk in a plastic cup. Patiently, slowly, May showed him how to hold the cup with both hands and raise it to his mouth. Leslie picked up the cup, banged it on the table, and milk splashed all over his face.

"No, no, love. That milk is to drink!" May said over and over again in the next few days. Then she carefully showed him again how to hold the cup and lift it to his mouth so he could drink by himself.

May noticed that Leslie seemed to be listening more to what she was saying. Often, he turned his head toward her as she spoke or reached his hand toward her. He seemed to be trying to understand.

She gave Leslie the cup again. He banged it on the table. May was pleased that he was getting so much movement. "No, no, love," she said. "That's beautiful, but that's not the way to do it." And she showed him once more.

A few weeks later Leslie finally held the cup by himself and raised it to his mouth. But instead of drinking, he blew—hard—and the milk ran down his clothes. Again, with infinite patience, May responded, "No, no, love. Not like that. You don't blow it out. You drink it down."

Since nothing else seemed to work, May put a little sugar in the milk and a little more on the rim of the cup. The trick worked. Leslie liked the sugar, and the milk began to go down.

Her success at teaching Leslie to drink by himself gave May confidence that she could teach him to eat. She put a few bite-sized pieces of food on his plate. "Now love, I'm going to teach you to eat by yourself," she said.

She placed his fingers in the dish so he could feel the food. Leslie put his face down close to the dish and tried to suck the food up like milk. "Good for you, baby," May said. "One of these days you're going to eat right."

Day after day she offered Leslie a few bits of food on the plate. Slowly he figured out that pushing the pieces into his mouth with his fingers was easier than sucking them in. He still bent his face close to the plate, but he managed to scrape everything in. When he was finished, he wiped the plate with his fingers and licked them clean.

Gradually May taught Leslie to pick up a piece of food and put it into his mouth. His hand trembled—the procedure was clearly an effort for him—but soon he could eat almost all his food unassisted. Because of the palsy he could not manage a fork or spoon. But he rarely spilled anything or made a mess. He scraped his plate clean, licked his fingers, and obviously enjoyed eating.

# Chapter 9

## *New Sounds*

May began to wonder why Leslie could not talk. He never even made a sound. If he could hear, why was he unable to talk? She gently put two fingers into his mouth one day and moved his tongue around. All of a sudden Leslie made a gurgling noise. "You see," she said to him, "that shows you *can* make a noise."

She moved his tongue again and told him, "This is your tongue, and you use it for eating. But you can use it for talking, too."

She put his hands to her own lips, then put a piece of apple in her mouth. "Now I'm eating," she explained. In a few moments she put his hands to her lips. "Now, you see, love, I'm talking." She put her mouth against his cheek and sang a song. "Now I'm singing. Isn't it amazing how many things you can do with your mouth?"

Often when Leslie played the piano, May sat beside him, pressing her mouth against his cheek, singing the words to him. She explained to Joe, "Maybe I can teach him to talk by touch. When you touch someone's face or arm, you are showing affection—how you care about them. Maybe if I keep at it, I can get him to talk."

May worked every day, talking and singing into Leslie's cheek, moving his tongue, touching his lips, trying to get him to understand and to make some small effort toward language.

The only response was a flat, guttural grunt. *What else can I try?* she kept asking herself. *Maybe there's a clinic somewhere where they can teach him to talk.*

*Maybe I'll call my doctor and ask,* she was musing one day, when she became aware of a strange sound in the house.

*What was that?* She stopped washing dishes, hands poised in midair, in order to hear better. The sound was *singing*. Leslie was playing the piano, but who was singing? She tried to think where Joe was. *He went to the bank. He can't be back yet.* She knew the radio wasn't on. Nor was the television. Besides, this wasn't a trained voice. It sounded kind of flat, kind of throaty—like Leslie's.

"Leslie!" She ran to the porch. He was singing a song that Frank Sinatra had made popular—"I Did It My Way." The words were muffled and hesitant, but *Leslie was singing.*

May fell to her knees again. "Oh, God," she prayed. "Another miracle. Now I know why you put Leslie on this earth: to sing and play for people. Oh, thank You, God! Thank You!" She wept anew in gratitude for another gift, another miracle, another talent.

Leslie was nineteen years old when he started singing. He had never spoken a word.

From then on Leslie sang along with much of his music. At first his singing was indistinct, occasionally missing phrases. His tongue seemed to get in the way, twisting sounds rather than caressing or honing them. But like a child learning to talk, Leslie's voice developed and matured until at twenty, he had a strong, rich baritone. The talent added another remarkable dimension to his emerging personality. As he listened to music he recorded both melody and words in his brain.

One summer day when Leslie was twenty-two, he was walking up and down the fence, singing an Irish song at the top of his voice. A half hour later, a man came walking up the road and knocked on the door. "I heard someone singing a beautiful Irish song," he said when May answered. "Do you know who it was?"

May explained that he was her son who was blind and retarded.

"Oh, what a beautiful voice," he said. "We just moved in, and I thought there must be another Irishman living around here."

Despite the range of Leslie's repertoire, May loved hearing Leslie sing the old songs she used to sing to him most of all: old English ballads, World War I songs, and her favorite hymns. Sometimes, she even joined him in a duet.

May was fixing dinner late one afternoon when she heard Leslie playing something she had never heard him play. She stopped a moment and listened. Suddenly her eyes welled up with tears. The music was the first song she had sung to him as a baby. She had changed the words from "two lovely eyes" to "without any eyes."

*Only a baby small,*
*Dropped from the skies.*
*Only a baby small,*
*Without any eyes.*
*Only a baby small,*
*Never at rest.*
*Small, but how dear to me,*
*God knows best.*

Three years passed. Leslie was nearly twenty-six years old.

May had more questions, new expectations. "If he can sing, then why can't he talk?" she asked Joe one evening. "Words are words, whether they're spoken or sung."

She began again with the method she knew, pressing her lips against his cheek, forming words and talking through his cheek. She thought if he could hear the sounds and feel her lips, he might get the idea. The technique had worked before. He certainly was singing beautifully. Again May worked long hours for weeks, then months, trying to get Leslie to form words—moving his tongue, touching her lips, trying to get him to understand.

One day the following summer May was planting petunias while Leslie walked up and down the fence, listening to the three children next door. They were playing in the yard, and occasionally they called out to Leslie.

"Hi, Leslie. Are you having fun?"

"Hey, you're almost running today!"

"We heard you singing last night, Leslie."

Then they went back to their play.

May, too, engaged in one-sided conversation with her son.

"These petunias are beautiful, Leslie. Some are pink, some a lovely lavender. I'm going to plant my Easter lily to see if it will bloom. Are you too warm, Leslie? Shall I take your shirt off? School's out now, you know. You'll be able to hear the children all summer. Won't that be fun? And what are you doing now, love?"

"I'm having fun." The voice was flat, mechanical, unfamiliar. May looked up. *Who said that? Is one of the children being silly and trying to confuse me?*

"I'm having fun." There was no question this time. The children were down by the lake, playing in the boat. It was Leslie! He wasn't singing those words. *He was talking.*

"Oh, God! Oh, God!" May said as she looked at her son. "Now You have given him words so he can speak. I'm overcome with joy. Thank You from me! Thank You from Leslie! Thank You, God!" Exhausted with emotion, she fell to her knees.

Leslie continued to talk, on and off, very primitively at first. With practice, his words became more distinct, his sentences more complete. He was unable to carry on a conversation, but he could respond to simple questions. He began to repeat what he heard: television commercials, thoughts that May had spoken to him. He called Joe "Daddy" and referred to May as "Honey-love." He could tell people what his name was and who his parents were.

May had read to Leslie since he was a small boy— stories about the sun, moon, and stars, stories about Jesus, about nature—topics she thought might interest him. When they spent time outside, she tried to explain these things to him.

As Leslie talked, the ideas and concepts that May

had read to him came back to her through him. One evening Joe told Leslie that the moon was out. Leslie startled his parents by saying, "Yes, that silvery light is shining through the window."

"And where did you hear that?" May asked.

"I can see it," Leslie replied.

"You know, Joe, maybe he 'sees' more than we think he does," May said, reflectively. "How do we know what's going on inside his head?"

The following two years were filled with new accomplishments for Leslie—feeling his way around the house, brushing his teeth, bathing and dressing by himself. There were also new experiences—flying to Arizona, taking overnight trips, attending weddings.

May and Joe provided motivation and encouragement. Leslie came up with the courage to try.

Leslie began to tell stories to May. His voice still had a flatness about it, with little intonation or expression. But he seemed to enjoy communicating and being part of a conversation.

"I guess I'm going to a wedding," he said to May one morning. May's granddaughter was to be married the following April. "They're going to have a big wedding cake and some cool lemon juice," Leslie went on. "And Mary's going to be there. And I'm going to play the piano."

Later that day May said to Joe, "Leslie's got the whole wedding planned, and I don't even have an invitation yet!"

One winter evening, the family was sitting around the living room in front of a crackling fire. Leslie was slumped in his favorite chair as usual.

"What is that sniffing I hear?" May looked around and realized that the sound was coming from Leslie. "What is it, love?"

"I'm crying," he said matter-of-factly. Leslie knew what crying was because he had heard May cry and had felt her tears, but neither May nor Joe had ever seen Leslie cry. Leslie reached up to his own face this time, feeling his own tears. And then he began to sob, his whole body shaking.

He couldn't tell his parents why he was crying. "Oh, Joe," May said, "it's like a river, like something that has been inside of him all his life. I think he's crying a lifetime of misery—of pure agony!"

Finally Leslie was calm once more. Neither May nor Joe have seen him cry since.

May decided Leslie should walk alone—this time, for sure. After all, he was six feet tall and weighed one hundred fifty pounds. He wasn't a boy any longer; he was a man. Although he resisted losing the security of their shoulders, May was firm. "You can't walk this way forever. You've got to start feeling your way around the house by yourself now."

Again, she took him from room to room, putting his hands on furniture, mantles, and windowsills, showing him objects he could hold onto. They explored the house together many, many times. May pointed out doorways, chairs, plants, and dressers so that Leslie was familiar with the minutest details. She guided his hands from doorway to chair, chair to sofa, showing him how he could move around by himself.

He was slow and cautious at first, and very uneasy. Sometimes he couldn't find the window ledge or the doorknob and he would call out, "Honey-love!" Other times he simply uttered some indistinguishable sound of frustration. Yet, each day his body relaxed a little more, and he moved with greater assurance.

In a few weeks he was capable of walking throughout the house by himself: to the kitchen, to the bathroom, wherever he wanted to go. He called out his destinations loud enough for Joe and May to hear.

"I think I'm going to play the piano now."

"I'm going to sit in my chair."

"I'm on my way to the bathroom."

His voice was still mechanical and buried deep in his throat, but his body showed confidence and pride. No longer did he have to ask May or Joe for help. He could get around by himself.

About a month after Leslie had become adept at moving around the house, May heard a commotion in the living room. She poked her head in and there was Leslie, feeling his way around the room, moving in circles.

"Whatever are you doing, love?" May asked, a bit puzzled.

"I'm exercising," Leslie replied. From then on, "exercise" was a part of Leslie's regimen. Whether he walked up and down the fence or circled the living room, it was always the same. He was "exercising."

"Leslie should begin taking care of himself," May said to Joe one evening. "I'll teach him to brush his teeth and dress himself. I do wish we had a bathtub so Leslie could sit and scrub himself." The Lemkes' tiny facilities had room only for a shower.

"I've got it!" May said, after a few minutes. "Why don't we have a tub built into the shower? Couldn't they just weld it in, Joe? You'd just need a little dip in front to step over."

*May does have ideas*, Joe thought to himself. *She's always thinking of something!*

After being told by several welders that the idea would never work, the Lemkes found a man who said he would do it. He took the measurements of the shower stall and arrived a week later with a three-foot-high tub that fit perfectly. He welded it to the frame, and the tub sat inside the stall, exactly as May had imagined.

"It's perfect," she said excitedly. "Now, Leslie can sit in the water and enjoy his bath like other children."

May filled the tub the next morning after breakfast and helped Leslie over the edge, into the warm water. Cautiously, he held onto the side and felt the water, splashing a little to get used to it. Each time May helped him into the water, he grew a little bolder until he was splashing grandly and putting his head under, having a wonderful time.

"I'm going to my adventure bath," Leslie said whenever he heard May filling the tub. "Robin and Batman are coming in, too."

"He always talks to Robin and Batman when he's in the tub," May told Joe over lunch. "He must have heard them on TV."

A few months later, May had the welder return to install a pull-down shower so Leslie could wash and rinse his hair.

The next lesson for Leslie was how to brush his teeth. When he first tried, he brushed so hard that his gums bled.

"No, no, love," May said encouragingly. "That's

too hard. Be more gentle." May went out and bought new brushes with the softest bristles she could find. She took away the toothpaste because he tried to eat it. Instead she gave him a bowl of clean, warm water to rinse his brush in. Slowly he learned to brush up and down more gently, and May was satisfied.

Learning to dress himself took a little more time. Because of the palsy he had poor muscle control; consequently, getting a shirt over his head, pulling up a pair of pants, or slipping on socks and shoes took a long time. But Leslie worked hard at the tasks, and May was always there to give him a hand if he became frustrated. He learned to feel the labels on his clothing to tell the front from the back. The last thing that Leslie learned was to fasten a button. May replaced many of the buttons on his clothing with larger sizes and enlarged the buttonholes so that Leslie could manage them himself.

The more Leslie accomplished, the more he structured his own life. He sensed when nine o'clock came every evening and rose from his chair to announce, "I'm going to bed now." Before the Lemkes knew it, he had undressed, said his prayers, and was fast asleep.

He said his prayers aloud, reciting a litany all his own: the Lord's Prayer, followed by prayers from his church and churches where he had visited. To close, he prayed for all the people he knew.

May taught Leslie a prayer that seemed to speak for his own existence. He liked to recite it for visitors.

> *Dear Lord,*
> *I hold in my thoughts today*
> *The good health and happy things*

*I wish in my own future.*
*I call upon the limitless power*
*Of my Creator.*
*My body expresses that power.*
                              *Amen.*

Leslie's morning routine was as predictable as bedtime. At seven o'clock he got up, went to the bathroom, dressed himself, and arrived in the kitchen for breakfast.

As Leslie's progress continued, the special times—birthdays, Christmas, visits with relatives—took on more significance.

On his birthday, January 31, Leslie always had his favorite cake, topped with whipped cream and strawberries. As he matured he appreciated more fully the gifts of candy, clothing, books, or records.

Weddings and church services were an adventure, because Leslie always assumed he was there to play the piano. At one family wedding the friends and relatives were going through the receiving line when they heard music—loud music! Nobody knew how Leslie had done it, but he had found a piano and was playing and singing at the top of his voice.

By 1975 the Lemkes felt confident enough to fly with Leslie to Arizona, to visit May's son and family. May and Joe prepared Leslie for the flight by explaining how he would be going up in the air. It might feel strange at times, they warned. Leslie was a model passenger, enjoying the snacks and the special attention he received from the stewardesses.

When they landed and were met by May's son, Leslie said, "Oh, it was awful! We were thirty thousand feet in the air!"

"He heard the pilot say that," May laughed. "That boy doesn't miss anything!"

Leslie was reluctant when May took him to the strange bed in her son's home that night.

"This isn't my bed," he told his mother.

"No, love, this isn't your bed." She took his hands and let him feel the mattress. "But we're visiting now, and you've got to get used to another bed. So just do like you do at home. Take off your clothes, get into your pajamas, and go to bed." Leslie obediently went to bed and fell asleep at once.

During their visit they decided to go shopping in Mexico on a Sunday morning. Shortly before they reached the border, May saw a tiny church on a hill. "Let's stop there and go to church," she suggested.

They drove up to the church to find that it was filled with Indians and Mexicans. May asked the minister if he would like to have a blind and retarded boy play and sing for his people.

"I'd be delighted," the minister said. "These people don't speak much English, but they sure know what music is!" The minister led Leslie to the piano, and he played a few hymns. The people sat spellbound, tears rolling down their faces.

When the service was over, people congregated around the Lemkes to thank them for coming. An old Indian woman approached May shyly. "I haven't been to church in twenty years," she said in broken English, "but something kept telling me to come today." She reached out and took May's hands in her own. "I'm so glad I came today, my dear lady, because I feel like I've just seen a miracle."

The Lemkes also began taking Leslie out to eat occasionally. Knowing that some people are offended by disabled people, May frequently made a public announcement before they sat down.

"Folks," she said, "I'd like to talk to you a few minutes. I have brought a blind, spastic, and retarded boy here today. He has to eat with his fingers, and he has every right to eat his own way. That's the only way he can learn to do things for himself. I have to feed him occasionally, but he's very polite, and he eats and drinks nicely. He never spills anything, and he won't annoy any of you. But if you think it will bother you, you might rather sit across the room."

There were times when she had to take Leslie in the ladies room; she simply made a similar announcement and walked on in. "You'll have to excuse me, ladies," she called out, "but I'm bringing in a blind, unfortunate boy who needs a little help."

One fall evening in 1980 Joe and May were sitting by the lake, reminiscing over the years.

"Think of it, May. In a few months Leslie will be twenty-nine," Joe mused.

"Do you remember what he looked like, Joe? You know, the day the nurse brought him."

They were both silent, locked together in the memory of that helpless, forlorn-looking infant. "He's going to die anyway," the nurse had said so matter-of-factly. "He's going to die. How could anything live, looking like that?"

May suddenly straightened. Enough looking back. She learned long ago not to look back. If she let herself live in the past, she'd go crazy. The war, the explosion, the deaths, leaving her mother, the fire, the tornado. You have to put those things out of your mind.

"Joe!"

Now Joe sat up. "What is it, May?"

"Leslie's not through learning yet, you know." Her old voice was back, with the familiar high, sharp staccato. "I've got a lot more things planned for him. I want to teach him to spell, to print his name, to open a door by himself, to get in a car. . . ." She went on and on.

Joe smiled to himself. "Do you really think he can do all those things, May?"

"Well, we can't give up, you know. How do we know what might come next?"

She looked up at the sky. It was clear, with a full moon and a panorama of stars.

"It's like waiting for Jesus," she said. "We don't know when He's coming, but we never quit waiting for Him. It's that way with Leslie. We don't know when it's coming, or what's coming. But we know it always does, don't we, Joe?"

# Chapter 10

## *The Savant Syndrome*

While Leslie enthralled me with his musical precocity, he also piqued my interest in his rare, somewhat elusive condition known by the unfortunate name *idiot savant*. The term, which originated in France about seventy-five years ago, is an irritant to readers, viewers, and parents of the retarded—including May Lemke, as I soon discovered.

When the term appeared in my *Milwaukee Journal* story on the Lemkes, one annoyed reader wrote:

> The Journal's beautiful story on Leslie Lemke, the brain-damaged boy who plays music by ear, was spoiled by only one thing—a psychiatrist's characterization of Leslie's condition as "idiot savant."
>
> Why is it that doctors cannot see how cruel and prejudicial it is to use such terms as "mongolism" instead of "Down's syndrome," or "gargoylism" instead of "Hurler's or Hunter's syndrome," or "idiot" instead of "brain-damaged" or "retarded?"

I decided to visit Dr. Darold Treffert, the psychiatrist who had been the source of my story. We had talked only by telephone, and I wanted to know more about Leslie's condition, more than a simple definition.

Face to face with Dr. Treffert, I found a trim, casually dressed young man who looked as if he had just graduated from medical school. I discovered he had been practicing psychiatry for twenty years.

"Can't we call this phenomenon something besides *idiot savant?*" I began. "That term is extremely offensive, you know, to parents of retarded children."

He nodded in agreement. "It's an unfortunate term. I'm all in favor of dropping it for *savant syndrome*. The word *savant* means 'knowledgeable,' and the term is used to describe a person who has an area of subnormal intelligence with spectacular islands of intelligence. In other words, that person likely will display unusual aptitudes or brilliance in some special field, incongruous with the rest of his mental abilities."

Dr. Treffert told me that only a handful of such cases are reported in scientific literature, although obviously all cases have not been written up. Neither have they been studied in any depth, he added, although it has been established that male savants far outnumber females.

"What kind of skills do they have?" I asked. "Are they all musical or do they have other abilities?"

"Most often, they excel in either mathematics or music," Dr. Treffert explained, "but other talents show up as well." He listed some specific skills: calendar calculation (the ability to tell the day of the week of a particular date in any year), mathematical computation (usually done without paper and pencil with amazing rapidity), sensational powers of recall, mechanical ability, and exceptional ability in art.

He cited some cases he had observed in his own practice over the years. One was a boy who could calculate exactly where to stand for shots in basketball. He was able to throw the ball endlessly and rarely miss a basket. "Some professional basketball team could have used him!" Dr. Treffert said, laughing.

Then there was the boy who studied the Milwaukee bus schedule until he had it memorized. "If you told him the time of day and the bus number, he could tell you the corner where you would be standing to catch that particular bus," Dr. Treffert related.

"Why did he pick a bus schedule to memorize?" I asked. "Could he have done the same thing with an encyclopedia or a dictionary?"

"That's one of the things we don't know. Maybe it was happenstance—he just picked up the right piece of literature and really zeroed in."

Dr. Treffert went on to describe a case of mathematical manipulation. This particular savant could stand in front of a fast-moving train and add the numbers of the cars instantly. He came up with the correct total every time.

Later, at the library, I read of a case where a man used this same ability in a different way. He was taken to the theater and later stunned his host by commenting, not on the performance, but on the exact number of words spoken by the actors and the number of steps taken by the dancers.

I spent most of an afternoon on that trip to the library, poring over some fascinating studies of this small but remarkable psychological group.

I found that two of the most publicized savants are identical twins named Charles and George (last names were not included) who, although clearly re-tarded in most areas, are geniuses when it comes to calendar calculations. They can rattle off the years in which a given date will fall on a Sunday or which month in a given year commences on a Monday. They can identify in almost an instant the day of the week for dates as far in the future as A.D. 7000 or for dates hundreds of years in the past.

I also read of a Boston woman who was tested in 1970 and found to have phenomenal music history abilities. She could identify the period in which vir-tually any piece of music was written and play any composer's tune as if it had been written by another, in addition to reciting extensive information about music *per se*.

Few savants have managed to use their talents to become self-supporting. One who did is a Japanese artist named Yoshihiko Yamamoto. Despite an IQ of 40 and speech and hearing impairments, Yamamoto has become a nationally known artist.

I had more questions for Dr. Treffert. "What causes this strange phenomenon? Where do savants get this spectacular island of intelligence that we're talking about?"

"Again, we don't know enough about the human mind to really understand the phenomenon," Dr. Treffert responded, "but several theories have been explored in an attempt to explain its existence."

He pointed out that one of the most recent theories concerns the dominant and nondominant hemi-spheres of the brain. According to this hypothesis, in savants the dominant hemisphere of the brain has been affected, while the nondominant hemisphere has been left relatively intact. The dominant (the left hemisphere in a right-handed person) measures intelligence, verbal skills, and speech; the nondominant is associated with music and abstract ability.

Another theory suggests that savant syndrome is the result of a selective area of the brain being spared from the injury that caused the general loss of mental capacity. Either through constant exercise of this one functioning area, or perhaps because it is the only area to receive and process outside sensations normally, its ability to perform is greatly enhanced. The principle is the same as in a blind person who has developed extraordinary hearing to compensate for lack of sight.

Organic factors play an important role in the latter theory. Currently, some psychologists are looking outside environmental influences for the pieces to the puzzle of the brain's protein chemistry.

In my reading on the savant syndrome I had come across the expression *computer brain* several times. I thought of Leslie hearing a song once and recording it instantly in his memory. I thought of the hundreds, perhaps even thousands, of songs that he can recall instantly and play.

I asked Dr. Treffert if he thought computer brain an apt description.

"Normally man has a phenomenally creative and abstractive ability," he replied. "We can create, we can abstract, we can think, we can dream, but we have a very poor memory. A computer has a phenomenal memory, but that's all it is. When we refer to a computer brain, we're saying that the brain develops greatly in the area of memory, but it never broadens the scope of its abilities. There is depth, but little breadth.

"The savant syndrome is characterized by a narrowing down—a funneling effect—of the kind of abilities that get deeper but never spread. There is very little generalization of those abilities. This is, of course, in sharp contrast to a normal genius, who has intellectual abilities in many areas and talent spread over a broad spectrum."

Dr. Treffert explained that people like Leslie, with exceptional musical ability, are unable to learn to play their instruments by reading music.

"What about people who learn music by ear?" I asked. "They don't read music, either."

"But they can if they choose to," Dr. Treffert said. "Playing by ear is a talent, like knowing how to draw, but people with that talent also can learn to read music. A savant can't."

I was always intrigued by the way Leslie listened to music. Sometimes he looked as if he were sleeping. Other times he assumed an expression of great seriousness. Often he shielded his eyes or face with one hand. What would have been distractions for others did not bother him.

One afternoon I took my children to visit the Lemkes. Lynn, my oldest daughter, played a song that Leslie had never heard. While she played and Leslie listened, the rest of us in the room continued our conversation, making no effort to lower our voices. When Lynn was finished, Leslie moved over to the piano and played the same piece. With *no* mistakes!

"In all my years of practice," Dr. Treffert said, "I have never come across a case with such an incredible musical ability. What makes it even more striking is that Leslie is also blind and suffers from cerebral palsy."

It occurred to me that I had been so involved researching the savant syndrome condition, I almost had overlooked the cerebral palsy.

I read in my medical encyclopedia that cerebral palsy is a condition that affects the brain centers having to do with muscular control, *cerebral* meaning "brain-centered" and *palsy* meaning "paralysis." People with cerebral palsy have a great deal of trouble controlling their muscles. They sometimes are afflicted with chorea (involuntary jerking movements) or a slow, writhing type of constant movement, chiefly in the fingers, along with poor sense of balance, tremor, and spastic muscles.

I tried to relate the definition to Leslie. He has a poor sense of balance and muscle spasms. He still can't walk more than a step or two alone without grasping for something to hang onto. Maneuvering food or a cup to his mouth requires a great deal of concentration and effort, and he is unable to use a fork or spoon. He is also unable to use a cane or to learn braille.

I talked with Dr. Rona Alexander, director of a cerebral palsy project in Milwaukee. She said classifying specifically the type of cerebral palsy Leslie has is very difficult without evaluating him. There is a considerable range in both the severity and the symptoms of cerebral palsy. It is not a single condition, but rather a group of conditions with a common denominator: some form of injury to motor control centers in the brain.

"What are the causes of cerebral palsy?" I asked.

She listed a few possibilities: birth injuries, infections of the mother and the embryo, problems in natural development. "But the causes really haven't been established, except for the fact that there is always some cut-off of oxygen to the brain, causing brain damage," Dr. Alexander added.

I was surprised to learn that the incidence of cerebral palsy has decreased significantly in the past twenty years. "What is responsible for this?" I asked.

"Partly the development of the rubella vaccine, which virtually has eliminated German measles, a common cause of cerebral palsy," Dr. Alexander explained. "Other factors are better prenatal care, improved neonatal conditions, more sophisticated equipment, better nutrition, and greater understanding of drugs."

I told Dr. Alexander how May had warned me not to come on too strong the first time I met Leslie.

"Absolutely true," she said. "Many cerebral palsied people are hypersensitive to stimulation. They should be approached slowly in order that they may be forewarned. When touching or shaking their hand, a firm, slow, steady kind of touch is recommended—not so light that it tickles but firm enough to give them some feeling.

"Body placement also can be threatening to a person with cerebral palsy. We suggest not approaching the person too fast or leaning over them. Because of Leslie's blindness, a person really ought to speak first before approaching him."

One of the things I had noticed about Leslie in the year I had known him was the improvement in his speech. "When I first met Leslie," I said to Dr. Treffert one afternoon, "his vocabulary consisted of yes and no. But now he answers many of the questions I ask. He seems to be developing a larger vocabulary and to be answering more intelligently."

Dr. Treffert agreed that from what May had described, a generalization had been occurring with Leslie in the past year. "His abilities do seem to be spreading out. As I said earlier when we discussed the computer brain, this does not often occur.

"The most logical explanation for this is May Lemke herself. Since most of our savants are in institutions, the care and example of the Lemkes is a rarity."

He used a tripod to demonstrate his point. "You see, for the savant the first leg of the tripod is the limitation. The second leg is an area from which he gets a lot of reinforcement—positive "strokes." In Leslie's case, this area is his music, of course. The third leg, which so often is missing, is a person in that child's life who is motivating—one who will look beyond the limitations to find the one or two areas of intactness or beauty and zero in on them."

*Looking beyond the limitations.* That phrase reminded me of something I couldn't quite grasp. Then I knew. May had said it one day so matter-of-factly that I always would remember it.

"We've always tried to treat Leslie like a normal child," she said. "Joe and I never worried much about what was wrong with him. We just tried to teach him to do whatever he could do. And whatever he couldn't do, we did."

But Dr. Treffert was speaking. "You know, we have something here that is far beyond an interesting scientific story. This is the incredible story of an amazing woman and her unshakable belief in her foster son. The story of an extraordinary, dedicated mother who, with a great deal of love, concern, care, effort, and patience, has worked with this youngster. It's really a melding of these two circumstances—Leslie's condition and May's care—that makes this story unique."

I half-wondered where Leslie would be today had it not been for May—or May had it not been for Leslie. Strange, I couldn't imagine one without the other. Or the two without Joe—silent, steady, faithful Joe. The balance wheel.

"Without May, Leslie might have been presented as some sort of oddity. But May has turned his story into one of inspiration. She has overshadowed the scientific elements and turned us all into believers.

"She is so enthusiastic, so bubbly, so full of belief that she makes everyone else believe in Leslie. She is also very humble. She says, 'It's not me. It's Leslie.' That's what motivation is all about. You can't motivate anybody without believing in them. When you do believe in them, you cause them to believe in themselves.

"This case ought to be presented as a scientific study somewhere. . . . Yet, maybe it shouldn't be. There is always the risk that scientific analysis might rob it of its beauty. And that would, indeed, be a tragedy."

# Chapter 11

## *The Concert Circuit*

It was inevitable that Leslie would one day be led out of his tiny enclosed porch onto the concert stage. But six years passed—years of playing and singing for visitors who came to the Lemke home as well as performances at nursing homes, hospitals, and churches—before his first formal concert in 1974.

Leslie's first recitals were held right on the porch of the Lemke home. Word spread quickly throughout the small community that something had happened on Pewaukee Lake. Friends, ministers, doctors, children, and townspeople hurried over to see and hear May Lemke's "miracle."

One day an old man came to the door and asked if Leslie could sing "The Old Rugged Cross." The time was close to Easter. May invited him in, and Leslie played the hymn.

Tears streamed down the old man's face. As he left, he said, "If God ever showed His presence, it was here today, hearing that boy sing."

On one of their hospital visits, a nurse came down to the central lounge. She had been tending a patient who was going to die, and he wished to see Leslie. They brought the man in on a long stretcher and moved him right up next to the piano. He asked Leslie to sing "A Closer Walk With Thee." When the song was over, the man was crying, and he reached out to hold Leslie's hands.

He died two days later.

Leslie's first public concert, at the 1974 Waukesha County Fair, was more like a "happening." Headlines boasted he drew the largest crowd ever assembled at the county exposition grounds.

I talked about the Lemkes one afternoon with Stance Bergelin, community education coordinator for the Fond du Lac County Department of Social Services. He mentioned attending that first concert.

"What was it like?" I asked. I had read the account in the *Waukesha Freeman* and had wondered if the concert was really all that fantastic.

"It was absolutely incredible!" he said, without a moment's hesitation. "I knew Leslie was retarded and handicapped, but I had no idea how severely until I saw him. He had to be led over to the piano, and he was wobbling, his sense of balance was so bad. He sat kind of slumped over at the keyboard.

"Then his mother spoke to him, and he started to play. It was as if someone had turned on a switch. From the moment he started singing he had the audience in the palm of his hand. The ballads that he sang brought tears to the eyes of the audience. His amazing imitations of Tiny Tim and Louis Armstrong prompted rounds of standing cheers, applause, and laughter.

"The audience absolutely did not want to leave. He had standing ovations after each number and he was brought back for two encores. It was an unbelievable experience."

After the County Fair, the Lemkes continued to perform sporadically for small groups in and around Pewaukee—churches, schools, women's clubs, and civic organizations.

In June of 1980, Stance Bergelin invited the Lemkes to perform at a large, well-publicized benefit for foster parents in Fond du Lac. Like the County Fair in 1974, the concert was another unforgettable evening of applause, encores, and for the first time, television cameras.

"I called a television station, requesting that a reporter and cameraman be sent to the concert," Bergelin recalled. "They agreed to come but made it clear they had only fifteen minutes of shooting time. Once they started interviewing the Lemkes, they got so excited, they stayed for an hour and a half!"

That night marked the Lemkes' foray into television. A brief segment from the concert was shown on the ten o'clock news.

The concert was attended by more than four hundred people, who couldn't get enough of Leslie Lemke.

"When it was over, people just would not leave," Bergelin said. "They gave him a standing ovation. Leslie played more. Another standing ovation. Leslie played again. People wouldn't let him quit! My contract expired at 9:30 P.M., and I almost had to throw people out!"

The more I heard about these Lemke concerts, the more I wanted to go to one. I had been interviewing

May for several weeks, and after our tapings, I always was entertained with a short performance. I had brought my family and a few friends to hear Leslie, but I had not yet attended a real concert, one of those "Evenings With Leslie Lemke."

I learned from May that Leslie's next concert was Sunday night at Atonement Luthern Church in the neighboring town of Muskego.

My husband Lee and I arrived early that night. As we walked into the church vestibule, Lee grabbed my arm and pointed me in the direction of a large bulletin board. "Hey, how about that?" he grinned. "What's it like to be a celebrity?"

There was my story from the *Milwaukee Journal*, and over it, in huge black letters, read the words, *Have you ever seen a miracle? Come and hear Leslie Lemke on Sunday night at 7 P.M.*

Inside the sanctuary we were astounded at how many people were already there. We had to settle for seats near the back. We sat down, joining an audience that was not talking, just waiting. A feeling of expectancy was in the air.

People now were pouring in. The pews were filled, so chairs were hastily assembled for additional seating. Those who came in last had to fend for themselves. The pastor's wife walked onto the platform and told of the amazing Lemkes, May's love and devotion, and the power of God working in their behalf. Then she introduced her guests.

I was wondering where they would enter when something came flying down the aisle, long full skirts swishing and swirling everywhere. Without even looking, I knew May Lemke had arrived. She was waving now, thanking everyone for coming and asking where they were all from in that clipped British accent I had grown to know so well.

Coming along behind in measured steps and utter contrast were Joe and Leslie: Joe in front, walking ever so slowly with Leslie behind, both hands holding on tightly to Joe's shoulders.

The audience rose, almost as one person, slowly and solemnly. Then suddenly, as if the emotions of the crowd had just caught up with the events, the people broke into a thunderous ovation, applauding until Leslie was seated safely at the piano and May obviously was ready to begin. The audience sat down reluctantly, wanting this gesture not to diminish in any way their admiration for the young man who already had won every heart and evoked a good many tears.

While Leslie sat hunched over the piano, waiting quietly, May chattered excitedly about her years with him, what raising him during those years was like and how she had worked with him and prayed for him.

She was a whirlwind in miniature as she dashed around the stage, pointing, pausing, demonstrating—serious for one moment, joking the next. Joe sat quietly in the background while Leslie waited for his cue.

"I believe in Jesus Christ, and I expected Him to do something for Leslie," she was saying. "After all, I prayed to Him over and over again, day after day. I think I was getting to be a real nuisance. 'Lord,' I prayed, 'You said everybody has a talent. Won't you please do something for Leslie? He has no eyes, no voice, no nothing.'

"And after that, the miracle came.

"Play it for them, Leslie," she went on, "what you played that night."

You could hear a collective gasp from the audience as Leslie's fingers struck those first few chords—such fullness of sound, such inexplicable skill. By the end of his powerful, brilliant rendition of Tchaikovsky's piano concerto, we were all believers.

"Well, He finally gave Leslie a gift, didn't He?" May said after the first number. "He really knocked me off my feet. But isn't it wonderful how God answers prayers and takes care of us?

"Now, would you like to hear Leslie do some imitations?" Of course we would. Leslie broke us up with impersonations of Louis Armstrong, Jimmy Durante—and Jeannette McDonald and Nelson Eddy, where he sang *both* parts!

Next he played his own favorites, "I Believe" and "I Was Nobody's Baby But I'm Somebody's Baby Now." He did an Italian aria, a German waltz, an Irish folk tune, and "The Entertainer" from the movie *The Sting.* I looked at the faces around me and saw emotions change as quickly as the tempo: tears to laughter, laughter to looks of incredulity.

"Leslie never needs a microphone," May broke in. "He's such a powerful singer. And you know, you can sing or play anything to him and he'll sing it right back to you, only a whole lot better!

"Who would like to hear something?" she called out.

Hands shot up.

" 'Moonlight Sonata.' "

" 'How Great Thou Art.' "

" 'Hello, Dolly.' "

*"Ave Maria."*

" 'Bridge Over Troubled Waters.' "

He played them all. "Can you play something by Mozart?" someone asked. "Do you know any marches by John Philip Sousa?" said another. May looked as surprised as anyone when he came up with the right song. One man only hummed a tune. Leslie refreshed his memory—and played the song in full harmony.

A little girl stood up. "Leslie, can you play 'Puff, the Magic Dragon'?" While Leslie played, Joe collected all the kids in the audience and led them through the room in a conga line, up and down the aisles. After that, May told Leslie to perform a couple of commercials for the kids. He mimicked the Electrolux vacuum cleaner ad and a spot for Hush Puppy shoes. The children—young and old—loved it.

May and Joe jumped up and swayed to a couple of waltzes, then May did a solo production while Leslie played a hand-clapping, foot-stomping number. She also enticed the audience into several sing-alongs on some of the old favorites. I had the feeling we were at a good old-time movie, and nobody wanted it to end. I saw no one yawning or looking at their watches or fidgeting in their seats. There was rapt attention all the way.

When May was ready to wrap things up, she had Leslie play his beautiful, highly emotional rendition of "The Lord's Prayer," followed by "God Be With You Till We Meet Again."

Another standing ovation, except this time the applause did not die down. Everyone wanted more. Finally the pastor's wife announced that coffee and cookies were being served in the basement. She also said there was a piano below, so "perhaps Leslie would play a little longer during refreshments." More applause.

When my husband and I joined the crowd in the basement, the Lemkes already were surrounded. Questions were asked that May had answered a hundred times before. "Why were his eyes taken out?" "How can he play the piano that way?" "Where does he learn all those songs?" The questions tumbled all over one another, hopelessly interrupting each other.

After a minute to eat a few cookies, Leslie was led to the piano again. In no time people were crowded three deep, four deep, and more, calling out other requests. Leslie complied, loving every minute of it. Finally May managed to bring the evening to a close, but not without a great deal of reluctance from both Leslie and his admirers.

"What do you think the attraction is?" Lee asked as we got in the car. "Can you explain it?"

"No, I can't," I admitted, "and I've sure never seen anything like it. I've never, *never* seen that kind of emotion—the love that emanated from that audience."

We sat silently for a few moments, lost in our own thoughts. Lee hadn't even started the car.

"Somebody tried to explain it to me once," I offered. "Let's see. I think it was Stance Bergelin, the first time I met him. We were talking about the Lemkes and he said, 'You know, I have worked with Paul Harvey, Robert Schuller, Bob Hope, and many others. But I have never seen people respond the way they do to the Lemkes.

" 'I have sat on that stage with them and seen people really open up. It's as if we finally drop that big guard we all carry around twenty-four hours a day, and we see people for who they are. It's beautiful—beautiful—the way he reaches people. Like anything of value, you can't really explain it. It's like trying to verbalize the beauty of a rose. You just can't do it. That's the way a lot of people feel about Leslie.' "

That made me feel better. *He* couldn't explain it either.

"Lee, Bergelin says another question that often comes up is whether Leslie has any understanding of what he sings. Bergelin and Dr. Treffert discussed that once, and both felt he must have some understanding. Otherwise how could he sing with so much meaning, so much emphasis? When Leslie sings, people *feel* the meaning, the intensity, the emotion of the song. So where does it come from, if not from him?"

I decided to follow up on Leslie's concerts. I soon realized that each was different: a different audience, different requests, different messages from May. The two aspects they all had in common was May's pride in Leslie and May's love for Jesus Christ.

"A lot of you go around saying you're lonely and there's no love in your life," she said to a group of parents. "Then get yourself a foster child or a new baby and you'll have all the love you need. You'll have plenty to keep you busy, too!

"Look at Leslie. Sometimes I have worked twenty-four hours a day with that child. I never left him. I never neglected him, because he needed that love.

"He couldn't let me see it, but how could I know

*May's Boy*

what was inside of him? We can't ever give up on our handicapped children. Who knows what they can become?''

Then she turned to the subject of institutions, and I saw fire in her eyes.

''We don't need institutions! We need *foster mothers*. Those poor little crippled and retarded children need *mothers* to love them. They need the feel of a mother's body.

''Go into some of those institutions and see the children lying all over the floor, dirty and helpless. Nothing to do. No one to love them. Is this the way we're supposed to treat God's children? Why did He put them on earth? They're here for us to love—a way for us to learn the many lessons we must learn. 'Love ye one another as I have loved you,' Jesus said. If we can show love for these unfortunate children, we can show love to anybody.''

Leslie's itinerary at that time included a concert in front of five hundred teenagers. ''I can't miss that one,'' I laughed. ''I want to see you handle five hundred kids, May!''

May was more than up to the task. A tiny bundle of energy, she flitted all over the stage.

''Children,'' she began, with her characteristic bluntness, ''I brought you a miracle today: my boy, who is blind, spastic, and retarded. He's going to play and sing for you.

''Look at him and then look at yourselves—how beautiful and talented you are. And just see how much better you can do. There is no need for any of you to be failures. Ever.

''I brought Leslie here because he's never had

much fun in his life. He's never had much of anything. But now he has something, and he's going to give it to you. So let's all join in and sing with him and have a little bit of fun together. Let's make Leslie happy."

The kids loved him. They clapped and sang and stomped and called out requests and had a glorious time.

An opera singer who recently had escaped from Russia by way of Germany happened to be in the audience. He asked to sing a German song for Leslie. When he finished, Leslie, who had never heard the song before, sang it back to him. The kids were astounded, and so was I.

Then the gentleman asked Leslie to sing "The Impossible Dream." Leslie did, and most of us were wiping away the tears.

Of all the concerts Leslie does, I think I like the children's concerts best. The children are so open, so wide-eyed, so spontaneous. At one of these concerts, a small boy asked what had happened to Leslie's eyes, a common question.

"They were scooped right out," May said. "And just think of all the nice things you can see. You can read and write and this boy can't do any of those things. Just think how privileged you are to have a beautiful pair of eyes."

An adorable little girl ran up to May with tears streaming down her face. "Doesn't Leslie have any eyes at all? Can I look?"

May opened one of his eyelids and said, "You see, no eyes at all."

May told the children not to forget to pray for all

the blind children in the world when they said their prayers that night. "And there are many retarded children who can't talk, and crippled children who can't run around," she continued. "We, the able ones, are here on this earth to do like Jesus did. Our duty is to look after them and to love them. That's one reason Jesus came: to teach us to love one another."

At another concert, a child asked, "Well, where is God? I never see Him around."

I found May's answer simple yet eloquent. She held out her hands. "Look at your hands," she said. "There is God's creation. The greatest tool on earth— a pair of hands. The grass growing. That reflects God. The trees and flowers. God is there. The fruit on the trees. There is no place on earth where you can look without seeing God."

May also loves to talk about America to the children. As I think about her own childhood, the war, the hunger, the explosion, tears well up in my eyes.

"You know, children," she said, "I have been in many other countries in my life, but nowhere in the world have I seen a country like America.

"Look at what a wonderful school you have, a wonderful way of living, a mother and father and a nice home. I had a lovely home, too, but the war came along and destroyed it all. I was shipped over to this country to marry a man I'd never met, but he loved me and he was a good man.

"And even when I was left alone, I didn't go around moping. I just went out and did the things I knew I ought to do."

When both parents and children are present, May frequently asks the children if they'd like to sit up front. Many of them do. At a church concert, a little boy went up to the rostrum and asked, "Please, Mrs. Lemke, could Leslie play 'Jesus Loves Me'?"

"Of course he can, dear. And Jesus surely does love you." The child stood awestruck by the piano as Leslie played and sang.

May turned to the three hundred parents who filled the church. "Okay, parents. Now it's your turn. When a little boy can come up like this and say 'Jesus loves me,' I want you all to let him know how much Jesus loves you." So while the boy stood watching, we all sang "Jesus Loves Me." It was a precious moment.

I think one of the most enthusiastic and touching responses the Lemkes have ever received was at the Children's Home in Milwaukee. The children adored Leslie. They were calling out songs, singing, and dancing. May clearly loved and believed in every one of them.

"I wish I could play like Leslie," one small boy said to May. "My mother always wanted me to learn music."

"Then start right here," May said to him emphatically. "Somebody might be able to teach you, and then when you go home you can play and sing for your mother."

When it was time to leave, the children would hardly let them go. They hugged and kissed May until she kidded, "Now children, don't be too rough with me. I have to have something left to get out of here!"

One of them said, "Oh, Mrs. Lemke, please don't go back to Hollywood!"

May burst out laughing. "Hollywood? I've never

been there, and I'm never going. I'm staying right here where I belong!"

I suppose the toughest concert experience for me took place at the Veterans Hospital in Milwaukee. May's own eyes were pools of tears as they wheeled in a number of badly wounded men. When Leslie played the poignant "Over There," I could almost feel the torment going through her.

"Here I am," she said, "a little war baby. I've gone through it, too, so I know something about what you're feeling. I was battered from head to foot in an explosion in England. I wasn't anything to look at, at all."

But this was a concert, not a wake. As soon as May had established her credentials, she switched moods. "We'll push all that aside now. Come on, boys. Tell Leslie what you want to hear. He'll play anything you want!"

As Leslie's reputation grew, so did requests for concerts. With a musical repertoire that included everything from classical to ragtime, there was no group that Leslie could not accommodate. He played for realtors, physicians, senior citizens, conventions, and correctional homes, as well as for weddings and anniversaries.

One of the largest concerts was for two thousand senior citizens in Milwaukee County. Joe Fibeger, organizer of the event, said it was the best attended program ever sponsored for the group. "They swarmed around the piano afterwards, wanting to hear more from that incredible boy. Everyone was talking about the Lemkes. I had chills up and down my spine. It was unbelievable!"

Bob Ripp, a real estate executive, invited the Lemkes to perform for more than three hundred realtors at an annual motivational breakfast.

"Leslie was totally different from any program we had had in the past," Ripp said. "But I had seen him on television and thought, 'If that boy can achieve what he has, each of us has tapped only a fraction of our own potential.' "

Instead of the traditional introduction, Ripp showed tapes of Leslie from a television show. "When I brought him out, there was a standing ovation and not a dry eye anywhere.

"I had it planned how I was going to handle everything. But of course, I had never operated with May Lemke before. The moment I introduced her, I lost control. She was flying all over the stage, hiding behind me, cutting up with the audience, totally in charge. I finally did what everybody else does. I sat back and enjoyed the concert! May never lost the audience for a second. She bowled them over.

"It was the most gloriously successful thing we'd ever done. The impact was tremendous. We always ask for evaluations, but we never got them like we did from that program. People were unable to express their feelings. It was absolutely incredible!"

The Lemkes frequently perform in concerts supporting foster parents, pro-life causes, and handicapped children. Stance Bergelin, who promotes some of these appearances, said, "I invite the Lemkes because I like to show foster parents a real accomplishment. I'm not saying, 'Hey, this can happen to you,' because it's too rare. Most foster parents work terribly hard and see little accomplishment. But I like to show them something that did happen under the most extraordinary circumstances.

"There's no question that the Lemkes are motivating. They seem to instill the belief in people that we can all be better than we are."

May believes strongly in the value of these concerts and will keep them up as long as people want to hear Leslie. "I think it's wonderful that Leslie can sing and play for people. In the dark days, they used to hide these children and never let them out of the house. They need to be noticed, just like normal children. Leslie loves the concerts, and he even loves getting there. He'll say, 'Oh, I'm going out in a car today.'

"There were years and years when he didn't go anyplace. We had to physically carry him everywhere. And now he can enjoy a bit of fun and give a little pleasure to others.

"What Leslie's doing is reaching out and doing God's work. I have scores of letters from people saying that Leslie has brought them closer to Jesus Christ. If you ask Leslie what music means to him, he says it means *love*.

"Everything I do is for Leslie and the retarded children. I don't want anything for myself. Nobody has to pay to see him.

"We're just plain people," she adds, looking at her foster son. "Nothing fancy. We just do what we have to do, don't we, love?"

# Chapter 12

## On to Television

Producers of Terry Meeuwsen's morning talk show, "A New Day," were busy making preparations for a five-day series of programs recognizing the handicapped. The series was to be called "A Special Week for Special People."

They signed up a physician to talk about adaptive physical education and an attorney to point out the legal rights of the handicapped. Two houseparents were called in to discuss group homes, while a director from Goodwill Industries was asked to describe the employment picture for the handicapped.

Executives from the Association for Retarded Citizens, Special Olympics, and other programs for the handicapped were scheduled to appear. A remote was taped at the office of the *Milwaukee Citizens Newspaper*, a local enterprise staffed with handicapped people. Other remotes were scheduled at Penfield Children's Center, the Curative Rehabilitation Center, and Pleasant View School for retarded children.

Four award-winning athletes from Special Olympics would be interviewed on Friday, the last day of the series. Who else could they feature on that day? Bud Reth, executive producer of the show, mentioned Leslie Lemke. "Who's Leslie Lemke?" Jill Bishop, associate producer, asked.

Bud explained that his wife, Marcia, had seen Leslie sing and play the piano six months earlier at a community concert in Jackson, Wisconsin, a small town near Milwaukee. The auditorium had been packed, and Leslie had received a fantastic response. Marcia, a teacher of the handicapped, had come away highly impressed with this blind, retarded musician.

Reth drove out to Pewaukee to meet the Lemkes. As soon as Leslie touched the piano keys, Reth knew he wanted him for the show. His viewers would not forget this guest for a long time! He asked the Lemkes to appear on the final segment on Friday, June 13, 1980.

That was the morning Terry came for our interview and told me about the Lemkes. I had not seen the show, but later, when I began interviewing the Lemkes, I called the studio to ask if I could see a tape of the program.

A few days later I curled up in an overstuffed chair in a darkened room at the studio and watched the tape.

The studio audience consisted of children who had competed in Special Olympics. Terry interviewed four handicapped children who had won medals in several different events. They squirmed in their places, fought off their shyness, and managed to speak a few sentences and answer a question or two.

There was a remote from the *Milwaukee Citizens* office, and more commercials; then at last Terry introduced the Lemkes.

Once again May talked about how she had worked with Leslie, her faith in Jesus Christ, and the miracle. Then Leslie played: the Tchaikovsky first, then "Hello, Dolly" and "Everything Is Beautiful"—all the crowd pleasers.

Terry had been right when she described the show. Emotions ran high. People were wiping away tears; the children sat transfixed. Terry's mouth was trembling and her eyes were full. Meanwhile Leslie played on, his spastic fingers flying over the keyboard, his powerful voice overflowing the studio.

People looked as if they were watching an illusion. Whoever heard of a boy, unable to walk by himself, barely able to talk, performing like that? But Leslie was no illusion. He was human, he was playing, and he was in control. No wonder everybody was crying. They'd been talking about the handicapped all week, and suddenly, here was Leslie, a severely retarded youngster who is brilliantly gifted. His very existence was uplifting.

The audience was almost as smitten with the tiny, elf-like lady who was hopping around, calling out to the children and telling fabulous stories about this remarkable son of hers who could sing and play anything he heard.

The appearance was the Lemkes' first on Milwaukee television, and according to the phone calls and letters that followed, they were clearly a hit.

The series won the Public Awareness Award in November of 1980 from the Association for Retarded

Citizens in Milwaukee County. Five months later, in April of 1981, the station received a second honor, Media of the Year, from the State Association for Retarded Citizens.

Terry Meeuwsen remembers the show well.

"People always seem to enjoy human interest features, but nothing we'd ever done had received attention or prompted a response like that of Leslie Lemke's appearance on our show. We were still receiving phone calls from viewers weeks later."

In dozens of different ways viewers described how they were moved by Leslie's appearance that Friday morning.

> What a beautiful testimonial to the indomitable spirit of a human being who was considered a vegetable and hopelessly retarded.

> I'm writing while I'm watching Leslie Lemke play the piano and sing. Thank you, Terry, for showing Milwaukee another miracle worker, May Lemke. Today is my thirty-ninth birthday, and no gift could make me happier than to have heard Leslie.

> Your program on June 13 was special!
> The Lemke family is special!
> And I feel special having had the opportunity to view such God-given talent!

> Friday's program on the Lemkes was the most touching thing I have ever seen on TV. If God places people on this earth to do His work, May Lemke has got to be one of them.

A few months later the *Milwaukee Journal* published its account of the Lemkes. The story was picked up by the Associated Press and appeared in newspapers all over the country. Letters and phone calls began arriving from Texas, New York, California, Hawaii, Utah, Tennessee, and dozens of other states. Some of them read as follows:

> This young man, in giving a private concert for his parents, is giving one of the few things he can give. But how beautiful it is! What beautiful people! What a beautiful story!

> Mother Teresa is my heroine and May Lemke is a close second!

> This loving, selfless woman has devoted her life to teaching a twenty-eight-year-old child whose eventual response might have been, in all probability, non-existent. Her rewards, in his special gift of music, are perhaps greater than the rest of us may ever know.

> Mrs. Lemke, your story brought joy to my life today. Your courage and love shine like a star.

And from an eleven-year-old boy:

> Dear Leslie,
> Mom saw the article in the newspaper and read it to me. It told that you can play anything you hear note per note on the piano.
> You see, I have cerebral palsy, too. I play the piano for Bible class and I play by ear, too. I am legally blind. I really like playing for people. I don't play classical music, but I play songs like Four Leaf Clover, Five Foot Two, Anniversary Walz [sic]. I also play Happy Birthday whenever there is a birthday celebration.
> I hope your Mom can read this to you.

Paul Harvey talked about the amazing Lemkes on his radio broadcast the following day. Local television stations hurried out to feature them on their evening news shows. And on December 19, 1980, Walter Cronkite introduced Leslie on his "CBS Evening News" with these words: "This is a season that celebrates a miracle, and this story belongs to the season. It's the story of a young man, a piano, and a miracle."

Leslie returned to Channel 4 and Terry Meeuwsen to tape a touching Christmas Eve special, "Leslie and Friends." It was a sentimental evening with Santa Claus, an audience of retarded children, music and dancing, a Christmas tree, and plenty of treats. The show was repeated on Christmas Day.

On January 18, 1981, the Lemkes were featured on a twenty-minute segment of the television show, "That's Incredible!" This was the show that, even more than Walter Cronkite's news broadcast, launched the Lemkes onto the national scene. "Of all the stories we've ever told," hostess Cathy Crosby said, "none has touched me as much as the Lemkes. Thank you, May."

The Lemkes discovered that taping a television segment is not quite like giving a concert. "It was a long, exhausting day," May remembers. "The camera crew came in the morning and didn't leave until nearly midnight. I was bringing out trays of cookies, nuts, bread, apples, pears, 7-Up, and candy all day!

"There were three or four cameramen and then a girl who asked all the questions. I don't know who she was. Well, they shifted furniture around, took pictures all over the house, told us to stand here, sit there, kneel over there. They even had cameras outside, pouring through the windows. It really was incredible!" May stops to chuckle at her pun. "We didn't get to bed until 2 A.M."

The show was beautifully, painstakingly, and tastefully done.

It began with close-ups of May feeding Leslie and talking about the tiny, helpless infant who was brought to her that day twenty-eight years ago. "I had a duty to do and I was going to do it, no matter what it cost me!" Then there were close-ups of Leslie, hands trembling as he lifted a glass of milk to his mouth with obvious effort.

Dr. Treffert gave a clear, concise explanation of savant syndrome; then May again. "I said to myself, 'This boy can't stand so I'm going to drag him around so he'll feel what I'm doing!'"

She talked about the piano and the miracle, then suddenly the room was filled with music: a magnificent concerto fashioned from the spastic fingers of that severely retarded boy. Incredible! With Leslie's music in the background, May told of falling on her knees, weeping and thanking God for the miracle. Leslie played on, reinforcing the reality and beauty of this miracle.

Next, May talked about the first time Leslie sang. Leslie confirmed that second miracle with a powerful rendition of "Everything Is Beautiful," followed by "You Light Up My Life."

Dr. Treffert was back then with another slant on the Lemke story: the incredible dedication of May Lemke—her love, concern, care, work, and patience—and the melding of the two circumstances—Leslie's disability with May's devotion.

May talked while Leslie sang a hymn in the background. "Leslie's gift is from God. It couldn't be from anywhere else. And I know that Jesus is going to do lots of things for Leslie."

Next was this exchange:

Interviewer: Leslie, what does music mean to you?
Leslie: Music means it's from the heart.
Interviewer: Does it mean love?
Leslie: Yes, love!
Interviewer: Show me with music what you mean by love.

Leslie sang "The Lord's Prayer" as the camera withdrew slowly from the tiny cottage. It was the end of the day and dark outside. A full moon glistened on the lake, and Leslie's rich, clear voice penetrated the stillness of the night.

May received an outpouring of mail following the program and another stack when the show was repeated three months later on April 27, 1981. She regrets that there was no way she could answer all the mail.

"I've been meaning to write a letter to 'That's Incredible!' and ask them to read it on the air. I wanted to say that I'm deeply grateful to all the people who sent the nice letters and that it's impossible for me to thank each one of them because I have too much to do with Leslie."

These are a few of the letters the Lemkes received:

It was such a pleasure to see Jesus Christ glorified on a television show. And He certainly was last night as Leslie Lemke sang and played "The Lord's Prayer."

I have never heard the "Our Father" sung so beautifully and with so much love and feeling. Leslie, you give handicapped people of the world courage and hope. When I get on my knees tonight, I will thank

God for smiling down on you and for reminding us through public television that He is always present in our lives.

I was so happy my whole family was home that night so my two sons, aged 14 and 19, could see that God is still performing miracles in this day and not only in Bible times. Please tell Leslie he plays heavenly and sings like an angel.

I've never been a particularly religious person, but after seeing Leslie's great talent and your great love, how can one not believe? It's people like you and families like yours that make this world a beautiful place to live.

Therese Martineau, a fourth grade religious education teacher in Dracut, Massachusetts, wrote that her class had been discussing handicapped people—how God chooses to give some people disabilities that they can't understand, but He also gives special gifts.

A few weeks later, most of the class saw Leslie Lemke on "That's Incredible!" They asked Mrs. Martineau if they could write letters to Leslie. Here are some of their thoughts, unedited:

It's amazing that you can play the piano when your handicapped. I heard you were on that's incredible and it is incredible. Your a real smart person.

We all have things we can do good and things we can do not so good. I play the clarinet good but I don't draw so good. I liked the story of your life. It makes me feel good.

I think you have many talents and I think you can increase them by yourself. I think you are the best piano player and singer in the world.

I admired your courage and enjoyed your singing and I loved the way you played the piano. You have a good mother and you should be glad to have her.

And from an eight-year-old boy to his mother after seeing Leslie on television: "Mom, if anything should ever happen to me, how could I give Leslie my eyes?"

# Chapter 13

## *A Plea for Understanding*

---

I was driving home from the Lemkes one afternoon when the thought struck me: What did I *really* know about mental retardation?

I had come to know Leslie Lemke, but what about all those other retarded people out there, the ones who don't sing or play the piano? What kind of lives do they lead? What do they feel? What is their future?

I called the Association for Retarded Citizens in Milwaukee County and was directed to John Wilberding, citizen advocacy coordinator. When I arrived a few days later for our appointment, John led me to a comfortable, freshly remodeled sitting room on the fourth floor of an old building in downtown Milwaukee.

About thirty years old, John proved to be a serious, no-nonsense activist, and his strong convictions filtered through our conversation loud and clear.

"Please don't refer to them as *the retarded*," he offered first off. "*Retarded* should be used as an adjective, never a noun. We're talking about people who just happen to have a particular characteristic: mental retardation. How can I look at any other aspect of that individual's personality if he's called a retardate?"

I'd never thought of that. I tried to recall my *Journal* story about Leslie Lemke. Had I used "retardate"? I couldn't remember. But I knew I'd be more careful next time.

Wilberding moved on. He objected to the notion that all retarded people are children. "Until seven years ago," he said, "the Association for Retarded Citizens was called the Association for Retarded Children. It took us twenty-five years to admit that retarded people are not children all their lives.

"Do you know," he said, "to this day, there are *children's* toys and *children's* pictures in our institutions and nursing homes? Naturally, the general public reacts to these people as children. Even parents of retarded children have difficulty changing their attitudes when their children become adults. They've been told consistently, often by our professionals, that their retarded children always will be children."

I thought of the dedication to my book that I had been mulling over. I had considered dedicating it "to Leslie Lemke, to my nephew, Mark Turcin, and to retarded children everywhere, who are indeed God's Special Children."

"I guess you wouldn't approve of that, would you?" I asked, knowing full well the answer.

A look of dismay came over his face. "Well, I guess you can dedicate it any way you wish, but besides the word 'children,' I object to 'special.' To me, 'special' has a note of condescension in it. The term suggests that this person needs to be cared for constantly.

Now, how can I see this person as a functioning human being with abilities, potential, and feelings if I'm calling him one of 'God's Special Children'?"

"But 'special' can mean favored, too. It can mean something positive," I ventured. After all, I had a stake in this.

"You're right, it can. But I like to get people in the mainstream to concentrate on their likenesses, not their differences. I don't like seeing them singled out as people to be pitied. But remember, these are only my opinions. Professionals don't agree on everything. Some support things like the Special Olympics; others don't."

I was beginning to enjoy the exchange. Wilberding might be a few years ahead of his time, but he was making me think. And that was exactly why I had come.

"Are you ready for more?" He sensed that I was sifting through his ideas, thinking them over.

"I'm ready," I said quickly. "Tell me, are there more of these myths and misconceptions? I'd like to hear about them."

"Fine. Let's start with 'mental age.' A retarded person may be thirty-five years old, but people ask, 'How old is he *really?*' If that person reads and writes at, say, a five-year-old level, it is assumed he will be five years old all of his life. But what about the thirty-five years of experience that person has? If he's lived that long, then he has the feelings and emotions of a thirty-five-year-old. He's not likely to remain at a five-year-old level emotionally if he is encouraged to progress and is challenged to be independent. Retarded people learn more slowly, of course, but they can continue to learn for all their lives. They don't stand still."

"You know," I said, "I think I've always had a tendency to lock them in, to assume that academically, maybe even emotionally, they were standing in cement. They didn't move. I never thought of them as having the same needs that I have: to grow, to learn, to change."

Equally annoying to Wilberding is the assumption that retarded people are dangerous. He pointed out that this error stems from the fact that so many of them are institutionalized.

"It goes like this," he said. "Most communities have a place somewhere, probably hidden out in the middle of a cornfield, where they put their retarded persons. The only other people who live like that are prisoners. And we all know prisoners have committed a crime and are dangerous.

"But retarded people have never committed a crime. They are in no way dangerous. Yet, they are incarcerated, where they don't need to be and don't want to be. In most cases, they could develop, grow, and contribute to society by being allowed to live in our communities. I find that pretty heavy discrimination."

I was beginning to be convinced. Obviously, there are misconceptions. And problems. "How then," I asked, "are attitudes changed if we're all so caught up in the myths?"

"Not by speeches and media coverage," he said. "I can spend a month talking with groups, discussing problems, answering questions, and suggesting solutions. I doubt that my efforts change more than one or two people in any one group.

"But if we have contact with a mentally retarded person, if we make an attempt to get to know him as a person, then our attitudes begin to change.

"There's a group home for retarded people across the street from where I live. When the idea was proposed, the neighbors were scared to death of it. Now, five years later, they have seen that the home is not a detriment. It has not ruined our neighborhood. It's an accepted part of our community. Neighbors have come to know these people. I could have talked about acceptance forever with little effect. People had to experience it and see for themselves. Now the attitudes have changed, and changed favorably."

Group homes. A fairly new concept in the area of mental retardation. The idea has stirred plenty of controversy around the Milwaukee area in the past couple of years, but I had read little about it.

"Those are only for the mildly affected, aren't they?" I guessed.

"Absolutely false," Wilberding asserted.

He pointed out that a number of people in group homes were diagnosed as severely retarded at one time. But given an opportunity to *do* something, rather than to sit around all day, their functioning ability can change dramatically. He added that eighty to ninety percent of the retarded population is only mildly retarded.

Before moving to Wisconsin, Wilberding, who was then single, worked in a group home in Michigan for seven and a half years. Half the people in that home were diagnosed as severely retarded, but they were able to do almost everything for themselves.

Sixteen people lived in Wilberding's household and everyone of them participated in the ongoing functions of the home. "Of course, we had problems," he said. "I don't know of any group of seventeen people living together who don't have problems. But we learned to work things out, and that's important. We must always keep in mind that these are individuals, just as your own children are individuals. There are those who learn to function more quickly than others. Some cook more easily, some learn to clean more easily. We all have our own areas of expertise."

Don't we all function better in a home, where we are free to make our own decisions and have some control over our lives? I shuddered at the thought of living in an institution and having my life regulated by other people. *How we prize our freedom,* I thought to myself.

"Another thing," Wilberding continued. "It seems to me the goal of some institutions is to keep people quiet and their emotions under control. In truth, many parents with a retarded child at home operate the same way. They walk around on eggshells so their retarded son or daughter won't get upset.

"But they allow their other children to get upset. Why the difference? A person who can't get mad, can't really be happy. He's just somewhere in the middle all the time, unable to experience the joy of living. This is another advantage of group homes. Retarded people are allowed to express their emotions. They cry, they laugh, they get angry. They aren't living in an emotional limbo."

Sometime earlier, I had seen a reference to a sheltered apartment. "Is that something like a group home?" I inquired.

"Somewhat, but it's even less restrictive. The apartment usually consists of five or ten units. Two people live together in each unit, and there is one apartment manager. This manager also provides whatever support the other residents need: assistance in budgeting money, advice on a personal problem, whatever. Ultimately, some retarded adults are able to move through the whole process: from an institution to a group home to a sheltered apartment and finally, to complete independence."

I discovered that community acceptance of retarded citizens varies greatly from state to state. Allegan County, Michigan, for example, with a population of one hundred thousand has forty-four group homes. Milwaukee County, on the other hand, with a population of one million, has twelve group homes. Other states like Nebraska now have people living in sheltered apartments who, only ten years ago, were expected to live out their entire lives in institutions.

"How about getting jobs?" I asked. "Does the resistance found in neighborhoods exist in the workplace?"

"Of course it does," Wilberding said emphatically. "That's why we've set up sheltered workshops." He acknowledged that some retarded adults need such workshops because they can't meet the expectations of competitive employment. But he added that many *can* grow and move on to a competitive job *if* given the opportunity.

"I suspect there are fewer and fewer jobs available to them," I observed. "After all, our society continues to become more complex."

"You're right. Mentally retarded people were probably better off in rural America, before farming became so mechanized. In an agrarian society, there was much more of a demand for unskilled tasks and farming jobs, where these people fit in more easily. As jobs have become more sophisticated, people who are the least able to keep up with technological changes stand out even more."

"What about young retarded adults leaving home when they're between eighteen and twenty like their brothers and sisters?" I had visited a couple who had recently found a group home for their eighteen-year-old retarded daughter. Mary was reluctant and fearful of leaving home at first, but after a few months in the group home, she began to blossom.

"The decision was not easy," Patrick and Marge Healy said when I talked with them. "We worried that Mary would not make friends and that she'd feel rejected by us. But we found an excellent group home where there were four men and four women with two wonderful people in charge. After Mary adjusted to her new situation, people who know her marveled at how independent she had become. Now, she and her friends go shopping, take short trips, picnics, all the things that young people do. Two of the people who worked with Mary were married recently, and Mary was even in the wedding!"

Wilberding agreed that many young retarded adults do grow more when they're away from home, as Mary did. "But parents have a hard time with that. It's scary to let go of a person whom you see as not being capable of fending for himself."

I decided to look into the cost differential between

institutionalized care and group homes. Figures published in April of 1981 by the Association for Retarded Citizens in Wisconsin showed a significant difference.

The average cost of institutionalized care in Wisconsin runs at least $80 a day, and up to $36,000 a year in some cases. Estimates go as high as $2 million for a lifetime of care. Nursing homes, by contrast, cost approximately $45 to $60 a day.

But group homes cost almost half that figure, around $30 a day. A foster home is closer to $20 per day and a sheltered apartment may cost as little as $10 to $15 a day. Those living in sheltered apartments also are likely to be gainfully employed, paying taxes and contributing to the economy.

Aside from the social and financial considerations, Wilberding is concerned about the human potential of this vast group of citizens.

"Leslie Lemke is an example of what is happening to a number of people who are retarded. They don't possess Leslie's spectacular single ability, but at the same time, they are proving they have abilities people never saw before. They can live more independently and be an integral part of society.

"For some people, success may be learning to ride a bus alone. That's no big deal for most of us, but for a retarded person, it means overcoming a huge obstacle and succeeding against the odds."

*Getting past the condition. Seeing that person for who he is.* I tried to assimilate all I had learned on my way home.

When I first met Leslie, I saw only his handicaps: his blindness, the palsy, his lack of response. I was so caught up in his disabilities I forgot he had thoughts and emotions—yes, even that he was a person.

But May wasn't so blind. So often, in those early days of our friendship, I talked only to May since Leslie didn't seem to understand. And over and over again she prompted, "Ask Leslie some questions. That's the only way he'll learn to talk."

I still see Leslie's handicaps, but I don't think much about them. I have learned to take his hand or put my arm around him to warn him when I'm going to plant a kiss on his cheek after a successful concert.

I know what he can handle conversationally, and I encourage him by asking questions. "How was your concert last night, Leslie?" or, "Hey, you've got a beard today!" or "By the way, Leslie, do you know Rachmaninoff's Prelude in G Minor? If not, you've got to learn it."

I suppose I didn't realize what was happening at the time. But I did what Wilberding was talking about. I got past the handicaps and discovered Leslie Lemke is, indeed, a person. He is funny, intriguing, a wonderful ambassador for Christ, and clearly one of the most gifted musicians I have ever heard.

# Chapter 14

## *The Lemkes, Today*

---

"How did you ever do it?"

I must have asked the Lemkes that question a dozen times, and I always received the same answer. I guess I couldn't bring myself to believe it, because I kept asking.

"Joe and I are different from other people," May said again and again. "We just accept things when God puts them before us. It's like accepting what you have to do in life. Things come at you and you don't say, 'Am I going to do it?' You say, 'Now, how am I going to do it?'

"I had been working for the rich all my life, taking care of their children. I thought to myself, 'Why not help this little one who has nobody?' "

Joe soon chimed in with his own philosophy. "I believe that our lives are all laid out ahead of us. Whatever God wants us to do, we just do it. We took Leslie and did the best we could with him."

I accepted that for a few weeks; then I was back at them again.

171

"But May, you had to be lonely! You got away twice in twenty-nine years—once for surgery and once when you went to England for three weeks. You *had* to get frustrated!"

May was never defensive, only amused. "Frustrated? I'm never frustrated! I just said to Jesus, 'This is what You have given me. I'm going to stick to it all my life until You tell me when to stop. I am Your servant, and I am happy to do the work You've put before me.' "

I don't know what I was after. I guess I wanted May to tell me that she pulled her hair and pounded the walls and screamed a lot. Maybe because that's what I would have done. But May never did.

Once, I used the word *struggle* in reference to her years with Leslie.

"Struggle?" May winced at the word. "It was no struggle. We were learning so much beautiful love all those years with Leslie. Our house is filled with it. And people see it when they come to visit. Loving someone is never a struggle."

May was right, of course. You do feel love in the Lemkes' house. Love, acceptance, humor, friendship—a refreshing place to visit. The credos are relax; take me like I am; say it like it is; this is the way God made me so why should I try to be any different?

Another revelation came when I began to arrange interviews with people who had known the Lemkes over the years: attorney James Ward, social worker Paul Baumgartener, Stance Bergelin, Dr. Treffert.

"The Lemkes? Oh sure, I'd be happy to see you. Wonderful family! It's about time people found out what May and Joe have done all these years!"

I didn't have to wonder if they'd see me. I didn't have to explain *why* I was writing a book. I didn't have to worry about breaking the ice. I was accepted. I was on the team!

"The biggest miracle," Baumgartener said one day in his office, "is that those three ever got together. They totally complement each other. May is so gregarious, so determined—which is why she was able to do all those things with Leslie. Then there is Joe, who is such a gentle, quiet man, perfectly willing to stay in the background. Yet he's a fine, fine gentleman and a strong support for May and Leslie.

"I sometimes wonder," he said thoughtfully, "what would have happened to this young man if he had ended up at an institution and if he had never had access to a piano. I wonder if he even would have lived."

He told me about the first time he heard of the Lemkes. When Leslie turned eighteen, May called the Waukesha County Department of Social Services to see if he might be eligible for some kind of aid.

"They sent me out to the Lemkes, and it just blew my mind!" said Baumgartener. "Here was this boy who couldn't even talk to me (he kind of grunted at that time); yet he sat down at the piano and played like a professional pianist. I'm a weekend musician, so I could see right away that he was making key changes as if he were reading the music. He had fantastic timing. He was doing things that only a professional musician would do.

"When May told me she had been caring for this boy for eighteen years and had never received any aid, I was dumbfounded! She said they had expected him to die and when she called for help, she never seemed to get anywhere. I immediately signed Leslie up for SSI (Social Supplemental Income), and she's been getting help ever since."

Another topic frequently discussed in interviews was the change in Leslie over the years.

"When I first met Leslie, I asked him questions and he just sat there, like someone had turned off the switch," Bergelin recalled. "But when I call the Lemkes now, sometimes Leslie and I converse a little over the phone. If I'm giving May a message, I'll often hear him responding in the background."

Baumgartener, too, has noticed that Leslie seems to be developing socially since his visit ten years ago. "I think he's beginning to relate to people and to be more cognizant of who they are. When I talk to May on the phone, she'll ask, 'Leslie, who am I talking to?' and he'll say 'Mr. Baumgartener' very distinctly."

I thought of the many interviews I had conducted with May. When she couldn't think of a song or a person's name or some small fact, she asked Leslie to refresh her memory.

Sometimes, when the taping was long, Leslie grew impatient waiting for us to finish and called out, "Honey-love, I'm not shaved yet." Everytime, May answered calmly, "That will come later, love, when you've had your bath."

Then there was the first time I heard Leslie laugh. I had taken an editor to meet the Lemkes. A bit of a musician himself, the editor sang a duet with Leslie, tried some harmonizing, and then played a composition he remembered from years back. The song was not extremely difficult, and when the editor chal-

# The Cheating Spirit

God is a jealous God. He commands that we have no others before Him, including our spouses or our significant others. For both single and married women, we will discuss how the cheating spirit is a black problem and how it strives to ruin our lives. The cheating spirit of today seeks to have multiple sexual partners, is responsible for the transmission of life-threatening diseases, and drains the black woman's spirit. God created sex for the sanctification of marriage and we can enjoy the full pleasure of satisfying our spouses as long as we do so in the will of God. On the other hand, single women should live to please God. The Bible clearly stated:

> …An unmarried woman or virgin is concerned about the Lord's affairs: Her aim is to be devoted to the Lord in both body and spirit. But a married woman is concerned about the

affairs of this world—how she can please her husband (I Corinthians 7:34).

The purpose for briefly addressing single women and the cheating spirit is to identify the problems that women face when entangled with the cheating spirit and to enlighten single women of God's word and purpose concerning sexual intimacy. To begin, God is love, but He is dishonored when we engage in sexual relationships outside of marriage; it is a sin. God commanded, "Flee from sexual immorality. All other sins a man commits are outside his body, but he who sins sexually sins against his own body" (I Corinthians 6:18). Sexual immorality can lead to the destruction of our bodies and our spirits, as we could suffer with disease and broken hearts when we become entangled with the cheating spirit. God does not want single women to be hurt by the cheating spirit. He wants to love and protect unmarried women; however, the cheating spirit interferes and seduces single individuals to be unfaithful to God. Until I became a Christian, I did not understand that the act of "living together" with a man constituted a sexual relationship without the sanctity of marriage, whereby God was hurt and displeased. Any sexual relationship outside of a husband and his wife's marriage is against God's will and can be considered as a cheating spirit. Although we must date before we can marry, we should learn how to replace sex in our relationships with alternative behaviors. Since "The Fall" (Adam and Eve's first sin), we have had the knowledge to choose between good and evil.

We have choices as to whether we sin and displease God or whether we live righteous to please Him. The black problem is that the cheating spirit entangles African-American women in long-lasting, intimate, sexual relationships that rest upon us to the point of placing our lives at risk for bondage. We could face pregnancy outside of marriage, disease, or we could end up living with men for years without the full benefits of being their wives. We cannot enjoy the blessings that God has stored away for our lives when we continue in sin to please our black men before we strive to please God. Our bodies were created for God's use, not for us to misuse or for black men to abuse.

Some black women may feel that their bodies have the sexual power to keep their black men. In reality, black women weaken their chances of marriage when they practice pre-marital affairs because many black men will continue to expect sexual relationships without marital commitments. There are so many men who take pride in being bachelors. Likewise, single black women should take pride in abstinence. As long as some of our significant others are willing to provide some of us with Gucci goods, Prada purses, Liz luxuries, and financial freedom, we choose to allow our men to live with us for years. Jesus asked, "What good is it for a man to gain the whole world yet forfeit his soul" (Mark 8:36). Everyone is not looking for marriage. However, when we choose to live with men for years without the commitment of marriage, we should consider the fact that we are sinning against our own bodies. Also, we are hurting the Creator that designed our bodies for His glory. Not only does the cheating spirit operate in the lives of single individuals, but also the cheating spirit dwells in some marriages.

Marriage is a sacred covenant between one man, one woman, and God. As vows come up out of our souls, we should make every effort to fulfill those vows, for Ecclesiastes 5:5 stated, "It is better not to vow than to make a vow and not fulfill it." Once we recite our wedding vows into our spouses' eyes, we are now connected as one emotionally and spiritually. The spirits of two people have now become one according to the marriage ordinances of God. Although marriage should be holy before God, there may come a time in a marriage when one may have to deal with the cheating spirit. We need to understand that spirits are transferable; good and evil spirits have abilities to transfer from person to person or from host to host as God allows or disallows (Read Mark, chapter 5). Thus, when one person from the marriage chooses to commit adultery, the unfaithful person has just opened the family's door for an ungodly, deceiving spirit to enter the home. Yes, an adulterous spirit can also be looked upon as – a cheating spirit.

How does the cheating spirit operate? Let us look at a typical scenario as to how the cheating spirit may try to seduce your husband – your man. Let us just say that your spouse is at work one day, and perhaps you and he have had a bad argument (arguments are door-openers for the cheating spirit). Like many, you have left the situation unresolved. Your husband may not want to come home right away. You both feel anger, bitterness, and resentment. Now, here comes a sexy lady who knows how to reel your man in for the drowning of your marriage – watch and pray! Ladies, we would like to introduce you to what we call the three C's: caring, conversation, and compliments. These are the three C's initiated by some seductresses that can begin the ruin of your relationship with your spouse. God has blessed your husband with you and your beautiful breasts that he should enjoy. Cheating should never be a solution to marital problems. The Word of God stated, "May your fountain be blessed, and may you rejoice in the wife of your youth" (Proverbs 5:18).

Returning to our scenario, keep in mind that your man is angry right now. Your black man is thinking that this sexy devil is caring, has good conversation, and above all, she is complimenting him at a time when the two of you are arguing. It is at this point that your man may try to forget you—his family. The affair begins with heavy conversations, phone calls, luncheons, and private meetings. Immediately, your man has gone from conversation and compliments to an adulterous affair. Proverbs 7:21 - 23 declared,

> With persuasive words she led him astray; she seduced him with her smooth talk. All at once he followed her like an ox going to the slaughter, like a deer stepping into a noose... little knowing it will cost him his life.

The devil will ensnare and tempt your man. Without morals, principles, and God, it is highly probable that he will fall for the seductress and allow the cheating spirit to enter your home. Your man begins to change his attitude, his ways, even his habits are changing. At this point you will need to pray and talk to your husband and ask, "Is having an affair worth losing what God has blessed us with?" Get an answer - although we know for now that his answer may be, "Of course not, honey!" You will be able to hold him to his response. The Bible stated, "Houses and wealth are inherited from parents, but a prudent wife is from the Lord" (Proverbs 19:14). Yes, as his wife, you are probably aware of some strange spirit that has come between the both of you.

Suspicion causes you to ask questions. You may want to try to find out what your man needs and wants. If he is having an affair, it is evident that he feels he needs something more. What your man probably needs is to just be honest with you, get his flesh under control, and learn to be more disciplined. The black man may need more conversation, the finances may need addressing, or he may need more intimacy from you. Whatever the need, God has blessed him with the provision through you, and he needs to embrace you—not another woman! Now you may ask, "Are you happy with me? Are you alright?" and the all-time favorite question, "Is there someone else?" This is an opportunity for your husband to discuss his concerns. Most of the time he will not communicate with you concerning whatever shortcomings the marriage may face unless you earnestly initiate some conversation. He owes you a fair chance to listen, to speak your opinion, or to make the necessary changes within the marriage; nevertheless, adultery is against God's will for marriages. An important factor to understand is that the cheating spirit could care less about destroying you or your husband as long as it fulfills its lustful pleasures, regardless of the fact that it could carry around the human immunodeficiency virus (HIV) and other sexually transmitted diseases. Why is it so difficult for some men to understand that just because some women are willing to give themselves over to men, it does not mean that men have to take what is being offered? There may come a day when the man or woman may take home more than pleasurable memories of a cheating affair. The risks are too great. A man of great wisdom declared, "Food gained by fraud tastes sweet to a man, but he ends up with a mouth full of gravel" (Proverbs 20:17). Some black men should just get out of the mentality that the grass is greener on the other side and work to maintain green grass in their own yards.

A husband should not deceive or deliberately hurt his wife (his special gift). "Husbands, in the same way be considerate as you live with your wives, and treat them with respect as the weaker partner and as heirs with you of the gracious gift of life, so that nothing will hinder your prayers" ( I Peter 3:7). As you can see, God does not want your husband to mistreat you or ruin your family by allowing the cheating spirit to come in and disrespect you. The spirit of cheating needs to be exposed, convicted by the Holy Ghost, and the unfaithful one needs to come to repentance before God through our Lord and Savior, Jesus Christ. Some black men are stiff-hearted, hard-headed, selfish and simply greedy. Black woman, it is your choice if you want to live with the cheating spirit, as it could place you at risk for disease and depression. Whether you are married or living the single lifestyle, the cheating spirit can drain your emotions and take you for an emotional roller coaster ride. You will need God to help see you and your relationship through the ups and downs of infidelity regardless of your decision to terminate the relationship or your decision to remain married. Do not try to take matters into your own hands.

If a woman chooses to remain in her marriage, each day may be a struggle until seeds of healing and forgiveness sprout. Keep in mind that there would be no need for God's healing power if you did not hurt. We recommend fasting and prayer in humbleness to help with the healing process, as God would not be pleased if you were in constant quarrel and battle with anyone, especially your husband. You will need to seek God for guidance and answers. It is after your hurt, your pain, and your humbleness that God's grace and mercy begins to heal your wounds. Isaiah 58:8 encouraged, "Then your light will break forth like the dawn, and your healing will quickly appear; then your righteousness will go before you, and the glory of the Lord will be your rear guard." What God is saying is that as you hurt, He will have your back! Assuredly, you can trust God to comfort and deliver you from the pain. You do not have to accept the abuse that comes along with the cheating spirit.

Even though it may appear that your husband is not abusing you, he is physically abusing your body and your marriage is being spiritually disintegrated. In addition, children could be affected by the disruption of love and peace throughout the home due to the cheating spirit's presence. Children could grow up thinking that infidelity is a behavior that is acceptable and tolerable in relationships.

As African-American women, we should not tolerate the cheating spirit to live in our homes. God did not design marriage to include three or more people. Not only does settling to live with the cheating spirit ruin relationships and marriages, but also women may lose their self-esteem, self-respect, and godly personalities. We must have faith and seek God to help us develop plans to restore our souls from the damage caused by the cheating spirit. We may need to seek professional counseling from our pastors, marital counselors, or seek godly counsel from friends. Let us not be complacent with disrespect and infidelity in our marriages less our souls, spirits, and health become at risk for oppression and illness. God may be invisible through eyes of the flesh, but He is ever-present in the spirit, especially in the time of need. If your black man cannot earnestly repent, show you love, respect your body, and be faithful in your marriage or relationship, then do not continue to dishonor God or yourself and live knowingly with the cheating spirit. It is not God's will for us to be involved in marital unfaithfulness (Read Matthew 5:31). As black women, if we disrespect one another in this manner, then how can we anticipate respect from black men?

# Reflection Questions

1. Have you taken time to thank God for the good that is in your spouse or significant other, while praying that God grants you patience to cope with the person's shortcomings? Do you consider these shortcomings as draining to your well-being? (Explain)

2. When was the last time your spouse or significant other complimented you? What was the compliment and how did you feel afterwards? What was the last compliment you gave to your husband?

3. Do you tolerate the cheating spirit in your marriage – if so, have you sought marital counseling? Why is God displeased with the cheating spirit?

# He is Not Ready

God does not exist to please mankind. All human races have been created that their ways should please God. The only way to please God is through the righteousness that comes forth from His Son, Jesus Christ. Many of us know that we should serve God through righteousness, but since God does not instantaneously kill us when we commit sin, many of us have become immune to sin. Blacks are a group of people who have maintained close relationships with God, yet we find ourselves high ranking in many negative matters such as poverty and disease and low ranking in positive issues such as education and marriage. Many black women focus on men's financial status, job status, and other status quos that are traditional, but characteristics such as integrity, respectability, reliability, and uprightness are standards that few of us seek. The time has come for African-American women to uphold higher standards for relationships as we endeavor to please

God rather than invest so much energy into trying to please black men. There are many African-American men who demonstrate that they are not ready to make commitments to protect hard-working, God-fearing, African-American women. Black problems that many African-Americans face are the lack of education, the inability to show credit worthiness, problems with our actions when we feel disrespected, and many of us are spiritually immature.

There was a time when African-Americans were considered ignorant property. Certainly, our ancestors have fought and died so that our generation and generations to come could have rights to education, equality, and freedom. We dishonor the moves of God, Christ's death and resurrection, our ancestors, and ourselves when we act carelessly about education and liberty. Many black men and black women lack the necessary training, education, and life skills to be productive in society. Many of us do not search our souls and spirits to discover the gifts and talents that God has placed within us. We believe that God has blessed all of mankind with a special gift or talent that should be discovered and nurtured throughout life. The gifts are the talents that God has invested in our souls. God expects us to use our talents for the good of Christian services in the community and as a means of being productive citizens. The rise of a technological society places the black man in a situation where education is necessary and required to compete in today's job market. The U.S. Census Bureau (2006) reported that in 2002, of the 1,197,567 black owned businesses, black men owned 571,501 of the companies. Therefore, we thank God for the black men who do realize that they have been gifted with talents to provide for their loved ones and to serve their communities. Although black males owned nearly one-half of these black businesses, there are still so many black men who do not take their God-given talents to pursue education or their own businesses. Marketable skills or education is required if black men are to possess good jobs, operate successful businesses, and live productively.

Furthermore, some blacks have difficulty obtaining credit as many creditors look to loan money to consumers who already demonstrate that they have excellent to good credit. There are many blacks who do not regularly check with credit bureaus to protect their credit status. Blacks have been known to pay higher interest rates on loans due to lack of credit worthiness. Without a fair credit rating, the black man is not ready, and he may find that taking on the responsibility of a family will be difficult. Yes, all things are possible with God, but God granted us with His wisdom along with His word.

In addition, mankind has a nature that seeks lawlessness. There are many of us who have heard of the slogan "Birds of the same feathers flock together." Many black men flock together with others who possess their same types of characters. Some black men lack qualities and integral personalities that are necessary to possess respectable reputations. We thank God for black men who maintain steady employment, love their wives, and who protect their families. On the other hand, we should be praying for black men who have problems maintaining employment and praying for those who are neglecting their families and responsibilities. The Word of God commanded, "Our people must learn to devote themselves to doing what is good, in order that they may provide for daily necessities and not live unproductive lives" (Titus 3:14). Sin comes naturally, as many of us become angry when feeling disrespected. Once angered, we allow Satan to tempt us with seeking revenge. God declares that vengeance belongs to Him (Read Deuteronomy 32:35). When a man takes his angry matters into his own hands by taking revenge on others, he attempts to take revenge out of God's hands. God forbids! Some black men and their friends instigate matters and make unwise, immature decisions that cause black men to put their lives at risk for incarceration or death. The black man is not ready for the black woman when he acts lawlessly.

Last, many African-Americans attend church, but we do not all have personal relationships with Jesus Christ. Spiritual immaturity can be seen in our neighborhoods as many of us take apathetic attitudes about drugs, violence, and crime throughout our communities. Laws, including God's commandments, will always govern our actions whether we choose to act responsibly or irresponsibly. When the black man acts immaturely and lawlessly, he jeopardizes his soul, spirit, and freedom, not clearly understanding Jesus' words, "...Satan has asked to sift you as wheat" (Luke 22:31). No man was made to be disconnected from God. Satan has exposed man to sin and death, as he has caused man to be divided from the goodness of God. Mankind cannot survive in the world peacefully and righteously without Jesus Christ. Some black men are not ready for black women, as these black men are prime targets for Satan's destructive plans when they act spiritually immature.

# Reflection Questions

1. Do you associate with positive individuals, or do the people you socialize with hinder your prosperity? Who is your man's best friend? What are some of the same characteristics that your husband and his best friend share?

2. If you could change three things about yourself, what would you change? Why are these changes important to you or to your relationship with others?

3. How important is education in your life? Is education important to your spouse or significant other? How do your children feel about education?

# More Excuses

$S$ ome men resort to any excuses and lies that they think black women will believe in order to fulfill their lustful pleasures. We set ourselves up for feelings of distrust and for relationships that fail when we continue accepting bogus excuses from some black men. Lies and excuses for thoughtless, selfish behaviors create strife and discord in relationships and marriages. Sisters, we should not be so naive when it comes to these "false-truths" – false because they are lies, truths because we believe them. We should not be so quick to believe each and every excuse or lie that people tell. We need to seek God for discerning spirits, praying that He reveals to us the truth about the relationships that we have chosen. The following are a few excuses to be aware: "She is just a friend. Oh, she is just my prayer partner. No, I am not married." or "It is too early to talk about marriage (yet it is not too early to engage in a sexual relationship)." Let us not forget the world's favorite, "I was working late."

Women listen, believe, and forgive black men for their fake explanations and tales to the point of broken hearts. We allow foolishness to enter our lives and we become entangled in bondage that holds us so tightly that we cannot experience liberty until Jesus makes us free. Although God tells us to forgive one another, we should learn to forgive and move forward when necessary if black men demonstrate that they cannot be trusted. The Bible asserted, "It is for freedom that Christ has set us free. Stand firm, then, and do not let yourselves be burdened again by a yoke of slavery" (Galatians 5:1). There are some binding situations that we will never be freed from until we obey God's word and face our fears. Although I am married now, I clearly remember a time when I heard God speak to my spirit, "This cup will not pass unless you drink it" (Read Matthew 26:42). Regardless of our fears, there will come a time when we will have to drink what is in the cup that God places before us if we ever want to become free. Sometimes, we will just have to trust God and drink!

Another problem is when some black men apologize and promise not to commit the same offenses, but they allow the enemy to use them to engage in the same behaviors time after time. We continue to forgive our black men in hopes that we can change their behaviors to satisfy our desires. Godly sorrow means that we repent and not continue to practice the offenses. We waste precious time trying to change some of our black men. In doing so, we allow others to drain our spirits and we find little peace in our lives. God commanded, "Turn from evil and do good; seek peace and purse it" (Psalms 34:14). True, behaviors can be manipulated and changed, but the practice of changing behaviors should be left in the hands of professionals and even more so – God. Notwithstanding professional help, we should remember that God has the power to make changes easier for us through the Lord Jesus Christ.

Some black men look for African-American women who will take second place in their lives. God did not create black women in His likeness that we should expect to be second best. God wants us to have His best! Some black women have lost their identities and their self-esteem after investing so much of their souls into stagnant relationships. As we love our black men, we should understand that we cannot love them above hurting God and above destroying our own lives. The book of Proverbs gives us a great example of the type of virtuous character that women should possess:

> She is clothed with strength and dignity; she can laugh at the days to come. She speaks with wisdom, and faithful instruction is on her tongue. She watches over the affairs of her household and does not eat the bread of idleness. Her children arise and call her blessed; her husband also, and he praises her: "Many women do noble things, but you surpass them all." Charm is deceptive, and beauty is fleeting; but a woman who fears the Lord is to be praised. Give her the reward she

has earned, and let her works bring her praise
at the city gate (Proverbs 31:25-31).

We need black men to stop making excuses and
to get into the will of God so that we can take our
rightful places as women. God created women to
be help-mates to men, and He created us for men
that they find some support and pleasure in our
companionship as their wives. We should be able to
look toward our black men to provide for us, to love
us, to support us, and to protect us in a world where
God created men to love their wives as Christ loves
the Church.

# Reflection Questions

1. How much time have you invested trying to change someone you care about? Can you notice any positive changes in that individual? List a few below:

2. How do you feel when others drain your spirit?

3. What is your plan to stop others from taking advantage of you?

# The Black Woman's Cry

According to the 2000 Census, African-Americans make up a small percentage (about 13%) of the population in the United States; yet, African-Americans lead the nation with alarming statistics concerning incarceration, HIV, and poverty. African-American males are over represented in the correctional system and as a result, we believe that some African-American communities are unstable and have unhealthy infrastructures. There are many problems facing black communities that not only cause black women to cry, but also these problems grieve God's Holy Spirit. God's word commanded, "And do not grieve the Holy Spirit of God, with whom you were sealed for the day of redemption" (Ephesians 4:30).

Many black men do not protect themselves in a society that we feel deliberately tries to undermine the success of black men. There are some black men who do not love and protect their families and communities, as black mothers live single lifestyles, head their own households and carry the burden of raising their children alone in communities filled with gang violence, drugs, and criminal activity. Black women face the HIV disease at alarming rates in comparison to other ethnic groups of women. There was a time when African-Americans depended on one another and God, understanding that limited support was available from governmental programs. Black men should not be absent from their communities, act immature about women's decisions to abstain from pre-marital affairs, or allow their children to grow up without their financial and emotional support. Also, we believe that the lack of mandated educational programs for the incarcerated, black, male population helps to keep recidivism rates high and adds instability and unhealthiness to African-American communities.

Data shows that the United States' incarceration population has grown tremendously in the last few decades from about 500,000 to over 2 million people. Today, statistics reveal that there are more black males in correctional facilities than there are black males in higher learning institutions. Black communities feel the effects of this black problem as few black, male, teens graduate from their high schools and even fewer attend colleges. Unfortunately, even with the newly adopted educational policies, many young, black males have been left behind; they do not graduate from high school. In the future, will there be enough black male graduates so that educated black women can look forward to dating and marrying black men with like status? Today, African-American men make-up about half of the total prison population, with about 1 million black males being held within the U. S. Correctional System.

There are many who contribute the massive increase of inmates in correctional facilities to America's war on drugs initiative. Black males are incarcerated about 7 times more than Caucasian males. The U. S. Bureau of Justice Statistics reported that at the end of year 2005, approximately 3,145 black males per 100,000 were sentenced to prison in comparison to 471 white males per 100,000. One may ask, "How is the war on drugs responsible for the incarceration increase of African-Americans?" A country's citizens can face serious socio-economic hardships when both husband and wife work full-time, earning the country's minimum wage, yet they are unable to find affordable rent or unable to purchase a home in the United States. A full-time employee in the United States who earns $5.15 an hour will earn $10,712 annually before taxes are deducted. Based on the minimum wage, a married couple's total monthly income would be about $1500.00 after taxes; yet, the Federal Housing Finance Board (2006) announced that the national average purchase price of a single family home was $306,258. Even at a very low interest rate, a mortgage for the average home in the United States would be about $2000.00 a month. We thank God and honor noble black men who work two and three jobs to handle their family affairs. Unfortunately, there are some individuals who may turn to the selling of drugs as a way of life or as a means for earning a living in a society where the cost of living has gone up annually, but the country's minimum wage has not increased in 11 years.

Nevertheless, many black men act irresponsibly and lawlessly when they choose to distribute drugs or engage in illegal methods of gaining money rather than finding legitimate means of taking care of their families and responsibilities. Black men should begin to take their rightful places in their homes and in their communities knowing that when they are absent from their communities due to incarceration, their neighborhoods and their children are affected. Keeping violence and drugs out of our neighborhoods are very important to our safety and health. However, some of the drug laws in which state and local governments enforce have had negative impacts on black communities, as many young, black children are raised without the proper fatherly guidance. We believe that without God's intervention, the black community may not be able to recover from what others call—public safety.

Black women cry as their loved ones who are felons face major obstacles when trying to find employment in America to provide for themselves and for their families. The government is so strict on employing felons that living successful lifestyles after incarceration can be extremely difficult for ex-offenders in some states. Neither can felony drug offenders obtain educational grants to attend higher educational institutions, nor can they obtain satisfactory employment to pay for educational expenses on their own. Some ex-felons do not qualify for services such as food stamp programs and public housing. Certainly, these restrictions have negative affects on the lives of African-American families. Felons need good jobs too if they are to remain in society and strive to live changed lifestyles. Many ex-offenders are prohibited from voting. Clearly, political outcomes are affected by American politics, which exclude a massive number of African-Americans (males and females) from participation in governmental elections. The United States of America was founded on Christian principles; however, some government officials do not find themselves "morally responsible" for rehabilitating criminals for the successful re-entry into society. The government should be held accountable by laws, policies, and its citizens to design and implement rehabilitation plans and programs that are researched based and effective to solve the high recidivism problem in black communities instead of creating laws that keep ex-offenders from being productive members of society.

Black women cry when they suffer from disease, financial hardship, and they cry when their African-American children lack fatherly love and discipline. There are times when some African-American women may experience male loneliness. Ultimately, we may feel the need to be provided for, protected, and loved; thus, we may surrender our love to black men who have no moral intentions of marriage. The high HIV status for black men and women is certainly a major black problem. Among women, African-Americans have the highest HIV rate in the United States. The

Center for Disease Control and Prevention (2005) reported:

- 64 percent of black women were living with HIV/AIDS, in comparison to 19 percent of white women and 15 percent of Hispanic women

- African-American women were diagnosed with AIDS 23 times the rates of Caucasian women and 4 times that of Hispanic women

- Forty-one percent of black males were living with HIV/AIDS.

Fortunately, research has remarkably improved the advancement of HIV/AIDS treatment. Today, one pill helps to control the deadly virus; however, a month's supply of the one-a-day treatment costs about $1100.00. We can conjecture that it will be extremely difficult for some to obtain the high-priced drug and predict that the United States may face major medical health care problems as it deals with the expensive treatment of HIV/AIDS. The high HIV/AIDS statistics in the African-American community tells us that there are many blacks who do not practice protecting themselves or others from this deadly virus. As the disease is a major health crisis, we should include HIV/AIDS testing as part of our annual physicals if we do not practice abstinence (married couples included). Also, keep in mind that

HIV/AIDS is transmitted by means other than being sexually active.

Other reasons that some black women cry are that they have to become the head authority figures in their homes and many of them raise children in poverty, as they are single parents. According to the National Vital Statistics Report (2006), among African-American women who gave birth in 2004, 69.3 percent were unmarried Non-Hispanic black women. Whether we lack the knowledge of God's word, abandon our moral principles or whether we are simply careless, many African-American women have low expectations for courtship and marriage, resulting in black men obtaining what they want while we end up with broken spirits and children. In addition, the National Center for Children in Poverty reported that 35% of black children live in poor families. We should keep in mind God's word that informed us, "Children's children are a crown to the aged, and parents are the pride of their children" (Proverbs 17:6). Black men are to be protectors, providers, and the overseers of their families to ensure that their black children and black women live flourishing and healthy lives. Yes, God mandated that husbands be the head of their families and wives be the helpers.

The social impact that awaits America as a result of some black males not heading their families and due to some black males returning to their families and communities after years of incarceration (without access to educational programs) may continue to be harmfully felt throughout many more bloodlines. As a result of many of these black problems, our children and grandchildren will face major economical, medical, and social crises for years to come. The United States (one of the world's greatest super powers and richest economies) is a country known for solving world problems and proposing solutions to other countries; yet, we believe that America fails to solve its own problems concerning the needs of its African-American citizens.

# Reflection Questions

1. Do you feel that you have an apathetic spirit about the black problems that we experience in our communities? What are some major black problems that concern you? What can you do to live a lifestyle that is more pleasing to God?

2. What accomplishments would you like to see come to pass in your life in the next few months?

3. Do you have annual testing for the human immunodeficiency virus (HIV)? What are some of your fears about being tested for the virus? Have you prayed to ask God to help you face those fears – why or why not?

# Black Solutions

This section of the book explores solutions to many of the problems that African-Americans face in their lifestyles, families, and communities.

# Drink From Your Own Cistern

God created us with ears, yet we do not hear. Since there is nothing new under the sun and no problem too large for God, we can defeat the cheating spirit that tries to kill and destroy the black race. Genesis 18:14 asked, "Is anything too hard for the LORD...?" If we as blacks do not seek God to change our lifestyles and unite to crush the cheating spirit, we may as well join the list of endangered species that move closer and closer to extinction. God has already given us the instruction manual on living, but we are a people who are determined to live according to what is right in our own eyes. As the cheating spirit lurks to find numerous partners (regardless of how lives are threatened), the only way to ensure the quality of life is through practicing God's holy word that commanded, "Drink water from your own cistern..." (Proverbs 5:15). God has already informed us that we should drink from our own cisterns by being faithful to Him and to our spouses, but we allow the cheating spirit to entice us to death and to the grave because "Death and destruction are never satisfied, and neither are the eyes of man" (Proverbs 27:20).

The solution to the cheating spirit is to submit to God or to one spouse. We should learn to crush the cheating spirit through abstinence, which requires us to sanctify ourselves for God's use. The other solution is to protect our spouses by being sexually intimate with them only. A covenant to God, whether one is single or married, is an earnest agreement to keep a promise that one has made before God. We dishonor God, our spouses, and ourselves when we commit fornication over and over and commit adultery over and over. Mankind can be so self-absorbed that he strives to please himself regardless of how others may feel. A covenant to God requires commitment to the promise. We should stick to the promise, regardless of the situation and ask God for deliverance when we can no longer fight the enticement. God will make ways for us to escape the temptation and bless us in the end of the struggle (Read 1 Corinthians 10:13). Honoring a covenant will take discipline, which means to be trained on how to display proper behaviors. Respecting a covenant takes a kind, caring, and gentle spirit between those in agreement. If we are going to survive the cheating spirit, not only should we make a covenant to our spouses to forsake all others, but also we should expect nothing less than faithfulness from our spouses. We should remember our spiritual relationships with God, and realize that we are in jeopardy of being reduced to crusts of bread when we commit adultery. Proverbs 6:26 stated, "For the prostitute reduces you to a loaf of bread, and the adulteress preys upon your very life." Adulterous relationships cause our lives to crumble like crusty bread! Satan's job is to tempt us; God helps to strengthen us so that we can resist temptation.

As God commits to protect us whether we are celibate or married, so should we commit to protect ourselves and our partners if we are going to be a part of the black solution. Being strong vessels, exercising temperance in our daily lives, and keeping one another from harm is another solution to conquering the cheating spirit. God has made the black man the stronger vessel who should stand tall, head his household, and be faithful to his wife. The black man should protect his wife and preserve his heritage by following godly principles with commitment and dedication. None of us have the right to jeopardize others' lives through contact with several sexual partners when we should be in monogamous relationships.

As African-American women, we should not practice fornicating relationships; these relationships can be dangerous and can separate us from God's goodness. As African-American women, we can no longer listen to the married man who says, "I am going to leave my wife." We should say goodbye to that black man because a relationship with a married man would be ungodly, unproductive, and complicated. God holds both black men and black women accountable for faithfulness, and He requires that we be more responsible concerning protecting ourselves and our loved ones from the cheating spirit. African-Americans already find it difficult to take care of serious black issues, such as diabetes, hypertension, and obesity. How much more will it be to control and to conquer HIV/AIDS with its expensive medical treatment? We have to bring our own flesh under subjection to God's word. (Read II Corinthians 10:5). We should begin to say goodbye to black men who refuse to protect our precious lives from the cheating spirit. We were created by God for black men to love us and to keep us safe, not for black men to take advantage of our love and kindness. Let us all begin to remind ourselves that we must drink water from our own cisterns or drink none at all.

# Reflective Statements

Take some time to reflect on your relationship or marriage-Remember to thank God for your blessings and remember that you are worthy of marriage and faithfulness.

## Personal Thoughts

_____

_____

_____

_____

_____

# Prayer

*Dear God,*

*Thank you for Your word that teaches me that I should submit only to my spouse. Please strengthen my spirit and my mind that I may dwell on Your words in times when I am tempted. I bind fornication, adultery, and sexual immorality in the name of Jesus, and I loose a strong, faithful commitment to God's Word in my life. Help me to live a life that is pleasing to You so that I do not grieve your Holy Spirit or allow others to drain from me the essence of who You wonderfully created me to be.*

*In Jesus' name, Amen!*

# GOALS

**My personal goal(s) to be a part of the black solution is (are) to**

_____

_____

_____

_____

## Objective I:

**I plan to reach my goal(s) by committing to**

_____

_____

_____

## Objective II:

**Spiritually, I plan to**

_____

_____

_____

# Iron Sharpens Iron

R eady or not, here comes the black woman who says goodbye to the black man who drains her spirit. Most black men are not ready for fine, God-fearing, faithful, African-American women. For the black man who thinks that he is ready for the black woman, thinking is just that - a thought. Both the black man who is without a job with poor credit and the black man who earns a six-figure to million dollar salary with excellent credit are a part of the black problem, if they both have not learned to put away childish things such as being unfaithful in their relationships with women, avoiding commitment, lacking godly morals and principles, and acting lawlessly.

The black man can experience a more successful lifestyle when he finds good friends, employs good life skills, and pursues spiritual maturity. By the grace of God, the black man can get ready for the black woman. Foremost, the black man should change his lifestyle to please God, and he should choose friends who are uplifting. God tells us that as iron sharpens iron, so can the countenance of a man's friends sharpen his countenance (Read Proverbs 27:17). What does the scripture mean? Brothers need other brothers who can respect and support their positive visions by faith and by deeds. The black man needs a vision from God if he is ever to head his own household, live godly, and live as a productive member of society. Some black men need to disconnect from their friends who engage in menacing activities that drain black women and society. One can always go back and try to encourage and lift up a friend at a later time, but the black man should first set and pursue personal goals that will enhance and empower his life. The black man needs friends who are encouraging and who can lift him up in prayer when the enemy tries to destroy his life. Our brothers need friends who know how to be truthful and friends who can tell them when they are wrong or performing unrighteous acts. Ladies, seek out your man's good friends and you may begin to see a clearer picture of your man's character. Keep in mind the old slogan - you are as good as the company you keep.

In addition to good friends to help see his vision through, the black man should possess proper life skills to make the vision happen and to see the vision come to pass. When the black man maintains a job, pursues education, and protects his credit rating, he can begin to prepare himself to face the responsibility of getting ready for the black woman.

To compete in the future jobs of America, black men need to prepare themselves by educating their gifts and abilities in which they have been blessed by God. Education helps to build wealth, which allows the black man to support his own family and gives the black man a sense of confidence, as he pursues employment in today's aggressive job market. "... remember the LORD your God, for it is he who gives you the ability to produce wealth ..." (Deuteronomy 8:18). God and a good job allow a man to resist the temptation of committing illegal acts to provide for himself and his family.

Without Jesus Christ and His righteousness, no man can escape sin. God tells us that sin waits at our doors to overtake us all, but also He informs us that we can take rule over sin (Read Genesis 4:7). With God's power and righteousness, mankind can take rule over sin that causes some black men to kill their brothers, act with lawlessness, and lose their lives to death and an unforgiving penal system. The black man can earn respect by taking responsibility for his own household and by supporting his own family. Black women should not be proud and supportive of black men who engage in illegal activities to earn their living. We should fervently pray that God save and deliver these black men from lives that may end in jail or death. Ladies, here are a few qualities of a respectable black man in which you should watch for and pray:

*R* esponsible for his own home
*E* ducates his God-given talents
*S* ays, "Yes" to God's Will
*P* ays his child support
*E* arns his income by working an honest job
*C* hooses to just say, "No" to illegal drugs
*T* urns away from mischief and sin

Also, employers are beginning to request permission to check potential employees' credit reports as a determining factor for employment. Maintaining a fair-to-good credit rating can demonstrate that one possesses good life skills. God's word added, "A good name is more desirable than great riches..." (Proverbs 22:1). The black man should protect his credit if he plans to live a prosperous lifestyle. One day he will need to purchase a home, finance a car, or he may desire other credit. As disciples of Christ, we challenge women to implore their husbands or significant others to obtain their credit reports and begin analyzing the reports. The three major reporting agencies are Equifax, Trans Union, and Experian (See the resource page for contact information).

First, review the credit report to be sure the personal information is accurate. Second, look for any negative information that is more than seven to ten years old, and request that the credit bureau remove that information from the credit record. Third, set some goals as to how any delinquent (old-unpaid) bills will be paid. The black man can begin by paying off his small, old accounts. Next, he should save his receipts and inform all three of the bureaus that the debts have been satisfied. The credit bureaus will update the files and his credit scores will begin to increase. God can help the black man maintain a job and keep a good name through means of a satisfactory credit report so that he can provide a good lifestyle for himself and for his family. Not only is good credit required for purchasing a home and financing a car, but also a good credit rating is necessary to get loans from banks. One should try to stay away from using credit cards, as misuse will place one's credit rating at risk. Truly, the black man should allow God to teach him how to exercise good life skills to support the black solution, and he should allow God to show him how he can lead a more successful lifestyle through Jesus Christ. The Bible pointed out, "I can do everything through Him who gives me strength" (Philippians 4:13).

Another solution that the black man can use to sharpen his countenance is to exercise spiritual maturity. Why is spiritual maturity necessary for the black man? Spiritual maturity for the black man is necessary if he is to rule over sin and lead an abundant life. The black man's soul can be blessed and can grow spiritually when he establishes a more personal relationship with God, resist temptation, and learn how to be gentle in spirit. Black women need black men who are spiritually connected to God through personal relationships in hopes of having prosperous marriages and families. The black man can begin his spiritual relationship with God by acknowledging that there is a higher power than himself in existence who desires to guide his life choices and to lead him into eternal life. Any man can simply begin holding conversation with God by sharing the contents of his heart. Ultimately, the black man should repent and confess his sins, believe in his heart that God raised Jesus from the dead, and the Word of God says that he shall be saved (Read Romans 10:9).

God has the power to change a man's lifestyle. Black women, we do not have the power to change our black men. We only have potential power to initiate change in our own lifestyles. The black man should take time to sit in God's presence, if he desires to grow spiritually. Establishing a relationship with God is a lifelong decision. The decisions to talk, pray, sit in God's presence, and spiritually walk with God should be maintained unto death. In return, God has promised everlasting life. Romans 8:35 questioned, "Who shall separate us from the love of Christ? Shall trouble or hardship or persecution or famine or nakedness or danger or sword?" Spiritual wickedness that seeks to destroy the black man can continue to reign, but God has promised that as sin reigns, grace will abide (Read Romans 5:20-21). It is by the grace of God that the black infrastructure still thrives. When our basic needs are not met, natural instincts to survive can take precedence over rationality when we are tempted. As Jesus used rational thinking to keep Satan from successfully tempting Him to sin, so should the black man use wisdom in his thoughts and actions. When Satan tempted Jesus to turn stones into bread, Jesus replied, "It is written: Man does not live on bread alone, but on every word that comes from the mouth of God" (Matthew 4:4). Jesus exercised enough wisdom to know that His basic needs may have been met for a moment, but the consequences of giving in to the flesh and to temptation could destroy Him and His relationship with the one that meant the most to Him: His Heavenly Father. As a people, we should learn to resist the devil so that his sinful tactics fail. In the Bible, James encouraged, "Submit yourselves, then, to God. Resist the devil, and he will flee from you" (James 4:7).

When the devil tries to tempt us, we should be spiritually mature to fight back with the Word of God. When we are tempted to kill our brothers and sisters, we should remember, "You shall not murder" (Exodus 20:13). When we are tempted to fornicate or to commit adultery, we should be spiritually mature to know that we should honor our bodies, as they are godly temples. When we are angered, we should remember, "...Everyone should be quick to listen, slow to speak, and slow to become angry" (James 1:19). Jesus is the Way to spiritual maturity, and He possesses the power to help all of us take authority over sin. When we resist the devil by calling on the Word of God, we weaken the power of the devil and strengthen the power of our spirits. We grow in Christ as we feed our spirits with godliness and as we become more sensitive to the Spirit of God. Being sensitive and possessing a gentle spirit is certainly a way to please God and black women. Women are gentle by nature. When men understand and respect that women are weaker vessels in the marital relationship, then men can successfully lead their households through love and compassion (not through tyranny and demands). Until black men can experience the love that Christ has for their lives, it can be difficult for them to show godly love towards their wives. As God shows His love towards black men by providing for them, loving them, and protecting them, so will black men be able to duplicate some of that love to their beautiful wives. Before we attempt to say, "I love you," we should understand the meaning according to God who created the word and who gave us the perfect example of love through Jesus Christ. The Apostle Paul declared:

> Love is patient, love is kind. It does not envy, it does not boast, it is not proud. It is not rude, it is not self-seeking, it is not easily angered, it keeps no record of wrongs. Love does not delight in evil but rejoices with the truth. It always protects, always trusts, always hopes, always perseveres. Love never fails... (1 Corinthians 13:4-8).

"For God so loved the world that He gave us His one and only Son, that whosoever believes in him shall not perish, but have eternal life" (John 3:16). The Bible tells us that God so loved the world – God is saying , "So - I love you anyway!" We may confess, "God, I have stolen." God replies, "So, I love you." We may confess, "God, I have killed." God responds, "So, I love you! I love you enough to give you My perfect Son that you may have eternal life through Him." We cannot begin to love one another until we begin to seek spiritual maturity through more personal relationships with Christ. God is the Ultimate Lover! Until we can say that we have met African-American men who have learned to love from the Ultimate Lover, we should learn to petition God to help us control our flesh. We should learn to say, "No" to our own low expectations and learn to say, "No" to the demands of certain black men. We must learn to surrender to God's purposes for our lives, less we could find ourselves without morals, principles, integrity, and positive self-images.

# Reflective Statements

Take some time to evaluate and write down your good characteristics-Pray about those traits that you may need to change-Spend some quality time assessing you and your spouse's friendships with others-Take inventory of the places in which you spend time and determine whether God is pleased-Any changes you desire to see in your spouse, take them to God in prayer before discussing them with your spouse.

## Personal Thoughts

_____

_____

_____

_____

_____

# Prayer

*Dear Jesus,*

*Thank You for Your insight and wonderful, sound doctrine about the importance of having positive friends in my life. Please help me to be a good friend to others as well as help me to find good friends to sharpen my life. I pray for my friends, and I lift their lives up to You right now for You to bless them according to Your will. Remove those friends who constantly drain my life, and bless me with friends who can uplift my spirit.*

*In Jesus' name, Amen!*

# GOALS

**My personal goal(s) to be a part of the black solution is (are) to**

_____

_____

_____

_____

## Objective I:

**I plan to reach my goal(s) by committing to**

_____

_____

_____

## Objective II:

**Spiritually, I plan to**

_____

_____

_____

# Just Say, "No" and Shut the Door

The black woman should understand that one of the major problems facing blacks is the massive imprisonment of African-American males. The black infrastructure is weakening and the reason our communities still prosper at all is simply because of God's grace and mercy. "From the fullness of his grace we have all received one blessing after another" (John 1:16). What other ethnic group of people can survive when its race only makes up about 13 percent of the population, yet more than 1 million of the males in its population are locked away? Can this group of people be fruitful and multiply as God commanded? While the black male is locked-up, who else can lead the household except the black woman? What about disease? As we stated earlier, African-American women test positive with HIV more than any other group of women. Some of us have sexual relationships with men who care for us, but unfortunately in an effort to feel love, we lower our standards concerning marriage first. There are many men who give us false hopes of marriage, as they confess, "I cannot wait to marry you." In reality, some of these black men have no moral intentions of entering into marriages (Read Matthew 7.15-20). Remember that we are worthy of marriage and worthy of faithfulness in our marriages.

Some black men may feel that they can have multiple sexual partners because as African-American women, many of us knowingly accept that our men have other sexual relationships. Some black men expect diligent black women to accept their careless behaviors or be replaced by other black women. If black women came together to just say, "No", then it is possible that these black men (single or married) would realize that their unwillingness to commit to marriage and their thoughtless actions in marriage would change to better please God and black women. For instance, if a black man expects a sexual relationship with you without commitment and you say, "No", he would move to the next black woman who would say, "No", and then he would have to go on to the next black woman who would also say, "No". Soon, that black man would realize that single black women expect more than a pre-marital sexual relationship and that married black women expect faithfulness.

True, some of us may not know that the men we are involved with have other partners, but there are a large number of women who know that they are sexually sharing black men. We should not take on attitudes that as long as some black men will give up a few dollars, spend time with us, and fulfill our sexual desires, then disease, morals, principles, and integrity take back seats to our physical desires. African-American women should begin to just say, "No" and shut their doors by closing their ears to lies, learning to forgive and move forward, and by seeking self-preservation. The single woman may ask, "Why can't the black woman say yes to pre-marital affairs? He is fine; he has a job and a car; and he is not married." What black women should realize is that some black men may meet certain qualifications, but most of these men are determined not to marry. They will have sexual relationships with us without commitment as long as we allow the behavior. What they are really saying is that we (our bodies and minds) are not worthy of marriage. We give the same message that we are not worthy of marriage when we allow black men to continue having sexual relationships with us without marital devotion. As beautiful black women, are we not worthy of marriage? A married woman may question, "Why can't the married black woman knowingly allow infidelity in her marriage?" Her husband provides her with a comfortable home; he pays the bills; and he is present most of the time. First and foremost, unfaithfulness in marriage dishonors God's marriage principle and the person committing adultery disrespects the other spouse and puts that spouse's life in jeopardy of diseases and a broken heart.

Let us stop listening to black lies and let us not allow others to deliberately drain and kill our spirits with these painful lies. We should decide whether we want to entrust our lives to those who deceive us. Lies are meant to deceive one from the truth. Lies must be maintained by covering them with details. The devil is the father of lies and knows how to manipulate the details so the lies can appear to be true (Read John 8:44). The more we listen to these "false- truths" the more we succumb to the draining power of the enemy. Satan knows how to get a man or woman to tell a lie and mix it with some truth. Before we know it, we have a poison that when we are bitten, our spirits are wounded and our souls are drained. If we just say, "No" and shut our doors, then we could save our souls from these poisonous lies, which could kill our spirits and cause us to become depressed. If we do not want to be lied to, then we have to stop listening to the lies and begin listening to God. We deserve men who respect us and who care enough about our lives to be honest with us about their lives. Our health and our bodies are in danger when we allow stress and oppression from unhealthy relationships to drain our minds, bodies, and our spirits.

Next, let us not allow men to deliberately kill our spirits by continuing to expose us to foolishness. We may think that some black men love us and that we can change them, so lie after lie, foolish act after foolish act, we still believe that we can transform some black men in order to live happily ever after. We continue to forgive some black men, all at the sacrificial offering of our hearts and spirits. When women are drained in the spirit, they cannot effectively perform the roles in which God created them to fulfill. Ladies, when our spirits are drained, we will find it difficult to feel like women, mothers, sisters, aunts, daughters, teachers, doctors, lawyers and so forth. We may feel drained and helpless if we allow some black men to continue lying to us. God commands us to forgive; however, deceit is deliberate. First, the deceiver should repent (turn away from lying). Then, trust should be earned and one should respect the other enough to be faithful and truthful.

As we deal with black men who constantly drain our spirits, we should learn to take action by forgiving our black men while loving ourselves. Yes, we should take some action and decide whether we will choose to forgive our black men, or whether we will begin loving ourselves to the point that we refuse to allow black men to drain our minds and hearts. We must begin loving our own lives to the point that we stop our own foolish, desperate actions. Are we so desperate for men to love us that we allow them not to work honest jobs? If a man does not work an honest job, then his life and relationship with a woman are already at risk for failure. Choosing to forgive the black man is more than simple lip service. We can say that we forgive them, take them back into our arms, and accept what has happened. The issues that are most important here are whether some of these black men will continue their deceitful behaviors and whether we will have peace trusting our lives unto them. We need to make decisions about entrusting our lives to men who disrespect us with deceitful lies and unfaithfulness.

Many women choose to enter into affairs with married men, supporting their unfaithful lifestyles. If you do not remember much about this book, please remember: IT IS NOT THE JOB OF A MISTRESS TO SATISFY A MARRIED MAN! If he is married and unsatisfied, it is not our jobs to try to satisfy him. We should say, "No" and shut our doors! He chose his wife and no matter how miserable he may claim to be, we do not have the command from God to try to love or satisfy him. God's word declared, "But since there is so much immorality, each man should have his own wife, and each woman, her own husband" (I Corinthians 7:2). The responsibility of providing love to a married man belongs to his wife! As a mistress, what gives us that right? Do loneliness, sexual desire, financial hardship, and selfishness give us the right to have an affair with someone's husband? No, these situations do not! When women make the wrong decisions and engage in affairs with married men – God forbids! The consequences will come around to bite soon – in this lifetime or in the judgment before God! Would we want some mistress to seduce our husbands? No, we would not. Respect the golden rule. "So in everything, do to others what you would have them do to you…" (Matthew 7:12). The problem with people in respect to the golden rule is that many of us treat ourselves bad; therefore, we treat others like we treat ourselves—BAD! As long as we behave in unrighteous acts and allow others to commit unrighteous acts against us, our self-esteem diminishes. We should commit to specific morals and standards and practice them in our day-to-day living. The Holy Spirit of God can take control of our lives to stop Satan from destroying us. Again, we say, "Commit to the golden rule."

Self-preservation is crucial to survival. Self-control, self-respect, and perseverance are traits needed for self-preservation. The Apostle Peter encouraged:

> For this very reason, make every effort to add to your faith goodness; and to goodness, knowledge; and to knowledge, self-control; and to self-control, perseverance; and to perseverance, godliness; and to godliness, brotherly kindness; and to brotherly kindness, love. For if you possess these qualities in increasing measure, they will keep you from being ineffective and unproductive in your knowledge of our Lord Jesus Christ. But if anyone does not have them, he is nearsighted and blind, and has forgotten that he has been cleansed from his past sins (II Peter 1:5-9).

Self-esteem is when one feels confident and is satisfied with one's physical, emotional, and spiritual state in poverty or in financial security. We should love ourselves to the point that we make righteous decisions about our lives. The health of black women has declined with the taint of HIV. It is the quality of life for the black woman that is diminishing and we cannot allow our fate to rest in the hands of others that we cannot trust. We should take control of our own lives and protect ourselves from the danger that threatens the prosperous lives in which God intended us to experience. African-American women work very hard to please their spouses and to take care of their families, churches, and communities. We have always worked hard to please others. The time has come for many of us to raise our standards when entering into and maintaining relationships with black men. We should learn to protect our godly principles, our health, and our precious spirits by saying "No" to men who come to drain our souls outside of God's will. Yes, it is time for the black woman to stop trying so hard to please the black man. It is time for the black man to learn how to please God and learn how to protect and please the black woman.

## Reflective Statements

Consider terminating any draining relationships that you feel may be oppressive-Wait on God to provide you with someone who loves, cares, and who can protect you-Do not listen too long to lies and excuses, as they will deceive you from the truth.

### Personal Thoughts

_____

_____

_____

_____

_____

# Prayer

*Dear Jesus,*

*In reading Your Word, I pray that You grant me the courage to say, "No" to situations that are displeasing to You and to affairs that cause me to become distant from Your will. God, when the devil comes to tempt me or tries to trick me, please allow me to stand on Your Word that I may resist temptation. I pray that You strengthen my soul that I give no place to the devil, and I pray that You strengthen my husband's spirit that he may also escape the devil's temptations. Thank You for listening to and answering my prayers.*

*In Jesus' name, Amen!*

# GOALS

**My personal goal(s) to be a part of the black
solution is (are) to**

_____

_____

_____

_____

## Objective I:

**I plan to reach my goal(s) by committing to**

_____

_____

_____

## Objective II:

**Spiritually, I plan to**

_____

_____

_____

# Catch the Black Vision

W here is the black woman's knight in shining armor? Will he show up in time to save his family, or will he help the enemy to destroy his own castle? The black man should first learn to protect himself before he can protect his family and community. You may ask, "Protect himself from whom?" The answer is that the black man should learn to protect himself from - his own self. Some black men have become so absorbed with their own selfish needs that they are destroying themselves. There are some black men who need money, so they sell drugs. There are some black men who desire sex, so they have multiple partners to fulfill their lustful desires. Some black men need to protect themselves from the violent lifestyles that they have chosen, so they illegally carry guns. Also, there are black men who need to forget their responsibilities, hardships, and painful hearts, so they excessively drink alcohol. Black women are drained by these foolish actions!

There are even some black men who are tired of other black men! After all, there are many God-fearing, hard-working, loving, black men in America who take on the burden of trying to keep their communities safer places to live, while other selfish brothers tear down communities with their self-absorbed actions. The black solution to the black problem begins with catching the black vision: the black man should learn to protect himself, his family, and his community. After all, the Bible stated, "Be self-controlled and alert. Your enemy the devil prowls around like a roaring lion looking for someone to devour" (I Peter 5:8).

First, black men should surrender to Jesus Christ and petition God for strength to be better men, husbands, fathers, sons, brothers, uncles, cousins, and mentors. Can your black man protect you when he will not even try to protect himself from the many snares that try to entrap him? There are some black men who need Jesus to help protect them from sin, jealousy, anger, and most of all their out-of-control flesh, which has numerous sexual partners, use illegal substances, drink excessively, refuse to work, and harmfully utter negative words to their black women and families. One way that the black man can protect himself is by pursuing education. Education is one of the keys to a better lifestyle and is a solution to some of our black problems. Education is a great economic means to a wealthier lifestyle. Ladies, your black man should have a desire for knowledge, whether it is to learn a skillful trade, go to college, or just simply educate the talents in which God has blessed him. Also, research supports the premise that recidivism is reduced when inmates participate in educational programs so their chances for returning to the correctional centers decrease.

The Bible tells us that we drink to forget our misery, yet in the morning, we still hurt (Read Proverbs 31:4-7). Alcohol and drugs are not protectors; they can be destroyers. Drugs and alcohol cannot heal wounds or disappointments. We should look to Jesus for protection from pain so that He can allow His Holy Spirit to heal our souls. The Holy Spirit was sent and charged by God to comfort those in the world; let Him do His job! We need to terminate the alcohol, drugs, and the guns from being our protectors and allow God to protect us. Who else can better protect us than God who shelters us behind Jesus, the Holy Spirit, and a host of heavenly angels? Black men should find positive hobbies in which they can engage such as playing pool, swimming, weightlifting, basketball, and playing football. There are many men who participate in hunting as a sport; they hunt animals, not one another. Some black men need to stop hunting and killing other black men! If black men choose to use guns, then they need to find ways to use their guns legally! Ladies, our black men should learn to protect themselves first and then they can exist to protect us and our families!

Black men should catch the black vision of protecting their families, as the government is not responsible for protecting black men's homes beyond the regulations governed by federal, state, and local laws. The black men that we have decided to give our spirits to should be black men who can protect us and our families from divorce. They should love us as wives and put our needs before their own needs. They should be willing to die to protect us—their family, just as Jesus was willing to die for the church. Black men should protect their families from hurt and pain. At no time should black men strike their black women. If they do, then they do not demonstrate that they love us; they demonstrate that they have come along with the enemy to destroy us and our spirits. Let us not allow any man to strike us! When we allow black men to drain our spirits, we will begin to lose our functioning abilities. God's word asked, "Who can bear a broken spirit" (Proverbs 18:14)? Neither our spirits nor our bodies should be broken when our black men truly demonstrate that they love us. Our black men should be there to relieve stress from our lives. They should relieve stress from our lives by loving us, paying the bills, and supporting us and our children. When married, a black woman should not be made to feel degraded or blamed if she does not work or if she earns a small salary. God commanded that our men sweat to their brows (Read Genesis 3:1-19), not us! We already bear our curse, which is to look to our husbands for our needs and to bring forth children in pain. Yes, both of these curses cause black women much sorrow! We no longer have time to take on our own curse and then take on the man's curse as well by working part-time, overtime, anytime, and then having to live with unappreciative, insensitive, unfaithful spouses. The black man is the one who should be working diligently for his family,

# how to
## use this
# discussion guide

This discussion guide is meant to be completed on your own and in a small group. So before you begin, line up a discussion group. Perhaps you already participate in a women's group. That works. Maybe you know a few friends who could do coffee once a week. That works, too. Ask around. You'll be surprised how many of your coworkers, neighbors, and children's friends' mothers would be interested in a small-group study—especially a study like this that doesn't require vast biblical knowledge. A group of four to six is optimal—any bigger and one or more members will likely be shut out of discussions. Your small group can also be two. Choose a friend who isn't afraid to "tell it like it is." Make sure each person has her own copy of the book.

1. *Read* the Scripture passages and other readings in each lesson on your own. Let it all soak in. Then use the white space provided to "think out loud on paper." Note content in the readings that troubles you, inspires you, confuses you, or challenges you. Be honest. Be bold. Don't shy away from the hard things. If you don't understand the passage, say so. If you don't agree, say that, too. You may choose to go over the material in one thirty- to forty-five-minute focused session. Or perhaps you'll spend twenty minutes a day on the readings. If the book doesn't provide enough space for you to write, use a notebook or journal.

2. *Think* about what you read. Think about what you write. Always ask, "What does this mean?" and "Why does this matter?" about the readings. Compare different Bible translations. Respond to the questions we've provided. You may have a lot to say on one topic, little on another. That's okay—this isn't a test where you have to answer every question. When you're in your small group, come back to the topics that seem most significant. Let the experience of others broaden your wisdom. You'll be stretched here—called upon to evaluate whether your conclusions make sense. In community, that stretching can often be painful and sometimes even embarrassing. But your willingness to be transparent—your openness to the possibility of personal growth—will reap great rewards.

3. *Pray* as you go through the entire session: before you read a word, in the middle of your thinking process, when you get stuck on a concept or passage, and as you approach the time when you'll explore these passages and thoughts together in a small group. Pause when you need to ask God for inspiration or when you need to cry out in frustration. Speak your prayers, be silent, or write out your prayers by using the prayer starters we've provided throughout each lesson.

4. *Live.* (That's "live" as in "rhymes with give" as in "Give me something I can really use in my life.") Before you meet with your small group, complete as much of this section as you can (particularly the "What I Want to Discuss" section). Then, in your small group, ask the hard questions about what the lesson means to you. Dig deep for relevant, reachable goals. Record your real-world plan in the book. Commit to following through on these plans, and let the other women support you in doing so. Arrange some way of checking in with each other for encouragement.

5. *Follow up.* Don't let the life application drift away without action. Let other group members ask you how your plan is going and refer to previous "Live" as in "rhymes with give" sections often. Take time at the beginning of each new study to review. See how you're doing.

6. *Repeat* as necessary.

# small-group
# study tips

After going through each week's study on your own, it's time to sit down with others and go deeper. Here are a few thoughts on how to make the most of your small-group discussion time.

**Set ground rules.** You don't need many. Here are two:

*First,* you'll want group members to make a commitment to the entire eight-week study. A binding legal document with notarized signatures and commitments written in blood probably isn't necessary, but you know your friends best. Just remember this: Significant personal growth happens when group members spend enough time together to really get to know each other. Hit-and-miss attendance rarely allows this to occur.

*Second,* agree together that everyone's story is important. Time is a valuable commodity, so if you have an hour to spend together, do your best to give each person ample time to express concerns, pass along insights, and generally feel like a participating member of the group. Small-group discussions are not monologues. However, a one-person-dominated discussion isn't always a bad thing. Your role in a small group is not only to explore and expand your own understanding; it's also to support one another. If someone truly needs more of the floor, give it to her. There will be times when the needs of the one outweigh the needs of the many. Use good judgment and allow extra space when needed. *Your* time might be next week.

**Meet regularly.** Choose a time and place, and stick to it. No one likes showing up to Carmine's Cafe at 12:30, only to discover the meeting was moved to Salad Celebration at noon. Consistency removes stress that could otherwise frustrate discussion and subsequent personal growth. It's only eight weeks. You can do this.

**Talk openly.** If you enter this study with your Happy Christian Woman mask on, you're probably not alone. And you're not a "bad person" for your hesitation to unpack your life in front of friends or strangers. Maybe you're skeptical about the value of revealing the deepest parts of who you are to others. Maybe you're simply too afraid of what might fall out of the suitcase. You don't have to go to a place where you're uncomfortable. If you want to sit and listen, offer a few thoughts, or even express a surface level of your own pain, go ahead. But don't neglect what brings you to this place—that longing for real life and real connection. You can't ignore it away. Dip your feet in the water of brutal honesty and you may choose to dive in. There is healing here.

**Avoid fixing others.** Sometimes it's scary when another woman takes off her Happy Christian mask. We women have an instinct to want to "make it all better" for any hurting or angry person, whether child or adult. Also, we have varying levels of tolerance for other people's negativity. Please resist your mommy instinct. Give advice only when asked, and even then, use restraint.

**Stay on task.** Refrain from sharing material that falls into the "too much information" category. Don't spill unnecessary stuff, such as the sexual positions your husband prefers or the in-depth details of an argument you had with your mother. This is about discovering how *you* can be a better person.

**Support each other's growth.** That "Live" section isn't just busywork. If you're really ready for positive change—for spiritual growth—you'll want to take this section seriously. Not only should you personally be thorough as you summarize your discoveries, practical as you compose your goals, and realistic as you determine the support you need from the group, you also need to check back with the others in the group to see if they're following through. Be lovingly honest as you examine each other's "Live" section. Don't hold back—this is where the rubber meets the road. A lack of openness here may send other group members skidding off that road.

# my schedule

## the beginning place

Take a moment to think about your schedule. Grab that first reaction—when you read the word *schedule,* did you shut your eyes and wince? Hold your breath or let out a deep sigh? Feel like throwing this book across the room? Smile about the great plans you have to look forward to today?

Chances are that if you're married with children, you spend a lot of time shuttling kids here and there, or getting them ready to be shuttled. Laundry, meals, Back-to-School Night—your to-do list goes on and on, and that doesn't even count what your husband needs from you. Maybe on top of taking care of your family you've got a paying job because without your income, the mortgage wouldn't get paid. Wouldn't life be easier if you were single?

If you're single, you're probably shouting *No!* You work full-time, and unless you have a great roommate, nobody's sharing the bills, errands, and household chores with you. You're on your own, and you feel it. Furthermore, unless you can survive practically and emotionally as a hermit, you have to devote at least some time to friends and perhaps to "the quest for the Holy Grail," a decent husband. All this is hard enough if you're single and childless, but if you're a single mom, heaven help you.

So how's it going, really? Please don't say, "Fine." For the duration of this study, drop that word from your vocabulary. It's too easy to say, "I'm fine," when you're not, to say your schedule isn't that bad.

If you're exhausted, scared, frustrated, unhappy, please say so. Or if you're challenged, excited, well-rested, and motivated, say that, too.

Use the space below to summarize your beginning place for this lesson. Describe the reality of your schedule as well as your dreams. We'll start here and then go deeper.

# read   the end of a loooong day

From the *Today's Christian Woman* article "Not Tonight, Dear . . . " by Jill Eggleton Brett[1]

> **Note:** If you're married with children, start with the first reading, "Not Tonight, Dear . . ." If you're single, skip to the next reading, from *The Devil Wears Prada.*

I'd returned from running errands one afternoon when I walked into the house and saw my husband give me "The Look." The screen door banged behind me as my twin preschoolers ran over to me and wrapped themselves around each leg, squealing with delight. As I reached down to hug them, my husband gave me his signature shake of the head and said, "Hey, honey . . ." And I, as usual, rolled my eyes as I peeled the girls off my legs.

If your husband's anything like mine, you know what the "dot, dot, dot" means. Those little punctuation marks come at the most inconvenient times! I mean, come on, I'd just picked up the dry cleaning, bought his cousin a wedding gift, found new shoes for our twins, shopped for his favorite food for dinner that night. And now this—another chore. I was cranky and still had laundry to do. Not to mention I could hear my pillow calling in the distance.

But God had some lessons for me that night, and many more nights to follow. As I continued to shrug off my husband's sexual advances, tension continued to build. I grew colder, and he continually felt rejected. It was time to face the facts: I didn't want to have sex. I was too busy, too tired, and flat out didn't have the desire. I had two little people calling my name all day, wiping their noses on my pants, and vying for their turn on my lap. When the twins' bedtime arrived, I wanted personal space.

From *The Devil Wears Prada*, by Lauren Weisberger[2]

"How could you do this to me?" she hissed as she pushed me through *Runway*'s reception-area doors and we hurtled together back to our desks. "As the senior assistant, I am responsible for what goes on in our office. I know you're new, but I've told you from the very first day: we do not leave Miranda unattended."

"But Miranda's not here." It came out as a squeak.

"But she could've called while you were gone and no one would've been here to answer the . . . phone!" she screamed as she slammed the door to our suite. "Our first priority—our only priority—is Miranda Priestly. Period. And if you can't deal with that, just remember that there are millions of girls who would die for your job. Now check your voice mail. If she called, we're dead. *You're* dead."

I wanted to crawl inside my iMac and die. How could I have screwed up so badly during my very first week? Miranda wasn't even in the office and I'd already let her down. So what if I was hungry? It could wait. There were genuinely important people trying to get things done around here, people who depended on me, and I'd let them down. I dialed my mailbox.

"Hi, Andy, it's me." Alex. "Where are you? I've never heard you not answer. Can't wait for dinner tonight—we're still on, right? . . ." I'd immediately felt guilty, because I'd already decided after the whole lunch debacle that I'd rather reschedule. My first week had been so crazy that we'd barely seen each other, and we'd made a special plan to have dinner that night, just the two of us. But I knew it wouldn't be any fun if I fell asleep in my wine, and I kind of wanted a night to unwind and be alone.

## think

- How is your story like or unlike these stories?
- What stresses in your life come from children?
- What stresses come from paid work? What about from unpaid work (at home or volunteering)?
- What stresses stem from your husband, boyfriend, or lack thereof?

**think** (continued)

**pray**

Lord, please help me face . . .

## **read**  tell me how you *really* feel

### Job 7:1-4

Human life is a struggle, isn't it?
　　It's a life sentence to hard labor.
Like field hands longing for quitting time
　　and working stiffs with nothing to hope for but payday,
I'm given a life that meanders and goes nowhere—
　　months of aimlessness, nights of misery!
I go to bed and think, "How long till I can get up?"
　　I toss and turn as the night drags on—and I'm fed up!


### Psalm 6:1-7

Please, GOD, no more yelling,
　　no more trips to the woodshed.
Treat me nice for a change;
　　I'm so starved for affection.

Can't you see I'm black and blue,
　　beat up badly in bones and soul?
GOD, how long will it take
　　for you to let up?

Break in, GOD, and break up this fight;
　　if you love me at all, get me out of here.
I'm no good to you dead, am I?
　　I can't sing in your choir if I'm buried in some tomb!

I'm tired of all this—so tired. My bed
　　has been floating forty days and nights
On the flood of my tears.
　　My mattress is soaked, soggy with tears.
The sockets of my eyes are black holes;
　　nearly blind, I squint and grope.

## think

- How, if at all, do you identify with the words of Job? How about with the psalmist?
- What do you typically do when you feel "starved for affection"?
- How do you imagine God responding to the psalmist? To Job?
- How easy is it for you to complain to God about your life? Why do you suppose that's the case?

## pray

Father, what I most long for from you is . . .

**read**   too many worlds, too little time

From *The Connecting Church*, by Randy Frazee[3]

One of the underlying problems of the Johnsons and most people who live in the average American suburb (or international equivalent) is that they have too many worlds to manage. There are too many sets of relationships that do not connect with each other but all require time to maintain. Bob and Karen simply do not have enough time and energy to invest in each world of relationships in order to extract a sense of belonging and meaning for their lives.

Just think of the many disconnected worlds the Johnsons have to maintain: their own family, two places of work, church, a small group, the children's sports teams, the children's schools, extended family out of town, and neighbors. If we were to delve further into the Johnsons' lifestyle, we would discover many other worlds as well—old friends from high school and college, the last place they lived, and other relationship circles at church (for example, the women's Bible study group and the Mission Committee of which they are both members). . . .

If a true and workable solution is to emerge, it must involve a radical restructuring of our lifestyle. At the core of this restructuring is a new operating principle for living: *In order to extract a deeper sense of belonging, we must consolidate our worlds into one.* . . . The mission is to simplify our lifestyles in such a way that we concentrate more energy into a circle of relationships that produces a sense of genuine belonging. While this in no way suggests that we should be so narrow in our scope as to cut significant people out of our lives, it does reinforce the common-sense notion that we can go deeper with less to manage, and we *must* find a way to do this.

# think

- Make a list of the different worlds you have to maintain.
- To what degree do these worlds overlap? How does that affect the amount of time you spend with each person? How does it affect the depth of your relationships?
- How would your life be different if you had fewer worlds to maintain? For example, if your children's school friends and church friends knew each other?
- How do you respond to the idea of concentrating more energy into a circle of relationships that gives you a sense of genuinely belonging with those people? Does this mission seem desirable? Achievable? Wrongheaded? What makes you say that?
- What forces in your life make it hard to reduce the number of different worlds you have to juggle?

# pray

God, the challenges I'm dealing with here are . . .

## read   a really rough lifestyle

2 Corinthians 11:24-33

> I've worked much harder, been jailed more often, beaten up more times than I can count, and at death's door time after time. I've been flogged five times with the Jews' thirty-nine lashes, beaten by Roman rods three times, pummeled with rocks once. I've been shipwrecked three times, and immersed in the open sea for a night and a day. In hard traveling year in and year out, I've had to ford rivers, fend off robbers, struggle with friends, struggle with foes. I've been at risk in the city, at risk in the country, endangered by desert sun and sea storm, and betrayed by those I thought were my brothers. I've known drudgery and hard labor, many a long and lonely night without sleep, many a missed meal, blasted by the cold, naked to the weather.
>
> And that's not the half of it, when you throw in the daily pressures and anxieties of all the churches. When someone gets to the end of his rope, I feel the desperation in my bones. When someone is duped into sin, an angry fire burns in my gut.
>
> If I have to "brag" about myself, I'll brag about the humiliations that make me like Jesus. The eternal and blessed God and Father of our Master Jesus knows I'm not lying. Remember the time I was in Damascus and the governor of King Aretas posted guards at the city gates to arrest me? I crawled through a window in the wall, was let down in a basket, and had to run for my life.

## think

- What goes through your mind when you read the apostle Paul's description of his life?
- Do you ever play "My impossible schedule is worse than yours" with your friends or family? Why do you suppose some of us tend to brag about our stressed-out lives?
- Among many other trials, Paul mentions hard work, hard travel, struggles with friends and foes, betrayals by those close

to him, and anxiety for others. Describe your experiences with any of these.

- What does Paul's account of his life motivate you to do? Work harder? Thank God that your life isn't so bad? Feel guilty? Why do you suppose that's the case?
- What do you think about Paul's determination to "brag about the humiliations that make [him] like Jesus"?

## pray

Lord, thank you . . .

# LIVE

## what i want to discuss

What have you discovered this week that you definitely want to discuss with your small group? Write that here. Then begin your small-group discussion with these thoughts.

## so what?

Use the following space to summarize the truths you uncovered about your schedule, how you feel about it, and where you need to begin in dealing with your situation. Review your "Beginning Place" if you need to remember where you began. How does God's truth affect the next step in your journey?

## now what?

What is one practical thing you can do to respond to what you discovered? What concrete action can you take? Remember to think realistically—an admirable but unreachable goal is as good as no goal. Discuss your goal in your small group to further define it.

## how?

How can your group—or even one other person—help you follow through with the goal you described? What support do you need? (Sure, you're Superwoman, but . . . ) How will you measure the success of your plan? Write the details here.

# expectations

## a reminder:

*Before you dive into this study, spend a little time reviewing what you wrote in the previous lesson's "Live" section. How are you doing? Check with your small-group members and review your progress toward your goals. If necessary, adjust your goals and plans, and then recommit to them.*

## the beginning place

Why do we live like this, constantly on the run? Do we feel better on six hours of sleep than on eight? Does food taste better in the car? Does a relaxing evening with friends seem dull?

Certainly some of us enjoy the adrenaline rush of speed and dead-lines. But a lot of us don't. Instead, we're driven not by the pleasure of the chase but by expectations. Our children have needs and wants. Our bosses expect a certain level of productivity. The other women at church; the other mothers at our children's schools; our husbands, boyfriends, and female friends—they all look to us for something, and we really don't want to let them down. On top of that, we have our own dreams and standards.

Take a few minutes to list some of the people in your life and a few of the things they expect from you. Then add yourself, and write down what you expect from yourself. Read your list. What goes through your mind as you read it? "No problem!" or "I can't face this"?

## read  mothers who make the effort

From *I Don't Know How She Does It*, by Allison Pearson[1]

Homemade is what I'm after here. Home is where the heart is. Home is where the good mother is, baking for her children.

All this trouble because of a letter Emily brought back from school ten days ago, now stuck on the fridge with a Tinky Winky magnet, asking if "parents could please make a voluntary contribution of appropriate festive refreshments" for the Christmas party they always put on after the carols. The note is printed in berry red and at the bottom, next to Miss Empson's signature, there is a snowman wearing a mortarboard and a shy grin. But do not be deceived by the strenuous tone of informality or the outbreak of chummy exclamation marks!!! Oh, no. Notes from school are written in code. . . . Take that word "parents," for example. When they write "parents" what they really mean, what they still mean, is "mothers." (Has a father who has a wife on the premises ever read a note from school? Technically, it's not impossible, I suppose, but the note will have been a party invitation and, furthermore, it will have been an invitation to a party that has taken place at least ten days earlier.) And "voluntary"? Voluntary is teacher-speak for "On pain of death and/or your child failing to gain a place at the senior school of your choice." As for "appropriate festive refreshments," these are definitely not something bought by a lazy cheat in a supermarket.

How do I know that? Because I still recall the look my own mother exchanged with Mrs. Frieda Davies in 1974. . . . "You see, Katharine," Mrs. Davies explained later, doing that disapproving upsneeze thing with her sinuses over teacakes, "there are mothers who make an effort like your mum and me. And then you get the type of person who"—prolonged sniff—"don't make the effort." . . .

So before I was really old enough to understand what being a woman meant, I already understood that the world of women was divided in two: there were proper mothers, self-sacrificing bakers of apple pies and well-scrubbed invigilators of the wash-tub, and there were the other sort. At the age of thirty-five, I know precisely which kind I am, and I suppose that's what I'm doing here in the small hours of the thirteenth of December, hitting [store-bought] pies with a rolling pin till they look like something mother-made.

## think

- Do you agree that the world of women is divided in two—those who "make the effort" and those who don't? What makes you say that?
- In your experience, how are mothers (or people in general) who "don't make the effort" treated?
- Do you "make the effort"? If so, how? If not, what do you do and not do?
- How does making the effort (or not doing so) affect your stress level?
- How do you treat women who "don't make the effort"?

## pray

Lord, show me . . .

## read  a good woman is hard to find

**Proverbs 31:10-31**

> A good woman is hard to find,
>> and worth far more than diamonds.
>
> Her husband trusts her without reserve,
>> and never has reason to regret it.
>
> Never spiteful, she treats him generously
>> all her life long.
>
> She shops around for the best yarns and cottons,
>> and enjoys knitting and sewing.
>
> She's like a trading ship that sails to faraway places
>> and brings back exotic surprises.
>
> She's up before dawn, preparing breakfast
>> for her family and organizing her day.
>
> She looks over a field and buys it,
>> then, with money she's put aside, plants a garden.
>
> First thing in the morning, she dresses for work,
>> rolls up her sleeves, eager to get started.
>
> She senses the worth of her work,
>> is in no hurry to call it quits for the day.
>
> She's skilled in the crafts of home and hearth,
>> diligent in homemaking.
>
> She's quick to assist anyone in need,
>> reaches out to help the poor.
>
> She doesn't worry about her family when it snows;
>> their winter clothes are all mended and ready to wear.
>
> She makes her own clothing,
>> and dresses in colorful linens and silks.
>
> Her husband is greatly respected
>> when he deliberates with the city fathers.
>
> She designs gowns and sells them,
>> brings the sweaters she knits to the dress shops.
>
> Her clothes are well-made and elegant,
>> and she always faces tomorrow with a smile.

When she speaks she has something worthwhile to say,
>    and she always says it kindly.
She keeps an eye on everyone in her household,
>    and keeps them all busy and productive.
Her children respect and bless her;
>    her husband joins in with words of praise:
"Many women have done wonderful things,
>    but you've outclassed them all!"
Charm can mislead and beauty soon fades.
>    The woman to be admired and praised
>    is the woman who lives in the Fear-of-God.
Give her everything she deserves!
>    Festoon her life with praises!

# think

- Proverbs 31 has long been held up as the standard for Christian women. What thoughts and feelings go through your mind when you read this passage?
- What are the character qualities of the Proverbs 31 woman?
- How would you compare your own character qualities, work achievements, and family performance to hers?
- How might a woman misunderstand this passage and apply it in an unhelpful way?
- How do you think God wants you to respond to the standard set by the Proverbs 31 woman?

# pray

Father, I need to know . . .

## read   the superwoman syndrome

From the article "Women, Stress and Midlife," by Jeanne Mackin[2]

Raising perfect kids, working, keeping up a home, caring for aging parents—all while time is running out for dreams and youth. What's a woman at midlife to do? . . .

It's not just that so many people expect so much of [women]. It's that they expect so much of themselves. It's the superwoman syndrome, and it's very, very real. . . .

Part of the superwoman syndrome lies in the way women define success, which is different from the male definition, [Elaine] Wethington says. For women, success must include high achievement at home and on the job. Men define success in terms of their jobs; the kids matter—they are very important, in fact—but how well they turn out has more to do with the mother's work at home than their own.

"Women have this attitude that they have to handle every-thing and handle it well," she says. "They have to be tougher than men, work harder, and be morally superior. This generation of women now entering midlife was especially ambitious. They even made parenting a competitive sport. It wasn't enough to have and raise children. They had to have perfect children."

## think

- How important to you is high achievement on the job? At home? Why is that the case?
- What would or does high achievement at home look like for you? Are you hitting those standards?
- Do you aim for perfect kids? If so, how do you do that? If not, why not?
- If you don't have a husband and/or children, do you feel you're failing to meet expectations in that area? Explain.
- Do you know parents who treat parenting as a competitive sport? If so, how does that affect their families? How does it affect you?

**think** (continued)

**pray**

God, I want to put in your hands . . .

## read   thirteen men to feed

Luke 10:38-42

As they continued their travel, Jesus entered a village. A woman by the name of Martha welcomed him and made him feel quite at home. She had a sister, Mary, who sat before the Master, hanging on every word he said. But Martha was pulled away by all she had to do in the kitchen. Later, she stepped in, interrupting them. "Master, don't you care that my sister has abandoned the kitchen to me? Tell her to lend me a hand."

The Master said, "Martha, dear Martha, you're fussing far too much and getting yourself worked up over nothing. One thing only is essential, and Mary has chosen it—it's the main course, and won't be taken from her."

## think

- What were Martha's expectations of herself? Of Mary? What did Jesus want?
- When you put Proverbs 31 side by side with this passage, what picture do you get of God's desires for you?
- Are you more like Martha or Mary?
- In a given week, how much time do you devote to cultivating a personal connection with Jesus? Why is that?

## pray

Jesus, please strengthen me to . . .

**read**   professional jugglers

From the *Los Angeles Times* article "We're All Multi-tasking, but What's the Cost?" by Melissa Healy[3]

Multi-tasking, for most Americans, has become a way of life. Doing many things at once is the way we manage demands bearing down on us at warp speed, tame a plague of helpful technological devices and play enough roles—parent, coach, social secretary, executive—to stage a Broadway show.

But researchers peering into the brains of those engaged in several tasks at once are concluding what some overworked Americans had begun to suspect: that multi-tasking, which many have embraced as the key to success, is instead a formula for shoddy work, mismanaged time, rote solutions, stress and forgetfulness. Not to mention car crashes, kitchen fires, forgotten children, near misses in the skies and other dangers of inattention.

So turn off the music, hang up the phone, pull over to the side of the road and take note: When it comes to using your brain to conduct several tasks at one time, "there is no free lunch," says University of Michigan psychologist David E. Meyer. For all but the most routine tasks—and few mental undertakings are truly routine—it will take more time for the brain to switch among tasks than it would have to complete one and then turn to the other.

When the two get squished together, each will be shortchanged, resulting in errors.

And a prolonged jag of extreme multi-tasking, warns Meyer, may lead to a shorter attention span, poorer judgment and impaired memory. . . .

Indeed, complaints of forgetfulness among women in their 40s and 50s are so prevalent that Peter M. Meyer, a biostatistician at Chicago's Rush University Medical Center, in the late 1990s conducted a study intended to gauge how deeply the hormone changes of menopause disrupt women's memory.

Instead, he got a lesson on women and multi-tasking. The

tests of short-term memory and verbal memory stubbornly showed that women of this age, though they complained of forgetfulness, were not missing a step. Their forgetfulness appeared to be a function of depression, stress and "role overload"—the multi-tasking of many roles at once—Meyer concluded.

## think

- What tasks do you often try to do simultaneously?
- How does doing several things at once affect your performance or memory, if at all?
- Brain researchers say it takes "more time for the brain to switch among tasks than it would have to complete one and then turn to the other." How do you respond to that claim?
- If the research is right, then why do we try to do several things at once?

## pray

Father, these tasks I'm juggling . . .

## read    unforced rhythms

Matthew 11:28-30

"Are you tired? Worn out? Burned out on religion? Come to me. Get away with me and you'll recover your life. I'll show you how to take a real rest. Walk with me and work with me—watch how I do it. Learn the unforced rhythms of grace. I won't lay anything heavy or ill-fitting on you. Keep company with me and you'll learn to live freely and lightly."

## think

- What does your church expect of "good Christians"? Of you personally?
- What do you think "the unforced rhythms of grace" means?
- From this passage, what does Jesus seem to expect or want from you?
- Jesus says, "Watch how I do it." How would a person go about watching how Jesus does life?
- How do you respond emotionally to Jesus' words here?

## pray

Jesus, teach me . . .

# LIVE

## what i want to discuss

What have you discovered this week that you definitely want to discuss with your small group? Write that here. Then begin your small-group discussion with these thoughts.

## so what?

Use the following space to summarize the truths you uncovered about the expectations you live with, how you feel about them, and where you need to begin in dealing with your situation. Review your "Beginning Place" if you need to remember where you began. How does God's truth affect the next step in your journey?

## now what?

What is one practical thing you can do to respond to what you discovered? What concrete action can you take? Remember to think realistically—an admirable but unreachable goal is as good as no goal. Discuss your goal in your small group to further define it.

## how?

How can your group—or even one other person—help you follow through with the goal you described? What support do you need? How will you measure the success of your plan? Write the details here.

# limits

## a reminder:

*Before you dive into this study, spend a little time reviewing what you wrote in the previous lesson's "Live" section. How are you doing? Check with your small-group members and review your progress toward your goals. If necessary, adjust your goals and plans, and then recommit to them.*

## the beginning place

Some of us are profoundly aware of our limits. We notice we just don't have the stamina we did when we were younger. Or perhaps we have a physical disability. Others of us exult in pushing past the supposed limits to our achievement. We know we're bright and full of energy, and the world is our dance floor.

As you begin this lesson, pause to reflect on your limits. First, how do you feel about the suggestion that you have limits? Does something inside you say, *Yes, thank you for validating what I've known!* Or does your gut protest, *Why are you being so negative? I can do all things through Christ who strengthens me!*

What limits are you aware of? Think about physical, emotional, financial, mental, and spiritual limits, or any others that occur to you. How do you feel about your limits? If the whole idea of limits seems foolish and unhelpful to you, say so.

## read overload

From *Margin*, by Richard A. Swenson, M.D.[1]

Overloading is a phenomenon of limits. "Researchers," according to sociologist Alvin Toffler, "strongly agree on two basic principles: first, that man has limited capacity; and second, that overloading the system leads to serious breakdown of performance."[2] . . .

Performance limits are related to physical limits but also introduce the factor of will. The endpoint is not as objectively defined, and we often are not quite as willing to accept the fact that there are limits. This is where stress fractures come from—people want to push themselves beyond the limit of breakdown. . . .

Our performance increases with increasing demand and increasing effort—but only up to a point. Once we reach our limits, fatigue sets in, followed quickly by exhaustion and collapse.

Emotional limits are even more vague. How much straining can the psyche withstand before being overloaded? . . . You might be able to emotionally "carry" one person. But what about five? Ten? One hundred? Where should we draw the line? . . .

Mental limits are as difficult to define as emotional limits, but the existence of such limits is indisputable. Information overload soon results in mental short-circuiting. . . .

Some will respond: "I can do all things through Christ who strengthens me."[3] Does this mean you can fly? Can you go six months without eating? Neither can you live a healthy life chronically overloaded. God did not intend this verse to represent a negation of life-balance. Even Jesus Himself did not heal every case of leprosy in Israel. Think about it.

It is God the Creator who made limits, and it is the same God who placed them within us for our protection. We exceed them at our peril.

Stay with GOD!
   Take heart. Don't quit.
I'll say it again:
   Stay with GOD.

## think

- In Philippians 4, what does God promise to do if you pray rather than worry?
- If God doesn't promise to give us everything we pray for, then why pray?
- What happens when Christ displaces worry at the center of our life?
- What security does Psalm 27 offer? What portrait of God does the psalmist paint?
- How important to you is the "one thing" this psalmist seeks?
- Where are you now with regard to trusting God?

## pray

Father, instead of worrying, I want to ask you for . . .

# LIVE

## what i want to discuss

What have you discovered this week that you definitely want to discuss with your small group? Write that here. Then begin your small-group discussion with these thoughts.

## so what?

Use the following space to summarize the truths you uncovered about trusting God, how you feel about them, and where you need to begin in dealing with your situation. Review your "Beginning Place" if you need to remember where you began. How does God's truth affect the next step in your journey?

## now what?

What is one practical thing you can do to respond to what you discovered? What concrete action can you take? Remember to think realistically—an admirable but unreachable goal is as good as no goal. Discuss your goal in your small group to further define it.

## how?

How can your group—or even one other person—help you follow through with the goal you described? What support do you need? How will you measure the success of your plan? Write the details here.

# happiness

## a reminder:

*Before you dive into this study, spend a little time reviewing what you wrote in the previous lesson's "Live" section. How are you doing? Check with your small-group members and review your progress toward your goals. If necessary, adjust your goals and plans, and then recommit to them.*

## the beginning place

What do you want out of life? No, really. If you're like a lot of women, you may meekly whisper (or shout), "I just want to be happy." That doesn't seem like much to ask.

But what makes you happy? Surprisingly, research suggests that humans are poor predictors of what will make them happiest.[1] (The writers of the Bible would not find this surprising.) So to set the stage for this lesson, take the following quiz.

1. How would you define happiness?
   a. Good feelings
   b. Good feelings over a long period of time
   c. A life well lived, having pursued and reached valuable goals
   d. A fortunate life in which things generally go well
   e. A connection with God that makes me a citizen of God's kingdom
   f. Other: _____

2. How happy are you?
   a. Very happy
   b. Fairly happy
   c. Neither happy nor unhappy
   d. Fairly unhappy
   e. Very unhappy

3. When are you happiest? (Choose as many as are true for you.)
   a. Alone
   b. With friends
   c. With just my husband
   d. With just my children
   e. With my husband and children
   f. With other family members
   g. At work
   h. In a church worship service
   i. In another church activity
   j. Praying
   k. At the gym
   l. Doing a hobby
   m. Doing housework
   n. Doing volunteer work
   o. Resting/sleeping
   p. Having sex
   q. Watching TV
   r. Other: _____

4. What is it about the items you chose in question 3 that gives
   you happiness?

5. Which stressful aspects of your life, if any, drain away happiness?

6. How embarrassing do you think it would be for someone in your study group to admit she was less than "fairly happy"? How do you think others would view her?

## read   happiness at bargain prices

From the *Money* article "How to Buy Happiness. Cheap." by David Futrelle[2]

Make love, not money. That was the most unusual message of a research note this summer from stock strategist James Montier at Dresdner Kleinwort Wasserstein, urging his well-heeled clients to set aside thoughts of stocks for a moment and to focus instead on the things that really make folks happy—namely love, sex, exercise and sleep. . . .

Disposable income for the average American has grown about 80% since 1972, but the percentage describing themselves as "very happy" (roughly a third) has barely budged over the years, according to the University of Chicago's National Opinion Research Center.

Why is this? Well, as Cornell University economist Robert Frank notes, we humans are highly adaptable animals, quickly adjusting our expectations to new realities. As living standards increase, most of us respond by raising our own standards. Things that once seemed luxuries now seem necessities. Call it the "once they've seen Paris" effect. As a result, we're working harder than ever to buy stuff that satisfies us less and less.

How to snap this vicious cycle? New research in psychology and economics offers practical suggestions on how to increase your consumer satisfaction—without increasing spending.

- *If you can't be with the stuff you love, love the stuff you're with.* Research by Robert Emmons, a psychology professor at the University of California at Davis, found that people encouraged to keep "gratitude journals" were far more satisfied with their lives than those who weren't encouraged to accentuate the positive. So don't waste your life fretting over what you ain't got. Give thanks for what you have—it can actually do you good.

- *Spend selectively.* Splurge only on those things that really bring you lasting pleasure; skimp on the rest. If you're a true-blue cinephile with a DVD collection to rival Roger Ebert's, it might make sense to invest in a plasma TV. But for most of us, a cheaper alternative is more than good enough.

- *Don't buy things, buy freedom.* While people easily adjust to bigger houses and cars, stress is stress no matter how rich or poor you are. As Frank notes, commuting through congestion is miserable for most of us, whether we've been doing it for four months or 40 years, and an assortment of studies shows that commutes (even as short as 15 minutes a day) can have serious and measurable effects on health. (There's a reason bus drivers seem so grumpy all the time.) If you're working endless hours to finance a lifestyle that isn't making you happy, consider cutting back your hours and getting by on less. It may not be easy to do, but in the long run it's likely to make you far happier than a new SUV ever could.

## think

- This article says love, sex, exercise, and sleep make people happy. How do you respond to that?
- List ten things you're grateful for.
- How easy was it for you to list what you're grateful for? What helps or hinders you?
- What do you think about the advice, "Don't buy things, buy freedom"?
- What hinders you from buying freedom?
- Choose one of the things you identified as making you happy—friends, for instance. What would it take for you to invest more in friends (or whatever you chose)?

**think** (continued)

**pray**

Father, thank you for . . .

## read  and even deeper discounts

Isaiah 55:1-3,6-13

> "Hey there! All who are thirsty,
>> come to the water!
> Are you penniless?
>> Come anyway—buy and eat!
> Come, buy your drinks, buy wine and milk.
>> Buy without money—everything's free!
> Why do you spend your money on junk food,
>> your hard-earned cash on cotton candy?
> Listen to me, listen well: Eat only the best,
>> fill yourself with only the finest.
> Pay attention, come close now,
>> listen carefully to my life-giving, life-nourishing words.
> I'm making a lasting covenant commitment with you,
>> the same that I made with David: sure, solid, enduring
>>> love. . . ."
>
> Seek God while he's here to be found,
>> pray to him while he's close at hand.
> Let the wicked abandon their way of life
>> and the evil their way of thinking.
> Let them come back to God, who is merciful,
>> come back to our God, who is lavish with forgiveness.
>
> "I don't think the way you think.
>> The way you work isn't the way I work." God's Decree.
> "For as the sky soars high above earth,
>> so the way I work surpasses the way you work,
>> and the way I think is beyond the way you think.
> Just as rain and snow descend from the skies
>> and don't go back until they've watered the earth,
> Doing their work of making things grow and blossom,
>> producing seed for farmers and food for the hungry,

So will the words that come out of my mouth
  not come back empty-handed.
They'll do the work I sent them to do,
  they'll complete the assignment I gave them.

"So you'll go out in joy,
  you'll be led into a whole and complete life.
The mountains and hills will lead the parade,
  bursting with song.
All the trees of the forest will join the procession,
  exuberant with applause.
No more thistles, but giant sequoias,
  no more thornbushes, but stately pines—
Monuments to me, to GOD,
  living and lasting evidence of GOD."

## think

- How does this passage suggest we seek what we're hungry for? What are you hungry for?
- What is the "junk food" God warns against? To what degree do you think your stress is influenced by seeking and consuming "junk food"?
- How is God's way of thinking different from your way?
- God promises, "So you'll go out in joy, you'll be led into a whole and complete life." Why should you believe this?
- Why do so many women under stress find it hard to believe what this passage promises?

**think** (continued)

**pray**

Lord, I want to buy . . .

**read** but *she* has . . . !

From *The Art of Happiness*, by the Dalai Lama and Howard C. Cutler, M.D.[3]

Our feelings of contentment are strongly influenced by our tendency to compare. When we compare our current situation to our past and find that we're better off, we feel happy. This happens, for instance, when our income suddenly jumps from $20,000–$30,000 a year, but it's not the absolute amount of income that makes us happy, as we soon find out when we get used to our new income and discover that we won't be happy again unless we're making $40,000 a year. We also look around and compare ourselves to others. No matter how much we make, we tend to be dissatisfied with our income if our neighbor is making more. Professional athletes complain bitterly about annual salaries of $1 million, $2 million or $3 million, citing the higher salary of a teammate as justification for their unhappiness. This tendency seems to support H. L. Mencken's definition of a wealthy man: one whose income is $100 a year higher than his wife's sister's husband.

So we can see how our feeling of life satisfaction often depends on who we compare ourselves to. Of course, we compare other things besides income. Constant comparison with those who are smarter, more beautiful, or more successful than ourselves also tends to breed envy, frustration, and unhappiness. But we can use this same principle in a positive way: we can increase our feeling of life satisfaction by comparing ourselves to those who are less fortunate than us and by reflecting on all the things we have.

## think

- To whom do you compare yourself? Friends? Relatives? People you went to school with? People you see on TV? Famous people?
- What do you compare? Income? Looks? Clothes? Home and interior decorating? Achievements? Children? Husband or boy-

friend? Spiritual depth?

- How does comparing yourself to others affect your stress level?
- How competitive are you? When does competition spur you on to be more fruitful, and when does it make you less fruitful?
- Think of someone less fortunate than you. Compare your life to his or hers. How does doing this affect you?
- Think of someone you admire. Are you more inclined to envy that person or to see him or her as a role model of qualities you can aspire to? Why is that?

## pray

Lord, when I compare . . .

## read   better than happy

Matthew 5:3-12

"You're blessed when you're at the end of your rope. With less of you there is more of God and his rule.

"You're blessed when you feel you've lost what is most dear to you. Only then can you be embraced by the One most dear to you.

"You're blessed when you're content with just who you are—no more, no less. That's the moment you find yourselves proud owners of everything that can't be bought.

"You're blessed when you've worked up a good appetite for God. He's food and drink in the best meal you'll ever eat.

"You're blessed when you care. At the moment of being 'care-full,' you find yourselves cared for.

"You're blessed when you get your inside world—your mind and heart—put right. Then you can see God in the outside world.

"You're blessed when you can show people how to cooperate instead of compete or fight. That's when you discover who you really are, and your place in God's family.

"You're blessed when your commitment to God provokes persecution. The persecution drives you even deeper into God's kingdom.

"Not only that—count yourselves blessed every time people put you down or throw you out or speak lies about you to discredit me. What it means is that the truth is too close for comfort and they are uncomfortable. You can be glad when that happens—give a cheer, even!—for though they don't like it, *I* do! And all heaven applauds. And know that you are in good company. My prophets and witnesses have always gotten into this kind of trouble."

## think

- Jesus says, "You're blessed when you're at the end of your rope." Why do you think Jesus said that? What do you think about it?
- Why does contentment bring blessing? How is blessedness connected to or different from happiness?
- Do you consider yourself blessed? Why or why not?
- How does your view of happiness or blessedness affect the way you invest your time?
- If you had to choose between the things Jesus promises in this passage (such as "more of God and his rule") and other things you value (such as having a home as nice as your friends' or getting your kids into good colleges), which would you choose? How fair is it to pose this as an either/or choice?

## pray

Jesus, when I think about the blessing you offer . . .

## read   if paul's happy, why is he still running?

### 1 Corinthians 9:21-27

I've become just about every sort of servant there is in my attempts to lead those I meet into a God-saved life. I did all this because of the Message. I didn't just want to talk about it; I wanted to be *in* on it!

You've all been to the stadium and seen the athletes race. Everyone runs; one wins. Run to win. All good athletes train hard. They do it for a gold medal that tarnishes and fades. You're after one that's gold eternally.

I don't know about you, but I'm running hard for the finish line. I'm giving it everything I've got. No sloppy living for me! I'm staying alert and in top condition. I'm not going to get caught napping, telling everyone else all about it and then missing out myself.

### 2 Timothy 4:6-8

I'm about to die, my life an offering on God's altar. This is the only race worth running. I've run hard right to the finish, believed all the way. All that's left now is the shouting—God's applause! Depend on it, he's an honest judge. He'll do right not only by me, but by everyone eager for his coming.

## think

- In both of these passages, the apostle Paul speaks of "running" in positive terms. When is "running hard" a good thing?
- The 1 Corinthians passage comes from Paul's midlife. Does he seem happy to you? What makes you say that?
- In 2 Timothy, Paul looks back on his life as a man about to die. Why is he happy?
- When you are old and look back on your life, what do you hope to see?

- Do these passages inspire you? If so, what do they inspire you to do? If not, do they make you feel pressure, guilt, or something else?

## pray

Lord, at the end of my life, I want to look back . . .

# LIVE

## what i want to discuss

What have you discovered this week that you definitely want to discuss with your small group? Write that here. Then begin your small-group discussion with these thoughts.

## so what?

Use the following space to summarize the truths you uncovered about happiness, how you feel about them, and where you need to begin in dealing with your situation. Review your "Beginning Place" if you need to remember where you began. How does God's truth affect the next step in your journey?

## now what?

What is one practical thing you can do to respond to what you discovered? What concrete action can you take? Remember to think realistically—an admirable but unreachable goal is as good as no goal. Discuss your goal in your small group to further define it.

## how?

How can your group—or even one other person—help you follow through with the goal you described? What support do you need? How will you measure the success of your plan? Write the details here.

# rest

## a reminder:

*Before you dive into this study, spend a little time reviewing what you wrote in the previous lesson's "Live" section. How are you doing? Check with your small-group members and review your progress toward your goals. If necessary, adjust your goals and plans, and then recommit to them.*

## the beginning place

Rest. What we wouldn't give for some good rest! A month somewhere warm, on the beach perhaps . . . a day at a spa . . . even a good night's sleep.

The Bible has a great deal to say about rest. Unfortunately, a lot of what it says is about the Sabbath; that is, setting aside one day out of seven to connect with God and one another. In Old Testament times that day was Saturday, but the earliest Christians shifted to observing Sunday, the day on which Christ rose from the dead.

Today we do try to catch a worship service sometime on the weekend, but often it just feels like another item on a long to-do list. Getting kids ready to go to church is not exactly restful! And the idea of spending the remainder of Sunday enjoying family and friends or enjoying more time with God through prayer and study seems laughably out of reach. Our kids have soccer or music lessons; we have errands to run and homes to clean. If we didn't get things done on Sunday, when would we do them?

Besides, the Sabbath smacks of legalism to many of us. At some times and places in Christian history, children weren't allowed to play games on the Sabbath. That kind of Sabbath seems more burden than blessing.

To begin this session, then, reflect on what goes through your mind when you think of the Sabbath. Do you feel longing or guilt? Does it seem desirable or ridiculous? Legalistic or freeing? What aspects of modern life make the Sabbath difficult, if not impossible? Describe your starting point on the subject of the Sabbath; we'll go deeper from there.

## read   i'm a *former* slave?

### Exodus 20:8-11

Observe the Sabbath day, to keep it holy. Work six days and do
everything you need to do. But the seventh day is a Sabbath
to GOD, your God. Don't do any work—not you, nor your
son, nor your daughter, nor your servant, nor your maid,
nor your animals, not even the foreign guest visiting in your
town. For in six days GOD made Heaven, Earth, and sea, and
everything in them; he rested on the seventh day. Therefore
GOD blessed the Sabbath day; he set it apart as a holy day.

### Exodus 23:12

"Work for six days and rest the seventh so your ox and donkey
may rest and your servant and migrant workers may have time to
get their needed rest."

### Deuteronomy 5:12-15

No working on the Sabbath; keep it holy just as GOD, your God,
commanded you. Work six days, doing everything you have
to do, but the seventh day is a Sabbath, a Rest Day—no
work: not you, your son, your daughter, your servant, your
maid, your ox, your donkey (or any of your animals), and
not even the foreigner visiting your town. That way your
servants and maids will get the same rest as you. Don't ever
forget that you were slaves in Egypt and GOD, your God,
got you out of there in a powerful show of strength. That's
why GOD, your God, commands you to observe the day of
Sabbath rest.

## think

- What beliefs about God do you see reflected in these passages?
- Why is it valuable to pause and remember that "GOD made Heaven, Earth, and sea, and everything in them"?
- Here is one explanation of the Sabbath: "What happens when we stop working and controlling nature? . . . When we cease interfering in the world we are acknowledging that it is God's world."[1] What value, if any, would this weekly reminder have in your life?
- Deuteronomy says that the Sabbath reminds us that only God enables us to be more than slaves. What value would this weekly reminder have in your life?
- A Sabbath gives rest to servants and other low-wage workers. Does that matter to you? Explain.

## pray

Creator God, you made the world in which I work . . .

the door. The rain was coming down sideways and, out of habit, I reached for my hood. Unfortunately, the hood I needed was on the sweatshirt my mom told me to wear and that sweatshirt *was still hanging in my closet*.

"You should have worn a hood today," said T-Bone, as he lifted his hood from under his backpack straps.

I rolled my eyes.

As I stepped into puddles the size of small ponds, cold water rushed into my sneakers. I suddenly missed my old fireman rain boots.

"You wanna work on some ideas for our next New Jersey trip?" T-Bone asked as he jumped over a tiny puddle and landed in the middle of a huge one.

"Sure," I nodded as water dripped into my eyes. "Let's go to my house."

As soon as we walked in, I could hear my mom in the kitchen. She had just gotten home and was juggling shopping bags and the mail.

"Hi, Nick, I'm glad you're home. Can you give me a hand and get Emma and Maggie sippy cups before they have a melt down? And then can you put those puzzles by the door away? Thanks."

When I was done with the puzzles and sippy

11

cups, T-Bone and I went up to my room. He sat at my desk and started spinning the globe.

"Where do you want to go first?" he asked, giving it a good spin. As his finger brought it to a sudden stop, he read the name of the country he landed on.

"How about Morocco?"

"You do know we have to visit places in New Jersey, right?" I asked.

"Yeah, I know, but wouldn't it be great to see the world?" T-Bone wondered.

"Join the Navy," I said, as I opened a fresh notebook.

"Maybe I will," he shrugged. "Or maybe we'll do such a great job that the President will ask us to be 'Unofficial' Junior Ambassadors for the United States and we'll be able to see the country."

"Yeah," I laughed, "like that'll ever happen."

"Then, if we do a *really* good job," he continued, "the head of the Earth will ask us to be ambassadors for the whole planet."

"You're kidding?" I asked, hoping he knew there wasn't a president of the whole planet.

"I never thought about it," he said. "But it's kind of weird that no one is in charge."

"No," I said without looking up. "It's hard enough to get people to agree on pizza toppings and you want someone to be in charge of the Earth?"

"Well, that's a shame because it would be cool to be an Earth ambassador."

"Why stop there?" I suggested. "Why not just call the head of the galaxy and be a planet tour guide?"

"That's stupid," he said. "Who would read our reports? I doubt other planets can read English."

I rolled my eyes and then searched my bookshelf for an atlas. I paged through it until I found the New Jersey map.

"There she is," I said, holding up the map.

"She who?" asked T-Bone.

"New Jersey."

"Why did you call New Jersey a *she*? I think New Jersey looks like a man with a hat."

"Okay, then, there *he* is," I said, avoiding a discussion about whether New Jersey resembled a man or a woman. "Where should we start?"

"At the top?" he asked.

"I don't think we need to go top to bottom," I suggested. "Maybe we should call Billy at the Governor's office and see if he has any ideas."

"Are you crazy?" T-Bone asked. "If we call to ask where to start, they'll think we don't know what we're doing. They might even get someone else to do our job."

"I didn't think about that," I admitted, shocked that T-Bone made such a good point.

"Why don't we just do a report about the places we already visited?" he suggested. "We liked every place we went to last time and we'd even save gas money."

"I don't know," I hesitated, "we can go to some of the places we visited last time, but I think we should find some new places, too."

"Maybe we should go on the internet and see if New Jersey has a list of cool places for kids to visit," T-Bone said, forgetting one important issue.

"That would be fantastic," I explained, "*except we're making that list!*"

"Oh, yeah," he remembered.

"We could still look for ideas on the internet?" I suggested, heading to the family room.

"Why do we have to go downstairs to use the computer?" T-Bone wondered. "Why don't you have a computer in your room?"

"I'm not sure," I said, "but I think it had

something to do with a cop visiting my mom's school for a PTA meeting. He talked about internet safety and predators and told the parents that computers should never be in a kid's room."

"That stinks," T-Bone shook his head, as if I lived in a mansion and the family room was a mile away and not just at the bottom of the stairs.

"It doesn't really matter," I shrugged. "If it was in my room, whenever someone wanted to use the computer, they'd be at my desk. It's bad enough having Timmy in there all the time."

"That's why you should have *your own computer*, in *your own room*," T-Bone insisted. "I don't know how you get anything done, constantly running down to the family room."

"Hold on," I recalled, "I don't remember ever seeing a computer in *your* room."

"That's because I don't *have* a computer in my room."

"Well, then, how do you get anything done?" I asked in my most sarcastic voice.

"Computer in my room?" he laughed. "I don't even have a computer. I use my mom's laptop, but it's not in the family room…*it's in the kitchen*."

# Chapter Two
## Those Must Be Some Bananas

As we dragged an extra chair to the family room computer, I could hear someone knocking on the door. Suddenly, the door opened.

"Wait," T-Bone whispered. "You could be getting robbed right now."

"What?" I mouthed.

"Someone walked in," he said, frantically pointing at the door.

After thinking about it for a few seconds, I whispered, "Why would a burglar knock?"

"I don't know," he snapped, "maybe to throw you off!"

A moment later I heard my mom tell the mysterious visitor that she hadn't heard him knock. I took a deep breath and a sigh of relief. Even though I knew that T-Bone didn't make any sense, my heart did skip a beat or two when I heard the footsteps.

We headed to the front door, curious to see who it was, and we were happy to see it was my grandfather. I was sure he would have a few suggestions for day trips. After all, he's the one who always tells us that he's been around the block a few times. Hopefully, that block included New Jersey.

"Hi, Pop," I said, as I went over to shake his hand.

"N-i-c-k-y," he said in his usual, stretch-the-word-out-real-long kind of way. "How's my boy?"

"Good. You remember my friend, T-Bone, right?"

"Is this the friend that went on all your trips?" he asked, raising one eyebrow.

"Yup," I answered.

"Then, yes, I believe we've met and I know your father has mentioned him a few times," he nodded and smiled.

"So what brings you by?" I asked, hoping he might be on his way to a fantastic New Jersey destination, preferably one that kids would enjoy.

"Well, I went to visit an old friend in Columbus and, of course, stopped by the Farmers Market," he said as he handed my mom three plastic bags overflowing with produce.

"You must love fruit," T-Bone exclaimed.

"Of course, but why do you ask?" my grand-father wondered with one of those curious looks.

"Because Ohio is a pretty long trip for bananas," T-Bone smirked and threw my grandfather a high-five.

"No, Tommy, I didn't drive to Columbus, Ohio. I drove to Columbus, New Jersey."

"Never heard of it," T-Bone replied. "Are you sure you weren't in Ohio? Did you see any Buckeye shirts?"

"No, I'm sure it was New Jersey," my grand-father smiled.

"I'm just asking because every time I get in the car with my grandfather, he always ends up going somewhere he didn't plan," T-Bone explained.

"You wouldn't happen to be in the back seat talking to him when this happens, would you?" my grandfather asked, understanding how T-Bone could drive someone to distraction.

"That's *exactly* where I am when it happens," T-Bone answered, the sarcasm flying over his head.

"Anyway, there's a nice town north of here, called Columbus," he explained. "It's the home of the very popular Columbus Farmers Market.

18

Whenever I'm in the area, I always stop by and visit Bruce at Cannuli's Produce."

"You mean people go all the way to this Columbus just for apples and oranges?" asked T-Bone. "You know you can get fruit and vegetables at the supermarket, right?"

"Well, they have every fruit and vegetable you could imagine, including fresh Jersey corn, tomatoes, and blueberries when they're in season. They also have a huge indoor market and every Thursday, Saturday, and Sunday they have outside vendors. The Amish even have handmade wooden furniture, an unbelievable bakery, meat counter, and candy shop."

"I don't know who the Amish are," said T-Bone, "but if they sell candy, I'd like to meet them."

"You should go there one day. I'm sure they'd be equally excited," my grandfather joked.

"We should check it out," T-Bone agreed.

"If you make Columbus a stop on one of your day trips, you should also visit Burlington," said my grandfather.

"That's a great idea. The City of Burlington is lovely," my mom agreed. "There's so much history and it's right on the water."

"The Atlantic Ocean?" asked T-Bone.

"No, Tommy," my mom smiled. "The Delaware River."

"They have one of those up there, too? There's one by the Camden Riversharks baseball field. My dad took me to a game last year."

My mom and grandfather both laughed.

"What's so funny?" asked T-Bone.

"It's the same river," I laughed.

"Really?" he said, not sure if he believed us.

"It sure is," my grandfather smiled. "The Delaware River is a boundary between New York and Pennsylvania; New Jersey and Pennsylvania; and Delaware and New Jersey."

"Wow, you know a lot about the Delaware River. How'd you learn all of that?" T-Bone wondered. "Were you a fisherman?"

"No," my grandfather explained, "when we were kids we didn't have video games, nine hundred cable channels and huge movie theaters like you have now. We used to drive all over the state for fun. We even used to take our kids canoeing and tubing on the Delaware River."

"A friend of mine has a virtual canoeing game," said T-Bone. "It's awesome."

"How on earth would you know?" asked my grandfather. "Did you ever get wet while canoeing in his family room?"

"He did spill a soda all over himself when we were playing," T-Bone remembered. "So, yes, he definitely got wet."

"No, no, no," my grandfather shook his head. "I'm not talking about virtual canoeing. It was real canoeing. It was real people; real people in real canoes in real water. We didn't sit in the parlor and pretend to be outside: we really went canoeing."

"Did you get points?" T-Bone wondered.

"*Points*?" asked my grandfather.

"You know," T-Bone continued, "if you do tricks, you get points. If you make it over the waterfall, you get points. Points make it exciting."

"Tommy, you kids need to unplug those computers, video games, and televisions and get outside," said my grandfather. "You need to experience life firsthand and actually touch the water as you paddle, or feel the breeze as you walk. What could possibly be so great about *virtually* doing things?"

"Points," T-Bone said, grabbing a banana.

"I give up; he's all yours," my grandfather told my mom as he headed out the door.

I went over to shake his hand and he whispered, "I'm glad to see that you boys will really be visiting the state instead of virtually. If you need a ride or a guide for any of your trips, give me a call."

"You're hired," yelled T-Bone, "*unofficially*, of course."

"That kid's got some ears," my grandfather mumbled as he left.

"Hey, Nicky," T-Bone whispered, "your grandfather knows that *unofficial* means we can't pay him, right?"

I nodded.

We sat at the computer and started searching Burlington, New Jersey. I couldn't believe how many things were packed into one town. My mom was right about the history and the river. Even though I grew up in Philadelphia, I never paid much attention to American history. I used to live in the same neighborhood where Ben Franklin and Betsy Ross once lived and where colonists secretly met to declare our independence, yet I never really appreciated it. During my last year in Philadelphia, that started to change. Mr. Getty, my social studies teacher, loved history so much that everyone in his class started to enjoy it. He told us exciting stories about things that happened in our own city. By the end of the year, we were kind of proud that we lived in a city that was so important to our country. Now, I saw that New Jersey was pretty important, too.

We found a really cool website called www.tourburlington.org, which had everything you could possibly want to do in Burlington City. There were scheduled walking tours, ghost walks, and school field trips. There were descriptions of every famous house and famous resident, and even stories about famous visitors. And when they said famous, they weren't kidding. Some of the people who came to Burlington included: Ben Franklin, Abraham Lincoln, and Ulysses S. Grant. They called the tours *Time Travel* and we thought that might be something other kids might like to do.

"Look at that," T-Bone said, pointing at the screen. "It says that Abraham Lincoln arm-wrestled Ulysses S. Grant. That must have been something for that guy to arm-wrestle a president."

"Which guy?" I laughed.

"That Ulysses guy," said T-Bone. "He got to go up against a real president."

"You know Ulysses S. Grant became a president, too?" I asked since he wasn't in Mr. Getty's class.

"Really?" he said.

"Really," I answered.

"Then why isn't he on money, like Abraham Lincoln, George Washington, and Ben Franklin?"

"He *is* on money," I insisted. "He's on the fifty dollar bill. And not every person on money was a president. A couple of them were just really important, like Ben Franklin and Alexander Hamilton."

"Well, if we charged more money for our odd jobs, we might see who was on a fifty dollar bill," T-Bone laughed. "Do you think it really happened?"

"I don't know," I started reading. "It says they're called oral traditions. Stories passed down from one generation to another. There's no evidence to prove they happened, but there's no evidence to prove they didn't."

"So did they?" he asked, clearly ignoring my explanation.

"I don't know. I guess if they were both in town, it could have happened."

"Good, I'm going to assume it did happen. It's funnier that way," T-Bone nodded. "I just wish we knew who won. What else do they have?"

"This is cool," I said, pointing to the screen. "It says Elias Boudinot was the first President."

"Of what?" asked T-Bone.

"Of the United States," I read.

"I hate to break it to you, Nick, but George Washington was the first president."

"Hold on," I said, as I skimmed the paragraph. "The Revolutionary War ended in 1783 and George Washington was elected President in 1789."

"So?" T-Bone shrugged.

"So, there was no president for the first six years," I continued. "The Continental Congress was trying to set up the country and Elias Boudinot was the President of the Continental Congress in 1783 when the war ended. It says that he was even referred to as the First President in many newspapers."

"Does that mean he was an *unofficial* president?" asked T-Bone.

"Well, I'm not a history expert, but it sounds like he was in charge."

"Poor *unofficial* president," T-Bone shook his head. "He probably didn't get paid either."

# Chapter Three
## Greetings Meetings

The following week was very busy. T-Bone and I found ourselves spending every spare moment on the internet, searching different New Jersey cities and towns. We found everything from sports to history to the arts. The more we searched, the harder it was to decide where to visit and what we should see. It was also hard to believe that some of these places have been here all along.

We made a list of places and tried to figure out which ones were near each other. We figured if we had a good time, other kids would, too. And writing reports and taking pictures were the best ways to share New Jersey with other kids.

We called Billy at the Governor's Office and told him that we were planning all of our trips. He seemed really excited and told us how much he looked forward to working on a project with kids.

He suggested we take pictures and send him reports when we were done with each trip. He also invited us to come to the State House whenever we wanted. When we realized he worked around the corner from the Old Barracks, we decided to hand deliver our reports and pictures whenever we could.

It was a Tuesday afternoon and it was much hotter than it should have been. At least, that's what Action News reported. T-Bone and I decided to take my grandfather up on his offer to be our ride and guide. My dad was working extra hours at the grocery store, so we asked my grandfather if he could bring us on our first trip. He quickly agreed and even offered to help plan the day.

Around five o'clock we heard him walk through the front door.

"N-I-C-K-Y," my grandfather said, extending his hand. "How goes it?"

"It goes," I said, firmly shaking his hand. I remembered once hearing him complain about weak handshakes. Whenever it was time to shake his hand, I always made sure it was firm.

"So, when and where?" he asked, as we headed toward the kitchen.

"Tomorrow and Burlington, Roebling and

Columbus," I began. "Here are some of our ideas. If you think they're okay, we were hoping we could leave really early tomorrow. We thought we'd start with Burlington."

"The one on the Delaware River," T-Bone winked.

"And then," I continued, "we could drive through Roebling and go to the Farmers Market in Columbus."

"Columbus, New Jersey, not Ohio," T-Bone interrupted again.

"I get it," my grandfather said, shaking his head. "That sounds fine, boys. What have you planned so far?"

We both looked at each other and shrugged our shoulders.

"Alright," he said pulling a chair up to the kitchen table, "if these trips are for families, you should keep a few things in mind. First, not everyone likes the same things you do, so make sure the places you pick have something for everyone. Second, not everyone is rich, so include things that are free or cheap. And third, don't overbook a day. There's nothing more frustrating than realizing you booked twelve hours of fun into a seven hour day."

"That makes sense," I agreed, handing him some pages we had printed.

"Let's see," he said as he took a look. "The City of Burlington has so many great places. I recently read an article about how they're bringing the city's history back to life."

"We saw that on their website," said T-Bone. "*The past is their present to us.*"

"That's clever and true," my grandfather smiled. "Now, Roebling has a different kind of history because it began as a company town."

"What do you mean?" said T-Bone, wondering exactly what I was wondering.

"Well, in 1904, the Roebling Company built a steel mill on land between Trenton and Burlington. Charles Roebling, one of the Roebling Brothers, designed one of the country's first *company towns* when he created the Roebling Village. There were 750 brick homes for the workers, a general store, and a public school. They produced many products, including wire rope for San Francisco's Golden Gate Bridge. The town revolved around the company."

"That's pretty cool that they gave all of their workers a house," said T-Bone. "Did they give them a pool, too?"

"No," said my grandfather, "they didn't *give* them houses or pools. They *rented* houses to the workers."

"Too bad," said T-Bone. "Maybe we should put San Francisco and that bridge in our report, too."

"Except," I reminded him, "San Francisco is in California."

"Good point," he agreed. "That might be too far to visit."

Rather than explain to him that Junior New Jersey Ambassadors should really write about New Jersey, I decided to let it go. I noticed my grandfather did the same.

"Then we can stop by the Columbus Farmers Market and you can see a real New Jersey landmark," my grandfather continued.

"I don't know," T-Bone began, "maybe we should add some water parks or arcades or things kids actually like. Most kids don't really like vegetables or history and this trip is starting to sound like a lot of vegetables and history."

"You know, Tommy, you can have fun and still learn something," said my grandfather. "And I'm guessing a celery stalk wouldn't kill you, either!

"Or," T-Bone suggested, "we could visit

video arcades, miniature golf courses, and go-cart tracks and then read about history."

"There's a big difference between reading about history and seeing where it happened," my grandfather assured him. "People enjoy history more when they can visit historical places and learn about the interesting things that really happened."

"What interesting things?" asked T-Bone. "History is pretty boring and it's not like you can change it. Does anyone really care that we won the Revolution in 1776?"

"We *didn't* win the Revolution in 1776," I laughed. "The Continental Congress met in secret, in Philadelphia. They declared our independence from Great Britain, in 1776, with a little thing Thomas Jefferson and friends whipped up, called the Declaration of Independence. That was the beginning of the Revolutionary War and it didn't end until 1783 when British General Cornwallis surrendered in Yorktown."

Suddenly, the kitchen was silent. My grandfather and T-Bone both stared at me. My secret was out. I liked history. I blamed it on Mr. Getty and living in Philadelphia since we were surrounded by the Liberty Bell, Ben Franklin, and Independence Mall. Every day, horse carriages clip-clopped through the city, while drivers shared interesting stories and little known facts. My favorite was Ben Franklin's *Busybody Mirrors* which were three little mirrors, arranged just so, which hung outside a second floor window. When someone knocked at the door, a person inside could see who was knocking without being seen. I once heard a driver call them *mother-in-law mirrors*. He said a gentleman could see his mother-in-law at the front door and make a quick exit through the back door. It was impossible to live there and not know the history. Plus, the stories were pretty cool.

"Nick," said T-Bone, slowly turning his head. "How do you know all of that? You're not one of those history guys, are you?"

"What do you mean by *history guy*?"

"You know, you'll end up wearing a bow tie, always carrying a book under your arm. You'll spend your whole future thinking about the past."

"You watch too much television," I smirked. "And, no, I'm not a history expert just because I know we didn't win a war on the same exact day that it started."

"That's a relief," he sighed. "You know, it's a shame we can't turn our day trips into virtual trips that people could do from their computer. Then they could see those history things without leaving home. And, even better, they could turn it off when they got really bored."

"Is he for real?" my grandfather asked.

"Yeah," I laughed. "And you have no idea what you're in for, Pop."

"No, no, no, Nicky," my grandfather winked, "Tommy has no idea what *he's* in for. I have a feeling he won't be such a *history hater* by the time we're done with him."

# Chapter Four

## Greetings from Burlington, Roebling, and Columbus, Part 1

School had just started and we already had a day off for teacher workshops. We decided it would be a good day to visit Burlington, Roebling, and Columbus. T-Bone arrived nice and early and my grandfather pulled up a few moments later. I grabbed the papers we had printed, along with a map, and we were on our way.

We decided to change the order of our itinerary. The Columbus Farmers Market opened early so we made that our first stop. We didn't live too far away, so even with the traffic, it didn't take long to get there. As we drove north on Route 206, I could see the enormous sign and hundreds of cars.

"Look at all of those tables," T-Bone pointed.

"Those are the outside vendors," explained my grandfather as we searched for a parking place. "Some come once in a while, some come every week and inside are the permanent vendors."

"What do they sell?" I asked.

"What don't they sell?" my grandfather laughed. "You can buy anything from shoes to a gazebo to apples."

We parked the car and walked through some of the outside vendor rows. My grandfather wasn't kidding. A man selling baseball cards was next to a man selling antiques. Farther down the aisle we met a man named Rafi at the Krazy Korn booth. He was selling homemade kettle corn and it smelled great.

"Good morning," said Rafi.

"Good morning," we replied.

"Would you boys like to be official taste-testers?" he asked.

"I don't know," said T-Bone. "We're already Unofficial Junior Ambassadors working for the Governor. I'm not sure if we're allowed to be official taste-testers, too."

"I don't think he's making us a job offer," I whispered. "I think he's just offering us a sample."

"That's right," Rafi joked, "to be an *official* Official Krazy Korn tester you'd have to take courses at Krazy Kollege."

My grandfather and I laughed, but T-Bone was still thinking.

"Do you have to go to Krazy Kollege to be an *unofficial* taste-tester?" wondered T-Bone.

"I'll tell you what," Rafi leaned in and whispered, "I'll make you both unofficial taste-testers."

"You can do that?" asked T-Bone.

"Just don't tell Stephanie or Helen," he winked.

"Are they your bosses?" I asked.

"Kind of," he smiled, "Stephanie's my wife and Helen is my wacky mother-in-law."

"Wait," asked T-Bone, "do we have to write a report after we eat it?"

"Hmmm," Rafi pretended to mull it over, "how about a thumbs up or a thumbs down?"

We each took a mouthful and immediately threw him two thumbs up. When my grandfather asked us a question and realized the kettle corn made it difficult for us to speak, he ordered four bags. When we were finally able to speak, we thanked Rafi for the samples.

"Wow, Nick," T-Bone whispered, "your mom definitely wouldn't have given us Krazy Korn in the morning."

We made our way inside and it was packed. When we reached the end, we were standing in the Amish Market. It smelled like cinnamon buns and chocolate chip cookies, which I immediately decided was a great combination. My grandfather stood in line and walked away with three big bags.

"Hungry?" I asked.

"It's for your grandmother," he said.

"Sure it is," I laughed and rolled my eyes.

Our next stop was Cannuli's, where there were three produce companies right next to each other. While I wasn't a big fruit and vegetable fan like my dad, I could almost see why he loved it so much. Everything looked so colorful in the wooden crates. I suddenly started craving one of the plums. We followed my grandfather as he filled his cart. Soon he started talking to a man and woman behind the counter.

"Tim Abruzzi, who do you have with you today?" the woman smiled.

"This is my grandson, Nick, and his friend, Tommy," he answered.

"Nice to meet you," she extended her hand. "I'm Michele and this is Bruce. How are you?"

I gave them a firm handshake and told them about our project. They were impressed and wished us well. As Michele rang the order, she tossed us each a plum.

"Thanks," I smiled, sure she read my mind.

"You're very welcome," she replied.

As we pulled out, I was making a mental list of everything I was going to buy when we came back. On the top of the list, even before baseball cards, was Krazy Korn and more of those plums.

Our next stop was Roebling and I was pretty curious to see what a company town really looked like. As we approached the factory site, it was really quiet. There was a huge Flywheel out front and across the street began rows of homes once occupied by the employees and their families.

"This town was very important in our country's history," my grandfather explained. "The workers at this plant made the wire rope for some famous bridges like the George Washington, the Golden Gate, the Manhattan and the Williamsburg."

"What do they make now?" asked T-Bone.

"Sadly, the factory closed in 1974 and most of it is gone," he said as he continued the tour

"How do you know these things?" T-Bone wondered.

"I get around," my grandfather winked. "But the good news is that they just opened the Roebling Museum. That means you can visit the century-old gatehouse and learn about the company, the town, and the Roebling family, up close and personal."

"Bridges are nice," said T-Bone, "but iron rope and wire have nothing to do with kids."

"Don't be so sure," my grandfather laughed, "have you ever played with a Slinky?"

"Who hasn't?" T-Bone shrugged.

"Well, Roebling was the main supplier of spring wire for Slinkies."

"Really?" we both said at the same time.

As we drove through town there was a circle with a flag, a brick walkway, and a statue of Charles Roebling. I realized that he didn't just create a company town; Mr. Roebling created a *hometown* for kids who must have been proud to live there.

Next, we headed south on Route 130 toward the City of Burlington. I started looking over the papers we had printed from the internet, but before I could get everything organized, we had arrived. We parked in front of City Hall and I unfolded my map.

"Where to first?" my grandfather asked, checking his watch. "It's only 9:45; we have all day."

"I'm not sure," I said, slightly confused.

"Find the star that says YOU ARE HERE," T-Bone advised.

"There is no star," I replied.

"Look harder," he instructed, "most maps have a star to tell you where you are."

I shook my head, wondering if I should explain that when I printed the map, it had no idea where I would be standing when I opened it. I decided not to bother.

"Okay," I said, wishing I had joined the Boy Scouts when I was younger, "here's City Hall. That means the Visitors Center must be down the street."

"Which way?" asked T-Bone.

"Good question," I replied, noticing my grandfather was very quiet. I figured he was trying to let us handle everything ourselves. I was tempted to just hand him the map, but remembered that we were the ambassadors and this was our job. After a few moments, I noticed two men walking down the steps.

"Good morning," said the taller man. "How are you today?"

"Lost," T-Bone answered.

"We're not lost," I insisted.

"That's right," T-Bone agreed. "We just don't know where we are."

"Well, maybe I can help you. I'm Jim and this is Eric," he said.

"I'm T-Bone, this is my friend, Nick, and his grandfather, Mr. Abruzzi. We're Unofficial Junior Ambassadors working for the Governor," he explained. "We're checking out Burlington City and then we'll give the Governor a report for other kids."

Just like when we spent weeks collecting stickers at the mall, I was amazed at how easily T-Bone was able to speak to people. Remembering my own, less-than-wonderful speaking skills, I decided to say hello and let him do the talking.

"That's very interesting," Jim nodded. "You've come to the right place. There's plenty of history here. The City of Burlington was the first recorded European settlement in New Jersey and has had some amazing residents and visitors including Benjamin Franklin, Abraham Lincoln, Ulysses S. Grant, Captain James Lawrence, and Elias Boudinot."

"You must have gone on the same website we did," guessed T-Bone. "It said that Abraham Lincoln may have arm-wrestled Ulysses S. Grant at a tavern here."

"Actually, it's said to have occurred right down the street at the former Blue Anchor Inn, now the Visitors Center," Jim added as he pointed to a building at the intersection of Broad and High.

"I guess this isn't your first visit here," I said.

"No, it's definitely not my first visit."

"Boys," Eric laughed, "Jim is the Mayor of the City of Burlington."

"Really?" I asked.

"Really," he smiled.

I was shocked to see the Mayor just walking along the streets. I assumed most mayors had bodyguards, used back entrances, and avoided talking to people and kissing babies after the election was over.

"And Eric is the Business Administrator," said the Mayor. "We're walking down to meet the school busses. If you'd like to tag along, I can show you some pretty interesting things for your report."

"Wow," said T-Bone, "our mayor only comes to school during *Read Across America* week."

Eric laughed and explained that there were several schools visiting Burlington on field trips that day and when the Mayor isn't in a meeting, he likes to walk down and greet them. Nice guys, I thought.

"I've explained a little of your history to them and they've done some research on their own," said my grandfather. "I'm hoping to convince Tommy that history is exciting."

"Hmmm, a tough customer," the Mayor laughed, "I'll tell you a little secret. I wasn't particularly interested in history when I was your age. And now I dress up as Ulysses S. Grant for many of the town's events."

As we walked down High Street, he took us past the Burlington County Historical Society, the home of author James Fennimore Cooper, and Captain James Lawrence's house. He told us Captain Lawrence, as commander of the S.S. Chesapeake and mortally wounded, shouted to his men, "*Don't give up the ship*." Those famous words became the motto of the city and the United States Navy.

I couldn't believe we were getting a private tour from the Mayor and I was more shocked that he seemed to know everyone and everything in town. I took out my mom's camera and started taking pictures. We stopped by what was once Lyceum Hall, but was now a newly renovated Arts Center. It was huge and he was very excited about all of the programs that would be taking place. In fact, he was very excited about everything. I was convinced they picked the right guy to get other people excited, too.

When we reached the Visitors Center, T-Bone noticed the train tracks that ran right down the middle of Broad Street.

"You have high-speed trains in the middle of your town?" he asked. "That doesn't seem safe."

"No, this is the River Line," Eric explained. "It runs from Camden to Trenton. It's not a high-speed train, but it's a great, inexpensive way to travel from town to town."

We entered the Visitors Center and it was like traveling back in time. The bar was almost as long as the building and it was made of dark, heavy wood with a marble rail wrapped around it.

"Good morning, Jim," said a woman, popping up from behind the bar.

"Good morning, Maryann. I'd like you to meet New Jersey's Junior Ambassadors, Nicky and T-Bone. And this is Nicky's grandfather, Mr. Abruzzi."

"Excuse me, your Highness," T-Bone corrected the Mayor, "we're *unofficial* ambassadors."

"What exactly does that mean?" asked Eric.

"It just means they don't pay us," he said.

Everyone laughed and then we heard the door open. There were two bus loads of excited kids, teachers, and chaperones. They were pointing at the departing train as they made their way inside.

Maryann greeted them and turned on a flat screen television hanging on the wall. There was a short video and then the Mayor welcomed the group.

"Good morning, everyone, we are very happy that you can explore our city today. My name is Jim and I'm the Mayor of the City of Burlington. Where you are standing is the same place that Presidents Abraham Lincoln and Ulysses S. Grant once stood. This was the Blue Anchor Inn, a very important tavern in our city's past, where folks gathered to discuss the issues of the day. There are many great things to see in Burlington and I hope you enjoy each one. And be sure to come back with your families; we have great events all year long."

"Is this where Abraham Lincoln arm wrestled Ulysses S. Grant?" a boy in the front row asked.

"He must have gone on the website, too," T-Bone whispered.

"That's the legend," the Mayor smiled. "And it's possible since Abraham Lincoln campaigned here and Ulysses S. Grant moved his family to 309 Wood Street to keep them safe during the Civil War."

"My parents brought me to a festival here and we had ice cream at an old-fashioned ice cream parlor. Did Abraham Lincoln eat there?" asked a girl.

"No, you're referring to Ummm's Old-Fashioned Ice Cream Parlor. They weren't here back then, but they do make delicious homemade ice cream. Maybe if you have time you can stop by before you leave."

"Our teacher said she's not getting back on the bus until she has some," said a boy in the front row, pointing to his embarrassed teacher.

"I don't blame you," the Mayor laughed. "But, you've spent quite enough time in here, so go ahead and explore our city."

And, with that, the bus loads of kids were on their way. Unfortunately, T-Bone was so caught up in the excitement, he followed them outside. Before anyone noticed he was missing, I ran over and grabbed his elbow.

"Oh," he smiled, "I almost forgot that we're not here on a school trip."

"Almost?" I laughed.

I was sure the Mayor and Eric would be rushing back to City Hall, but instead, they offered to show us around some more.

"Let's walk down Broad Street and I'll show you the home of Elias Boudinot. Have you ever heard of him?" asked the Mayor.

"Actually, we read about him on your website. It said that he was the first president of the United States."

"Well, he isn't recognized as the first president, but he was the President of the Continental Congress, in 1783, when the war ended. So there are many people who considered him to be the first president," Eric explained.

"But what about George Washington?" asked T-Bone.

"He's the first President elected by the Electoral College after the Constitution was signed in 1789."

"So, Elias Boudinot was like an *unofficial* president?" T-Bone wondered aloud.

"I guess you could say that," Eric laughed. "Except, I'm sure he was paid."

We walked down Broad Street and stopped in front of the Boudinot-Bradford house. It was hard to believe that the *unofficial* first president lived right here. And he didn't just know the people who founded our country, he was one of them. As the Mayor explained, they risked their own lives in doing so and if they were caught, they could have been charged with treason.

"What's treason?" asked T-Bone.

"Participating in an act to overthrow the government was considered treason," said Eric. "Ol' King George enjoyed the tax money he received from the colonies and if those colonies won their freedom, he would have lost that money. Our founding fathers risked their lives to gain our independence and it's quite amazing that we were able to win the war."

"Why was it so hard?" asked T-Bone. "We had the home field advantage."

"Well, you have to remember that we were fighting Great Britain. They had well-organized, well-armed, and well-trained professional soldiers and the mightiest Navy in the world. We were thirteen separate colonies made up of mostly farmers and tradesmen, with no training, little organization, and our own weapons."

"Then how did we do it?" T-Bone asked, seeming much too interested for a kid who hated history the day before.

"Well, there were many times it didn't seem as if we could do it," offered the Mayor. "It wasn't easy. We lost many battles, our men were freezing during the winter encampments, and we needed help. Benjamin Franklin tried to convince France, an enemy of Great Britain, to help us and they agreed.

In any case, it was very difficult and colonial families made enormous sacrifices for a cause they truly believed in."

"Hey, look at that old cemetery," T-Bone said, pointing to rows and rows of graves. "Is Elias Boudinot buried there?"

"Yes, he is," said the Mayor. "In fact, the St. Mary's Churchyard is the next stop on your tour."

He pointed out the graves of Elias Boudinot, his wife, and some other famous people. I tried to listen to what the Mayor was telling us, but a couple of times I found myself busy reading the names and dates. Shockingly, T-Bone, *hater of history*, was just as curious as I was.

"You mentioned Benjamin Franklin earlier," I reminded him, "did he live here before he moved to my old neighborhood in Philly?"

"No, Benjamin Franklin was a visitor to Burlington on his way to Philadelphia. In fact, I can show you the Gingerbread House and tell you a story."

"Hold on," T-Bone interrupted, "you have a house made out of gingerbread?"

"If only," the Mayor laughed as he guided us down Wood Street, once known as Professor's Row. "No, the Revell House at 213 Wood Street is known as the Gingerbread House. It is undoubtedly the oldest building in Burlington County, and one of the oldest residences in New Jersey. It was constructed in 1685. Tradition places this as the home where Benjamin Franklin was sold gingerbread and given supper by a friendly Burlington City woman on his way to Philadelphia. He had arrived in town on Saturday but had missed the boat heading to Philadelphia and the next boat wasn't scheduled to depart until Tuesday."

"So he stayed here for four days?" I asked.

"No, the woman offered to let him stay in her home. But that evening he was walking by the river and met some folks in a boat heading to Philadelphia and they invited him to join them."

"Wow," T-Bone shook his head, "my mom would be furious if I got in a boat with strangers."

"Nowadays, that wouldn't be such a good idea," said my grandfather, "but back then life was very different. Don't worry, though, *they'd have returned you within the hour.*"

# Chapter Five
## Greetings from Burlington, Roebling, and Columbus, Part 2

As we approached the Revell House, I tried to picture Ben Franklin sitting inside eating his gingerbread. I took more pictures as we walked to 309 Wood Street, the home Ulysses S. Grant purchased for his family during the Civil War and the Carriage House at 13 Smith Lane, now the home of Burlington City's Historical Society. A friendly woman named Dorothy greeted us and gave us a tour of the house, carriages, and horse stalls.

It turned out that a Burlington man by the name of James Birch was a world-famous carriage maker. He was so famous that Henry Ford once visited his factory to discuss creating automobiles in Burlington, but Mr. Birch turned him down, confident nothing could replace carriages. Before we left, T-Bone noticed brochures on a table, grabbed one and pointed to the colonial woman on the cover.

"Hey, Nick, you're from Philadelphia," he whispered. "Is this Betsy Ross?"

"No, dear," Dorothy smiled, "that's me."

"Really?" said T-Bone. *"How old are you?"*

"Not that old," she said. "I'm a re-enactor. I dress up and tell stories as I give my tours."

"Are you famous?" T-Bone wondered.

"No," she laughed. "I'm just a history buff."

Before we could ask her any more questions, a large group of school kids knocked on the door. We thanked Dorothy and walked back down Wood Street toward the river. Since we arrived, I had noticed two things. First, the houses looked like the houses in Philadelphia's Olde City neighborhood, except many were private residences. I starting wishing that my house was three hundred years old and had great stories. I doubted the story about my dad saving $82.00 on last month's grocery bill would draw serious crowds. I wondered if one day I would do something so important that other kids would want to see where I grew up. Second, I noticed we were walking to everything.

"I don't see a lot of taxis," I pointed out.

"That's the great thing about our city," Eric explained. "We have so much history in one square mile. Visitors love that they can walk to everything."

"And," the Mayor added, "everything you see is original. These homes are not replicas; they are the actual homes and buildings that stood at that time. And, unlike some other great historical towns, our citizens live in and among all of this history, many in the exact homes."

When we reached the riverfront, or as they called it, the Promenade, I could see Pennsylvania on the other side. There was a time when I would have swam across the Delaware River to get back to Philly. It was funny that, as much as I liked living in Philadelphia, I really liked living in New Jersey, too.

He showed us an island in the river called Burlington Island, which was once an amusement park and then pointed to a large red house overlooking the river. The house once belonged to the Shippen Family. He told us that their daughter, Peggy Shippen married Benedict Arnold, the country's most famous traitor.

Docked in the water was a huge river boat, the *Liberty Belle*. He told us it sails the Delaware River for lunch, dinner, and special event cruises; the owner is a chef from Philadelphia. If he's from Philadelphia, I thought, he must be good. The Mayor told us that the food is so good it's not considered a riverboat with food, but a great restaurant that sails the Delaware River. There was a Green along the promenade and he told us that the city was hoping to construct a historical miniature golf course.

"That's cool," I said, "but what's historical miniature golf?"

"Maybe it costs three shillings to play," T-Bone attempted colonial humor.

"No, no," Eric explained. "The course would be built around replicas of our many famous houses, buildings, and landmarks," he answered. "We'd like to see this riverfront filled with families enjoying the view while appreciating the past."

"Do you win a free game if you get the ball in the alligator's mouth?" T-Bone asked.

"I don't think it will have an alligator at the last hole," Eric winked, "but we can see about winning a free game."

"What's that?" I asked, pointing to a large building across the green.

"That's Café Gallery," my grandfather smiled. "Your grandmother and I come up here for dinner once in a while. It's a wonderful restaurant with a great view of the river."

We followed the Mayor inside and he asked my grandfather if he had ever met Barbara.

"I really hate to date myself, but I've known her for many years. In fact, I had coffee with Barbara and Herman Costello last month. Good people."

"Who's Herman?" asked T-Bone.

"He was the mayor for thirty years," said Eric.

"Well, I sure hope he was the *official* mayor," T-Bone laughed. "That's a long time to go without a paycheck."

"Oh, he was official," my grandfather laughed. "He was Mr. Burlington City."

As we walked down High Street, the Mayor brought us to a house, opened the door, and walked inside. Eric was the only one to follow him. Realizing we were still outside, the Mayor returned and invited us inside.

"It's okay," he said. "This is the Lily Inn."

"What does that mean?" I asked.

"It's the only lodging in the city," said the Mayor. "It just opened and you'll feel like you've stepped back in time."

As we entered the foyer, I peeked around the corner. He was right. It looked like we were in a real colonial house, but instead of velvet ropes protecting everything, you could stay there and even sit on the couch. Very interesting, I thought.

"Murray, you in here?" the Mayor called out.

Suddenly a man emerged from a front room and started hugging the Mayor and Eric. Before I knew it, he was hugging all of us.

"Murray, this is Nicky, T-Bone, and Mr. Abruzzi. These fine boys are Unofficial Junior Ambassadors working for the Governor."

"I guess that means you don't get paid," he laughed.

"And this is Murray. He and his wife Eugenia are the proud owners of this bed and breakfast and Murray is also the Official Hugger for the City of Burlington," the Mayor continued. "Go ahead, Murray, show them your certificate."

"He's *official*, Nick," said T-Bone. "You think he's salary or paid by the hug?"

Before I could take a guess, Murray produced a resolution declaring him the Official Hugger of the City of Burlington. He and his wife gave us the grand tour. Everything really was as if we had stepped back in time, except for the modern kitchen and bathrooms with giant tubs and showers with glass doors. I assumed even history buffs would prefer to live in style rather than use an outhouse. When we returned to the foyer, we thanked them for the tour and continued down High Street.

"You must be getting hungry," the Mayor said as we approached a row of shops and restaurants. "We need to get back to work, but feel free to have some lunch and continue your tour. Wherever you eat, I think you'll be very happy. And stop by City Hall anytime you're in the neighborhood."

We shook their hands, thanked them and realized he was right; we were starving. There were restaurants called Francesco's, Taste It Creole, and Legends Pizza nearby. They all sounded great, but we decided to have pizza at Legends. T-Bone heard live music inside and I realized they had every topping you could imagine, even meatballs. As we entered, we saw a man named Cowboy Phil, wearing a cowboy outfit, playing a guitar, and singing cowboy songs. T-Bone was mesmerized and didn't speak a word. When he found out Cowboy Phil played Legends once a week, he made a note of it.

We looked at the map Eric left behind and planned what we should see next. We spent the rest of the afternoon checking out things like the Endeavor Fire House, the oldest fire company in the state; The Library Company, New Jersey's oldest continuously running library; the Burlington Pharmacy which was a stop on the Underground Railroad for runaway slaves looking for freedom; and the Quaker Meeting House. A woman who worked at the meeting house gave us a tour and then showed us to the grave of Chief Ockanickon.

"That's a funny name for a Fire Chief," T-Bone laughed. "The only thing that would make it funnier would be if it was *your last name;* Nick Ockanickon or better yet, when your brother calls you - Nick, Nick Ockanickon."

"Very funny," I shrugged.

Chief Ockanickon was a Native American Chief and a friend to the early settlers. On his grave sat a boulder with a bronze plaque that read: *"Be plain and fair to all, both Indian and Christian, as I have been."*

Our next stop was the Antique Emporium, which I'll admit, I didn't want to see. It reminded me of going shopping with my mom and I couldn't understand why my grandfather wanted to see it. I decided that since he offered to bring us out for the day, we should just pretend to like it. We weren't inside five minutes when I realized I just might like

"Then you've come to the right place," she smiled. "Today, you'll learn about the Wild, Wild West and you'll see what it was like to live back then. You won't just love the history, you'll *live* the history."

"Thank you, ma'am. We do love history," T-Bone proudly exclaimed.

"Well, good for you," Betty smiled. "You can learn a lot from the past. I know, I grew up in Philadelphia, myself; one very historic city."

"So did my pardner, here" T-Bone pointed at me. "His whole family is from Philly."

"Where abouts?" she asked.

"Fifth Street," I answered.

"Oh, I know it well. I have so many good memories of Philadelphia," she sighed with a smile.

"Me, too," I said. "But I'm also making some good New Jersey memories."

"Well, I'll bet today's memories will go right to the top of your list!"

I couldn't believe T-Bone met someone and didn't mention being an ambassador. That was a first. As we entered the park, we could see a train station on our left, and when we turned to our right, there was Main Street. I had to admit it was pretty awesome. It was a wide dirt road, with all of the buildings you would expect, including a jail, barber shop, general store, saloon, post office, and more. There were so many buildings on both sides of the street, it almost looked like a movie set. But unlike a movie set, these weren't just building fronts held up by two-by-fours, they were real buildings and each one looked like it would have back then. There were a couple of real horses hitched outside the Silver Dollar saloon and a few cowboys inside. Every time he saw a cowboy, T-Bone tipped his hat and said, "Howdy." One of the cowboys told us the jail cell was real, from a Scotch Plains jail.

"You ever find you any nesters on the dodge?" T-Bone asked, in some kind of crazy cowboy lingo.

"Not lately," the cowboy answered with a smile. "I usually ride the fence and only come across waddies and tenderfoots."

"What?" I asked, totally confused. "What are you talking about?"

"Just a little round up talk here, pardner," he said and winked.

"You learned this on the internet, didn't you?" I leaned in and whispered to T-Bone.

"Sure did, little doggie," he laughed.

At eleven o'clock the opening ceremony

started with horses, cowboys, and the raising of the flag. I checked the schedule and every fifteen minutes there was a live show in the middle of Main Street. They included a gunslinger, a cowboy competition, a bullwhip and dancing rope show, and the James gang. In between shows, we walked around the park. There was an area with picnic tables and behind it was the authentic 1880's one-room schoolhouse with a teacher standing outside. Next to that was a tiny chapel.

"What's that smell?" asked Timmy.

"It's probably the horses," said my dad, assuming he knew what Timmy was smelling.

"That there's Cookie's campfire," T-Bone corrected. "Let's mosey over to the chuck wagon."

We followed T-Bone over to a covered chuck wagon and a cowboy demonstrated how they cooked in the middle of nowhere. We walked to a mountain camp, where the mountain man explained how they survived on the frontier, and a blacksmith showed us how he shaped the horseshoes. When we reached the school, we were invited in for a lesson. It was hard to believe that all of the students, regardless of their age, sat in this one room. Although, for as small as it looked on the outside, it was amazing how much fit inside. Of course, they didn't have tons of supplies or computers like we have. In fact, each student had little chalkboard called a slate, instead of notebooks or paper. T-Bone sat right in the front row, introduced himself, and raised his hand.

"Yes, Mr. T-Bone," said the teacher. "Would you like to say something?"

"I would, ma'am," he began, "a couple of days ago, I became a history buff and now I reckon I'm startin' to notice things. For instance, you're missing some pictures of United States Presidents."

"Oh, dear," she pretended to sigh. "Which presidents are missing?"

"Well, I don't reckon I'm a big enough buff to know which ones yet, but you're missing a bunch."

"Tommy, Tommy" my mom whispered.

He didn't hear her.

"Psst, Tommy," she tried again, a little louder.

He didn't hear her, but the teacher sure did. It was funny to see my mom, a teacher herself, get in trouble for talking without permission.

"Is there something you'd like to say to Mr. T-Bone?" asked the teacher.

"I was going to tell him that you would only have pictures of presidents up to the 1800's," my mom explained, trying to get out of fake-trouble.

"Well, of course, we don't have pictures of presidents in the 1900's. How, pray tell, would we know who will be elected?"

"I have me a ruler that lists all of them there presidents," he told the teacher, "but you could also check out the History Channel."

"I don't believe I know what you're speaking of," she continued to speak in character.

"They must not get cable up here in the mountains," T-Bone whispered.

When the lesson was completed and we left the schoolhouse, I noticed the teacher looked just like some of T-Bone's teachers in our school. It wasn't a huge surprise that he could frustrate people in different centuries. *I always had a feeling.*

After school, my mom decided we should go to the Golden Nugget Saloon and eat lunch before it got really crowded. My parents definitely didn't know about the picnic area or we'd have been hauling a cooler in from the van. As we carried our trays over to the tables, a cowboy with a guitar stood on the stage and started singing.

"He sounds like Cowboy Phil," I noticed.

"Dinner and a show," said my dad. "Now,

when we're finished, let's take the train ride and the stage coach ride, then we can check out more shows, the petting zoo and the miniature golf."

"That there sounds like a plan, big fella," said T-Bone, as if my dad was waiting for his approval.

After lunch we headed to the train station. It was starting to get warm, but riding through the woods was nice and cool. We were just about to go through a train tunnel, when a bandit with a bandana over his face came out of the woods.

"I'll take all your silver and gold," he yelled, "and your valuables, too."

I guess T-Bone thought this was a real stick up and before I could stop him, he threw out his wallet and watch. Unfortunately, the wallet bounced off of the bandit's head and landed on the ground.

"What did you do that for?" asked the bandit, rubbing his head.

"Oh, I reckon you were gonna pass around a bag for us to put everything in?" T-Bone wondered. "I saw Jesse James do that in a western movie once."

"Is this kid for real?" the bandit asked the driver who laughed and shrugged his shoulders.

"Psst, Tommy," my mom whispered again. "It's not real. It's a show."

"Oh," T-Bone laughed while turning a few shades of pink. "Well, I'll be a donkey's uncle."

"I'll be a *monkey's* uncle," my mom corrected.

"I think you'd be a monkey's aunt, little lady," T-Bone said with a wink.

The injured bandit looked confused. He reached down, grabbed the wallet and watch, and handed them back to T-Bone who tried to apologize.

"No need to apologize," the cowboy sighed and let our train pass through the tunnel.

After the train ride, my mom told T-Bone that the cowboys were actors and we headed back to Main Street. We caught the Gunfight at the O.K. Corral and the big bank holdup. We headed over to take our stagecoach ride and ended up being part of the holdup. It was really exciting that regular people were involved. Unfortunately, T-Bone forgot my mom's discussion about the actors and ran out of the stagecoach, hands in the air, screaming, "Hit the deck." Because of his outfit, everyone watching thought he was part of the act and clapped for him.

After the show, we checked out the zoo, which Maggie and Emma loved and where they could have stayed all day long. Timmy, T-Bone, my dad, and I played a round of miniature golf while my mom brought the girls on a real Merry-Go-Round. They rode real ponies and I think they went on three times. When our golf was done, we decided to try our luck and pan for gold. T-Bone joined me and I knew with his luck, if there was even one tiny gold nugget, he'd find it. I wasn't completely wrong. After a few minutes he yelled, "Jumpin' jelly beans, I found gold!" Obviously, many people must try the same joke as no one even bothered to turn around. The way he said it seemed so real that I had to turn around. And when I did, there stood T-Bone, with a gold diamond ring in his hand.

"*Jumpin jelly beans*?" I asked.

"Yeah, that was pretty weak," he said, "but I'm running out of cowboy talk."

"You really did find something?" I asked.

"I found a diamond ring," he answered.

"Wow, that's some ring," said my dad. "Someone is probably very upset right now. Let's go see Betty at the ticket booth."

When we explained what happened, Betty said that a woman had just gotten engaged and didn't have the ring sized yet. Her fiancé begged her not to wear it, but she loved it so much, she started wearing it right away. When she and her nephew were panning for gold, it slid off of her finger.

"Her fiancé must have been furious," I said shaking my head.

"Oh, no, dear, she was much more upset than he was," said Betty. "Let me call Ed Stabile, one of our owners. I'm sure he'd like to meet such nice boys and keep the ring safe until we can reach the owner."

A moment later, Ed appeared. He smiled, shook everyone's hands, and thanked us for visiting Wild West City. He told us that his family purchased it in 1964. "My parents are no longer with us, but I'm one of six brothers and sisters and we all run it. But truthfully, everyone who works here is like family."

"That's what gives this place such charm and character," said my mom. "This is a family business and it reminds me of when I was a young girl. I think you have a wonderful park here and I'm so happy the boys found it."

"Thanks," said Ed. "I think you have some good, honest kids. I'm surprised you found the ring; I spent all morning looking and never came close."

"It only took me five minutes," said T-Bone.

"That's amazing," said Ed.

"Not if you know him it isn't," my dad shook his head. "Not if you know him."

We ended up staying until the closing ceremony; even though that meant we wouldn't sit down to eat dinner until 6:30 pm. To distract T-Bone, my mom bought everyone a giant, made-to-order cotton candy. As we pulled away, everyone was exhausted. It was nice to go somewhere you never heard of and have much more fun than you expected.

On the way home, my dad surprised us by pulling into the Black Forest Inn for dinner. We spent the whole meal talking about our day at Wild West City. T-Bone had taken a calendar of events and pointed out that there were special events going on every week, including Native American dancers.

Our waiter gave us even more ideas. He told us to come back and visit Tomahawk Lake, The Space Farm Zoo and Museum, and Mountain Creek Water Park. T-Bone grabbed our notebook and wrote them down. We decided that word of mouth was the best way to find out about New Jersey hot spots and best kept secrets. As we drove home, one thing was certain, *we all had a rootin', tootin' good time at Wild West City.*

# Chapter Eight
## Greetings From Millville

After our trip to Wild West City, we prepared our report, downloaded the pictures, and mailed them to Billy. It felt great to finish another report, but that also meant that it was time to choose another destination. We weren't sure how many reports the Governor wanted, so we were trying to make sure that the trips were spread around the state. After two days, we came up with our next day trip: Millville, New Jersey.

We learned that Millville was a huge art town in south Jersey and neither one of us had ever been there. We searched for things to do and found a place called Wheaton Arts. We didn't know anything about it, but their website looked pretty interesting. That evening, I decided to ask my parents.

"Mom, have you ever heard of Wheaton Arts?" I asked.

"I've heard of Wheaton Village," she said. "Is it near Wheaton Arts?"

"It's the same place," I explained. "They just changed their name."

"Then yes, I've heard of it," she said. "Why do you ask? Are you and Tommy thinking of doing a day trip there?"

"I'm not sure. Do you think it would be a good place?"

"Well, from what I know about it, they have a village and they show you how glass and other arts are made."

"T-Bone and I looked at their website and they have glass making, pottery, a glass museum, a playground, a general store, and wood carving."

"Well, do you know how those things are made?" she asked.

"No," I answered.

"Would you like to learn about them?"

"I think it would be cool to see how they make things out of a liquid that looks like lava," I replied.

"Then there's your answer," she smiled.

"Where's my answer?" I asked.

"Not every trip has to be an amusement park."

"What? Are you afraid you might learn something?" teased my dad.

"I guess it could be good," I said, still not sure that this would really be interesting.

"I'll tell you what; see if Tommy is available on Saturday and we can all take a ride to Wheaton," suggested my mom.

I called T-Bone and we prepared for our next day trip. When Saturday rolled around, I was anxious, but definitely not excited. I was really getting into colonial history, between the City of Burlington and Trenton and the frontier history at Wild West City. I couldn't imagine the history of glass being all that interesting, although I have learned that my instincts aren't great. Usually when I think I'll hate something, I end up liking it. And while I didn't expect to fall in love with glass, I decided I should give it a try.

The drive to Wheaton wasn't as long as I thought it would be, although I think my sisters would have disagreed. Every three minutes they asked if we were there yet. My mom put a movie on for them and it kind of worked; *they only asked every five minutes*. T-Bone was especially quiet and I wasn't sure if he was just tired or if he just wasn't very excited either. As we arrived in Millville we started seeing signs for Wheaton Arts. We pulled into the parking lot and headed toward the front gate.

"Before we go in there, I want everyone to look at me," said my dad. "This place is filled with glass, so you know what that means, right?"

"You break it, you bought it?" asked T-Bone.

"No," my dad said slowly, "it means you break it, *I bought it* and I'd rather not spend a few hundred dollars on fancy broken glass. Got it?"

"Got it," said T-Bone. "Be extra careful when we pick up the expensive glass."

"No," my dad said turning around again, this time much slower. "It means don't touch anything, anything at all, nothing. Look with your eyes, not with your hands. Got it?"

Sensing his frustration, we all answered, "Got it!"

My father paid for our admission and, to no one's surprise, had coupons from the internet. The man in the ticket booth handed us a schedule for the day's events. A nice woman named Janet suggested we start with the glass demonstration, so we headed toward the glass studio. The village itself was pretty cool and it was right in the middle of the woods.

We entered the studio and there were pieces of glass and equipment on display. As we turned the corner, there were a few rows of bleachers facing a huge brick oven. There were several people already seated up top, but we decided to go right in front. My parents used to sit all the way in the back, whenever we went anywhere, in case the girls acted up. They figured if they were in the back row, they could get out quick and easy. After a while they realized they were doing it all wrong. By sitting in the back, the girls couldn't see anything, got bored, and then acted up. By sitting in the front, going completely against their instincts, the girls had more fun and were usually too busy to act up. I thought it was funny how, by the fourth kid, they were still figuring things out.

"Welcome, everyone," said a woman near the brick oven. "Today we'll be showing you how glass is made. While our artists get prepared, let me tell you a few things about Wheaton Arts. The village sits on 65 wooded acres in New Jersey's Pinelands. Our artists are not only very talented, they are very friendly, so please feel free to ask them questions. And if you see them walking around the village later, go ahead over and talk to them or ask them questions. They love to talk shop."

As she started speaking, artists on both sides used long iron pipes to pull molten glass out of the oven. It was glowing bright orange and looked like lava. The woman with the microphone told us that the temperature in the oven was just over 2000° F. As the artists worked, blowing and shaping their forms, the glass was always cooling down and needed to be reheated. The artists were rolling the poles and sometimes blowing inside. I noticed one of the artists, Joe, re-dip the pole in the brick oven. The woman explained that adding more layers was called gathering. Blowing was the oldest method of working with glass, dating back thousands of years.

"As you can see," she said, pointing to Joe, "a ball of molten, or melted, glass is put on the end of a hollow iron pipe, the artist blows gently into the pipe like the way you blow soap bubbles, until the glass takes the shape and thinness the blower wants. During this process, the glass is constantly reheated to keep it soft and workable."

After blowing through the pipe, both artists rolled the pipe and used a wet rag to smooth the glass. When the demonstration was over we walked out the other side and saw different pieces of equipment and glass samples. The most interesting piece was a shopping cart with what looked like melted and cooled glass all over it.

My mom wanted to go to the ceramic studio next. T-Bone and Timmy were right on her heels, although I don't even think they knew what ceramics were. Inside, an artist, named Terry, was sitting at a spinning wheel. He grabbed some clay, wet his hands, and *threw* it on the wheel. Within a few moments the clay was getting taller and thinner. Amazingly, he was able to speak and work with the clay at the same time.

"How are you today?" he asked my family.

"Good, how are you?" said my dad.

"I'm great," he looked up and smiled.

"What are you making?" asked T-Bone.

"Right now, I'm throwing a pot."

"Tell me when to duck," said T-Bone.

"He's not really *throwing* it," my mom whispered. "That's the name of the technique he's using."

"Oh," he said. "That's a relief. I threw a bowl at my brother once and he dropped it on purpose. It was a huge mess."

We watched for a few minutes and even the girls were quiet. It was like the spinning wheel had hypnotized them. Terry told us how each piece needed to dry and then they were fired and glazed. We thanked him for the demonstration and he suggested we head down the hall to the lampworking station.

"I don't see any lamps," T-Bone whispered. "Do you think they're in the back?"

"Actually, lampworking isn't lamp-making," the artist who overheard him whispered back. "And it's also called Flameworking; the art of making glass objects from rods over a torch."

"What can you make?" T-Bone asked.

"Well, I make beads, marbles, and small sculptures," she said.

"Do you use the big oven?" I asked.

"No, I basically work with glass, the torch, and a large set of tweezers."

As she spoke, she took a glass rod and held it under the torch. She told us her name was Sue and that her ancestors worked in the Stanger Glass Factory, the first glass factory in Glassboro, New Jersey. She said she had flameworking in her blood and showed us a collection of marbles and beads that she had made. She was even wearing one of her own beads on a necklace.

We stopped by the 1876 Schoolhouse and the woodcarver studio, where the artists carved duck decoys and wooden toys. My sisters spotted the play-ground and my mom convinced my dad to bring them there so the rest of us could go inside the Museum of Glass. The man at the ticket booth told us that the Museum was kid-friendly, but my mom and dad were definitely too outmanned for a museum of glass. When we saw the two-story sliding boards, we told my dad to wait there for us. We may have been a little big for sliding boards, but there was no way we were leaving without giving them a try.

The museum had the first glass bottles made in America and some really huge pieces. When we finished touring the museum, without breaking anything, we headed to the playground to pick up the girls. Of course, we tried the sliding boards first.

We left the playground and headed to the Down Jersey Folklife Center. There were exhibits, programs, and performances about the culture and traditions of communities in southern New Jersey.

"What's Down Jersey?" I asked a woman inside.

"Down Jersey means the eight southern counties," she explained.

We had been so busy exploring the village, no one realized it was already three o'clock and we had missed lunch. Since my mom wanted to do a little shopping, my dad took us to the General Store for some snacks. My sisters immediately found the penny candy and had baggies of rainbow-colored Swedish fish in each hand. T-Bone, Timmy, and I had no trouble finding snacks, either. We were sitting outside waiting for my mom and enjoying the candy when Joe, one of the artists from the glass studio, came walking down the path.

"Hey, Joe," T-Bone waved.

"Hi, there," he smiled. "How are you kids enjoying yourselves?"

"This place is awesome," said T-Bone while trying to swallow a mouthful of candy. "You wanna talk shop?"

"Anytime," he laughed. "What would you like to know?"

"Oh, you want me to ask you a question?" said T-Bone.

"That's usually how it works," he answered.

"Have you ever broken any glass?" T-Bone asked, obviously uttering the very first thing to enter his mind.

"Have *you*?" asked Joe.

"All the time," said T-Bone. "I break so

much glass my mom only gives me plastic cups."

"Then imagine how much glass you'd break if you worked with it all day, everyday," he said with a chuckle.

"Good point," T-Bone nodded. "Your demonstration was really cool. So was the flame-work and pottery."

"Glad you're enjoying everything," he replied. "You should come back during one of our festivals. You'd have a great time."

"Do you think I could make some glass?" T-Bone asked.

"Once you're 16 years old you can come to one of our *make-it-yourself* programs. Then you can make your own paperweights, bowls, vases or flamework beads."

"Can we make marbles with Sue when we're 16 years old?" I asked.

"Absolutely," he winked. "And before you go back home, make sure you check out High Street."

"We will," I said, always happy to get a tip.

When we finally dragged my mom out of the gift shops and the Christmas store, we headed to downtown Millville. Our first order of business was dinner. We heard there was a family restaurant called *Oliver's Twist* where we could get sandwiches and ice cream. We talked to some people inside and found out that, like Burlington, Millville had river cruises, except these were on the Maurice River.

A woman overheard us and suggested we visit Village on High, which turned out to be a small village of cottages on High Street. My mom heard the word *stores* and led the way. We headed over to High Street and found the village.

My parents were amazed that in the middle of this city was a little village of cottages. It turned out that Millville was one of the top ten towns for artists in the country and each cottage was filled with things like art, soaps, jewelry, gift baskets, and candy. Of course, once T-Bone heard candy, he was right behind my mom.

We met a woman named Verna in the Marsh Hen Studio cottage. She was a painter and photographer. Just like we were amazed by the mural in Trenton, we were impressed to see Verna's work. And because it was a working studio, we were actually able to watch her paint.

My mom brought the girls into the Angels of Light cottage which had soaps, gifts, and children's books. Maggie and Emma were all smiles when they each got to pick out a book. The woman inside, Lettie, told us her daughter who owned the store was a teacher. Of course, my mom started talking shop.

We stopped by another cottage, called Gift Baskets Galore, which was filled with every kind of gift basket you could imagine. We spoke to Nanette, the owner, who made each gift basket by hand.

"Boys, you have to put this village in your report," my mom whispered. "This is how shopping used to be. It's so charming and I love the fact that they are artists *and entrepreneurs*."

"Entrepreneurs?" asked Timmy. "Does that mean they're from Europe?"

"No," my mom laughed, "it means they're business owners. They work for themselves and they create or hand-pick all of the products they sell. More people need to know that they're here."

"Nannette isn't just an entrepreneur," said T-Bone pointing to a shelf in the back, "she's a genius. She made a gift basket out of Kit Kats."

"That, too," my mom laughed.

Before we left, we met MaryAnn from LaBottega of Art, across the street from the village. She told us about 3rd Fridays. She said on the third Friday of every month, all year long, the town comes alive and the streets in the art district are filled with music, artists, food, and fun. She told us to visit www.3rdfriday.org and my mom told her we would definitely be back. T-Bone and Timmy pulled their money together to buy a bag of candy while my mom and dad grabbed a cup of coffee at the Steppingstone Café.

"So, what do you think?" I asked T-Bone.

"I think next time I'm bringing enough money for the Kit Kat basket."

On the ride home, every kid fell asleep except me. I leaned forward to talk to my parents. They said they were proud of us for choosing places that were fun and educational. My mom said she was thrilled that we included the arts. My dad said he thought we'd only want to visit arcades, mini golf courses, and candy shops. *He had no idea.*

# Chapter Nine
## Greetings From The Town Center

The next day we decided to get our pictures and reports together and bring them to Billy after school. My dad offered to drive us in, but warned us that he didn't have time to end up on another day trip. When my mom finished revising our reports and downloading the pictures, we were on our way. We parked behind the State House and the guard told us that Billy was out of the building at meetings. We were disappointed not to see him, but we left our folders and walked back to the parking lot. My dad said he needed to stop at the bank on the way home.

I noticed we weren't driving south and asked him if he was lost.

"No, I'm not lost," he said, shaking his head as if the whole idea was impossible.

"The GPS says we're driving north," I observed.

"That's because we're driving north," he pointed out.

"Mr. A., you do realize we live south of Trenton, right?" T-Bone tried to help.

"We're going to the bank," my dad answered.

"You just passed six of them," said T-Bone.

"I'm going to Roma Bank," my dad sighed and turned up the volume on the radio.

I wasn't sure why we were going to a bank north of Trenton, but got the feeling we should stop asking questions and just wait to see. When arrived I asked him where we were. He told me we were in Robbinsville.

"Robbinsville" yelled T-Bone. "For real?"

My dad turned around and looked confused. "Yes, Robbinsville. Why?"

"Do you know how to get to the Town Center?" T-Bone asked excitedly.

"Yeah, I do. Open the door and get out."

"I'm sorry, Mr. A.," T-Bone started to apologize. "I'll stop talking."

"No, Tommy," my dad laughed, "open the door and get out because you're in the Robbinsville Town Center. Why are you so excited?"

"You didn't tell him, Nick?" asked T-Bone.

"No, I thought my mom did," I shrugged.

"Mr. A., DeLorenzo's Tomato Pies is in the Robbinsville Town Center."

"What are you talking about?" asked my dad.

"It's true," I insisted. "We saw Sam's mom, Eileen, and she said he opened one in the Robbinsville Town Center."

"Really?" asked my dad, looking intrigued.

While my dad was busy thinking about tomato pie, we went inside the bank and asked to see a woman named Nancy. He told us that his grocery store was helping the bank raise money for a little boy from Hamilton. A woman at the reception desk told us to take the elevator to the third floor. The building was huge and reminded me of one of those old-fashioned banks. When we reached the third floor, Nancy was smiling and extended her hand to each of us. It turned out that a four year old little boy named Ryan was very sick. My dad read an article in the newspaper and spoke to his manager about helping Ryan's Quest, the foundation his family had started. We shook Nancy's hand and were then joined by Jane and Pam. I thought my dad would make us wait in the reception area, but surprisingly, even with T-Bone tagging along, he asked us to join him.

"Jim," said Nancy, "I'm happy you could join us today and that you reached out to us."

"Well, I have four kids and I hate to hear about any child being sick," my dad explained.

"What does he have?" T-Bone asked.

"Well," said Nancy, "Ryan has Duchenne muscular dystrophy. It's a rare form of muscular dystrophy and right now there isn't a lot of research for it. We're raising money to find a cure for Ryan and the other little boys who have this disease."

"How sick is he?" I asked.

"Well, it's the kind of disease that gets worse over time. Right now, if you met Ryan, you probably wouldn't know he was sick. But as he gets older, his muscles will stop functioning like they should and he'll end up in a wheel chair. Without a cure or treatment, boys with DMD only live to their late teens or twenties."

"That's so unfair," said T-Bone.

"We agree," said Jane, "that's why we're helping Ryan's family spread the word. We're also sponsoring some of their events so that we can help them raise money."

"But what good is money if he's still sick?" I asked, noticing a poster of Ryan on the wall.

"That's the key," Pam explained. "Right now, around the world, there are about 20,000 little boys diagnosed with this disease every year so the big drug companies aren't spending their money on research. Without money, there's no research and without research, there's no cure."

"That's a lot," I said, trying to imagine how long a line of 20,000 boys would stretch.

"Unfortunately, some diseases have hundreds of thousands of people diagnosed each year," said Nancy. "In the medical world, 20,000 isn't a very big number. If enough money could be raised, researchers could find a cure or a treatment while there's still time. They've never been closer, though, and the community is determined to help Ryan."

"That's why we're so happy you're here," said Jane. "Your dad read about Ryan and talked to his manager to see if they could help. When his boss agreed, we were very happy. That means the message is getting out there."

"But you're a bank," said T-Bone. "You're not a hospital."

"Well, Ryan's mom is a Hamilton teacher and his dad is a Hamilton police officer. We're part of the neighborhood, so we help our neighbors," said Jane.

"Can we help him, too?" I asked.

"Of course, you can," said Pam.

"We're Unofficial Junior Ambassadors for New Jersey," T-Bone announced. "We work for the Governor, but we report to Billy."

The room got quiet.

"It's true," said my dad, "believe it or not they write reports for the Governor."

"Really?" they all asked at once.

"Maybe you could include Ryan in a report or your school could do a fundraiser to help out. You should visit www.ryansquest.org and see some of the ideas they have listed," Nancy suggested.

Just then, there was a knock on the door and two men walked in.

Nancy introduced us to Former State Senator Peter Inverso, the president and CEO of the bank and Maurice Perilli, the Chairman of the Board.

We shook their hands and Nancy told them why we were there and about our *unofficial* job. They seemed very impressed.

"Are you savers or spenders?" asked Mr. Perilli.

"Uh, we're uh…" I hesitated, too afraid to say that we probably spent more money than we saved and too embarrassed to tell him about the sock where I saved the little money I did have.

"You're never too young to start, boys," he said. "Once you get a job, be sure you save more than you spend. It's one of the keys to your future."

"Actually," I said, "we just started our own odd job business."

"Perfect," Mr. Inverso smiled, "keep a little to spend and put the rest in the bank every week. Before you know it, it will really add up."

"Listen to my older brother," said Mr. Perilli, "it's good advice."

As they left the office, T-Bone and I were thinking the same thing and I guess everyone knew what that was.

"Mr. Inverso isn't his older brother," said Pam, as they all laughed. "They got you, didn't they?"

"Are they even brothers?" asked T-Bone.

"No, but I can tell you an interesting fact," Nancy smiled. "Mr. Perilli is *ninety years old.*"

"What?" T-Bone exclaimed. "He can't be ninety years old."

"Sure is," said Jane. "He still goes to the gym."

"I've never met anyone who was ninety years old," I said. "Does he go to the gym to people-watch?"

All three women started laughing and advised us to not get on the treadmill next to him. I guess he tears it up, I thought. Nancy handed my dad a large envelope and we were on our way.

We drove a couple of blocks down Route 33 and turned into the parking lot for DeLorenzo's. The new restaurant was really nice with old black-and-white pictures of Sam's grandfather and uncles hanging on the walls. We were hoping Sam was working and sat in a booth across from the pizza ovens. The menu was a little different than Hudson Street because he served salads, but the tomato pie was the same; it was fantastic. My dad ordered four large pies, one for now, three for home. When Sam emerged from the kitchen, he recognized us right away.

"Hey, Sam," said T-Bone. "Nice place."

"Thanks," he smiled. "I heard you were over at Hudson with your mom?"

"Yeah," T-Bone nodded. "We wanted to tell you about our new job."

We told him all about how we were working for the Governor and he was really happy for us. When we finished the first pie, we thought about opening one of the other boxes, but decided to bring them home.

We also told him about little Ryan and it turned out that he knew all about him and his family.

"Really?" T-Bone asked. "You know him?"

"Sure, he's a great kid," Sam smiled. "They usually come in early on Friday nights."

"What do you think we could do to help him and his family?" I asked.

"Tell other people," said Sam. "The more people who know, the more people that can help his family find a cure."

T-Bone nodded. "I bet his parents will move mountains to find a cure."

"They aren't just moving a mountain," Sam laughed, "Ryan's dad, Dave, climbed a mountain to raise awareness and money for research."

"What?" I asked. "Are you serious?"

"It's the truth," said my dad. "It was in the article I read. His dad climbed Mt. Rainier with other DMD parents, researchers and even some entertainers."

"That's some dad," said T-Bone.

"That's some family," Sam smiled.

# Chapter Ten
## Greetings From Morristown

The next morning, our friend, George, called early. We had met him that summer when we were hanging out at the mall collecting Wrangler Ray stickers for my parents' anniversary gift. George was about as old as my grandfather and ended up becoming a good friend. He also became one of our best customers. Not only did he hire us for his odd jobs, he told all of his friends to hire us. I figured he was calling to ask us to give him a hand with something.

"Hello," I said, grabbing the phone.

"Good Morning, Nick," said George. "Congratulations!"

"For what?" I asked, still half asleep.

"I saw your website."

"What website?" I asked, more confused.

"The New Jersey website," he said, probably shaking his head.

I wondered what made someone wake up at 5:00 am and start surfing the New Jersey website. Then again, this was the same man who used to sit on a mall bench all day, so go figure.

"How does it look?" I asked.

"Very professional," he said. "I'm impressed. You boys are really sinking your teeth into this project. I sure hope this doesn't mean you're out of the odd job business because…"

"Because we're so odd?" I interrupted, assuming he was going for the obvious zinger.

"No," he answered, "I was going to say because you're both so reliable, but… since you brought up being odd, that, too."

"Very funny," I replied. "And no, we're really busy, but we're still open for business."

"Great," he said, "I have a few jobs for you, whenever you get a chance."

"No problem," I told him, relieved that he still had work for us.

"I really enjoyed reading your reports," he laughed, "especially Wild West City. I used to bring my kids there."

"Really? I had never even heard of it until we came across their website. We had a great time."

"There are so many interesting places in New Jersey that people who live here don't even know about," he said. "You boys don't realize it, but you're doing a really good thing."

"Do you have any suggestions for a New Jersey day trip," I asked.

"I imagine I have quite a few," he said.

"Have you considered Morristown?"

"Which one?" I asked.

"I think you're confusing Moorestown in south Jersey, with Morristown in north Jersey," he explained.

"Oh," I said, "so which one?"

"They're both great towns, but I was thinking of Morristown. There's some great history, great sights, and great food."

"If I tell T-Bone there's history, he'll want to go today," I said.

"Really?" asked George. "I never figured him to be a history buff."

"That's a recent development," I laughed.

When we got home from school that day, I finished my homework and started googling Morristown, New Jersey. By the time T-Bone arrived, I had about thirty pages printed. The first thing I read was that Morristown was the winter headquarters for George Washington two times. There was also Fort Nonsense and Jockey Hollow. When I showed T-Bone the papers, he was definitely excited. We made a list of places to visit and decided to start at the Visitor's Center. Now, we just had to get a ride.

I called my grandfather and asked him if he wanted to check out Morristown with us that Thursday. We had another day off for parent-teacher conferences and I knew my parents would have to go to our school. Since kids weren't allowed, I could at least get Timmy and myself out of their hair. My grandfather, who must have really enjoyed himself on our Burlington City trip, immediately agreed.

We left bright and early Thursday morning, heading towards the New Jersey Turnpike. As we were driving, T-Bone was looking over the papers I had printed.

"Listen to this," he said, reading in his movie trailer voice. "*Morristown is the story of an army struggling to survive. During two critical winters, the town sheltered the main encampment of the Continental Army. In 1777, George Washington overcame desertion and disease to rebuild an army*

135

*capable of taking the field against William Howe's veteran Redcoats. In 1779-1780, the hardest winter in anyone's memory, the military struggle was almost lost amid starvation, tattered clothing, and mutiny on the hills of Jockey Hollow. George Washington was desperate to keep his small, ragged army, our country's only hope for independence, together."*

"I read somewhere that a lot of them didn't even have shoes," I nodded.

"It's amazing," my grandfather began, "the sacrifices so many people made for this country at a time when they had so little."

"I know," we said together.

"We're almost there," my grandfather announced a few moments later. "Where did you want to go first?"

"I think we should start at the Visitors Center," I suggested. We learned a while ago that this is the best spot for good advice and tips.

We parked the car and headed over. It was easy to find because it was across the street from the famous Morris County Courthouse. We walked inside and met Deidre. We told her about our project and she was impressed. She started filling a bag with brochures of things to do in Morristown and then made a list of things we could do that day. She handed us a walking tour of the town and suggested we walk to the Green. She said it was fun to do the scavenger hunt while visiting and gave us each a copy. We headed down South Street to the Green.

"Wow, it looks just like a park," said Timmy.

"Not really," said T-Bone, "there's no playground or basketball court."

"It's a park," my grandfather laughed. "It says here that in the 1700's it was used as a pasture for animals, a training ground for the local militia, and Arnold's Tavern was across the Green. That Civil War monument over there was erected in 1871. It's called *Soldier at Rest* and it honors those who lost their lives in the Civil War."

"Very nice," T-Bone said. "It's just a shame they didn't think about a playground."

We followed the map and checked out the churches, mansions, and famous houses. A month ago we didn't care who lived in old houses, but now we wanted to hear everything about them. I wondered if we were buffs or just really nosy.

My grandfather was right when he told T-Bone that it's one thing to read about history, but another thing to actually see where it happened. The walk took almost two hours and by the time we were finished, we were starving. We stopped back in the Visitors Center to ask Deidre to recommend a place for lunch. While we were looking at brochures, another woman came in and introduced herself. Her name was Carol and she was an historian.

"You mean your job is to know all of the cool things that happened in the past?" asked T-Bone. "And they pay you to do that?"

"That's right," she smiled. "And part of being an historian is learning the funny and odd things that happened in addition to the history."

"Really?" asked T-Bone. "We love odd things. We even started our own odd job company."

"That's because they're odd," Timmy laughed.

"Well, then you might enjoy this little fact," she began. "Are you familiar with Lady Justice?"

"The blindfolded lady holding a scale?" I asked.

"That's the one," she said. "Now, take a peek at the top of the Morris County Court House."

"Hey," I said, after staring at it for a moment. "She's not wearing a blindfold!"

"That's right," she smiled. "She holds the Scales of Justice representing a balanced judicial system in her left hand and a sword symbolizing protection of individual rights in her right hand. Unlike many of her counterparts, she isn't blindfolded."

"Very interesting," said my grandfather.

"I have a question for you," I asked, looking at a picture of soldiers from the Continental Army. "Why did one soldier play a drum? Wouldn't it be better to give him a musket or put him on a cannon? They thought it was that important to play music while they fought?"

"It's because they didn't have i-pods," said T-Bone.

"That's a very good question," she nodded, "but that's not the reason."

"The musicians used their instruments to boost the soldiers' morale and to provide cadence when they marched."

"So, it was just to keep time?" I asked.

"Well, there was one other reason," she explained, "and it was the most important reason of all. Their job was to convey orders and signals to the troops, as it was difficult to hear human voices on a battlefield."

"So they were like the third base coach in a baseball game?" asked Timmy.

"That's actually a very good analogy," she agreed. "Their music provided signals; just as a third base coach does in a game. And they usually wore the reverse colors of their regiment so they would be easier to spot if the officer needed to give them a signal in a hurry."

"Wow," I said, shaking my head, "it seems like there was a reason for everything back then."

"They may not have had the conveniences and technology we have today, but they were very, very intelligent," she smiled. "Do you have any other questions for me?"

"A very important one," said T-Bone, "where should we eat lunch?"

Deidre told us that there were many great restaurants and recommended a few, circling them on our town map. We thanked them for their stories and decided to try a place called the Famished Frog, mostly because we were famished ourselves and she told us the food was really good.

We left the Visitors Center, turned the corner and walked a couple of blocks. The restaurant was nice and I knew my sisters would have loved the frog murals painted on the walls and the little frogs sitting everywhere. Our waiter came over to take our drink order and we told him we were starving and ready to order everything at once. While we waited for our food, we talked about everything we had learned. I was anxious to see the Ford Mansion and Jockey Hollow. When the food arrived, we stopped talking. Our walking tour really did make us famished and the food was so good that no one wanted to stop eating to talk. When we were finished, Jimmy, the manager, came up and asked us about our meals. My grandfather pointed to our empty plates and told him everything was great. I decided to ask him if there was anything else we should see.

"Have you been to the Green?" he asked.

"Yes," I answered proudly. "We did the whole walking tour."

"No wonder you were so hungry," he laughed. "Do you have time to visit the Ford Mansion and Jockey Hollow? They're really very interesting."

"That's on our list," I replied.

"How about Fort Nonsense?" he asked.

"Is it a big army fort?" T-Bone wondered.

"No," he smiled. "Fort Nonsense rises about 230 feet above the Green and provides excellent views. Our troops were able to scan the eastern horizon over the Watchung Mountains for beacon fires alerting them that the British troops were moving out of New York City. You won't find an actual fort, but it's worth a ride to the top."

"Why was it Fort Nonsense?" I wondered.

"Well, in May 1777 the hill was busy with soldiers digging trenches and embankments on George Washington's orders. It was named Fort Nonsense because of the legend that George Washington ordered it built just to keep the troops occupied."

"No way," I gasped. "That's like when our teachers give busy work to let everyone catch up."

"That's a lot of busy work," T-Bone said in amazement, "or George Washington had a twisted sense of humor."

"That's the irony," said Jimmy, "George Washington was a pretty no-nonsense person. This is one reason many historians doubt that he would go to such lengths to merely keep morale high and troops busy. But like most legends; hard to prove, harder to disprove."

"Like the Lincoln-Grant arm wrestling match," said T-Bone.

"Exactly," I agreed.

We liked hearing all of the stories, but were anxious to see where they happened ourselves. We thanked Jimmy for his advice and headed to Fort Nonsense. He was right, the view was awesome and there were information markers placed all around to explain its story. T-Bone went over to the cannon while I stood there imagining soldiers digging trenches, not knowing if the British were heading their way. It suddenly hit me how scared these guys must have been. They weren't real soldiers, they were far from their families, and they were fighting in a war. We took some pictures and then headed over to the Ford Mansion.

We went to the museum behind the mansion to see when the next tour started. A woman named Anne told us the mansion was owned by Mrs. Jacob Ford, a widow, and her four children. She offered the hospitality of her home to George and Martha Washington, his servants, aides and officers.

"Martha Washington fought in the war?" Timmy asked.

"No, dear," Anne explained, "but she always

joined the General during his winter encampments. It was a morale booster for the General and also for the troops."

"Why did they stay in one spot during a war?" I asked.

"Well, after their amazing victories at Trenton and Princeton, the Continental Army arrived in Morristown for their winter quarters. It was the perfect place because they could see any British movement from Howe's army in New York City. This was a time for the troops to regroup. General Washington used his headquarters to solve the many problems facing his army; many of their enlistments were ending, there were food and clothing shortages, and diseases such as small pox were rampant. Thankfully, by the time spring would arrive, the army would be greatly reinforced. This was also the time to develop strategies."

"Did the Fords have to move out of their mansion?" I wondered.

"They didn't," Anne smiled. "Mrs. Ford, her children, and her servants settled into two cramped rooms of their home and stayed."

"They saw everything that happened and hung out with George and Martha?" T-Bone gasped.

"Well, they were witnesses to everything that

happened there, but I'm not sure how much they *hung out*. Remember, everyday chores didn't leave anyone, even kids, much free time and back then, they weren't even sure how the war would end."

"That must have been scary," said T-Bone.

"I'll say," I agreed.

We walked past the gift shop into a large room filled with so many interesting things. There was also a major research library on the Revolutionary War and a twenty-minute video. When it was time for our tour we entered the mansion. We were told that it was decorated in period and original furnishings and looked very much as it did when it was occupied by General Washington. It was weird to stand in the same room where he met with his officers during the revolution. It was even weirder that I cared so much.

"Did the Fords enjoy having the Army stay in their home?" I asked.

"Well, they stayed in cramped quarters, but for the children, it was very exciting to be in the midst of so much activity," said Anne.

"They were tutored and still had some time for games and activities. But suddenly, breakfast, lunch, and dinner consisted of thirty people and sometimes more when visitors were on hand. While both groups were cordial and respected each other's boundaries, having one large kitchen with two sets of servants, totaling around twenty-five in all, meant tensions started to grow."

"It's probably like Christmas at my house, when my mom and my aunts are all in the kitchen trying to get everything ready," said T-Bone.

"Except everyday," she smiled. "General Washington wanted to stop the friction, so he ordered the construction of a separate log kitchen. There were other changes, too; Mrs. Ford's visitors needed to use the outside entrance by the pantry, as sentries stood guard by the front door which was restricted to official army business."

We toured each room and really understood how difficult it must have been to have so many people staying in one mansion, even if it was a mansion. Before we left, we walked around the grounds and took more pictures. Having seen where the officers stayed, we were curious to see where the troops stayed during the two winter encampments.

We drove to Jockey Hollow and started at the Visitors Center where we saw a soldier life exhibit. It was an eye-opener. It made the cramped quarters of the Ford Mansion look like a luxury cruise. The troops arrived at the beginning of the worst winter of the 18th century. Bad timing, I thought. There were seven December blizzards greeting the exhausted soldiers. They cleared 900 acres of timber and built 1,200 log huts. Each hut had to follow General Washington's specifications of 14 feet wide by 15 to 16 feet long and 6.5 feet high. If a hut did not conform, it was torn down and rebuilt. The enlisted men's huts were built in rows of eight, three or four rows deep for each regiment.

The larger huts for captains and field officers were not built until the enlisted men's huts were completed, but they had two fireplaces, two chimneys, and windows. While the officers stayed two to four men in a hut, the enlisted men slept twelve to a hut on built-in wooden bunks stacked three to a wall. Their bedding was loose straw and this is where they also kept their personal belongings, like Bibles, playing cards, utensils, and journals. I wondered what they wrote about when they finally had a chance to sit down.

Walking through Jockey Hollow was really interesting. We were able to tour the 1700's Wick Farmhouse, which was used for Major General

Arthur Sinclair during the encampments. We also saw some of the soldiers' huts from the Pennsylvania Line. There was a guide inside who showed us around and explained everything.

"The fact that there were no battles in Morristown often results in the town's importance being forgotten," Anne said. "But the two winter encampments here were very important to victory. If General Washington had not been able to keep his troops intact, a difficult task to be sure, as many wanted to leave, he would not have been able to proceed to Yorktown and return victorious."

"Did thousands of men die that winter, like the winter in Valley Forge?" I asked, sounding pretty smart as I threw her a fact from Mr. Getty's history class.

"That's what makes this so interesting," she said. "In Morristown, during the worst winter of that century, less than one hundred troops died."

"Man, they were tough," T-Bone whispered. "You think we could have stuck it out?"

"Are you kidding?" I said, "Not a chance."

We spent more time walking the trails at Jockey Hollow and realized we were starving again. Earlier, my grandfather noticed a restaurant he thought we should try. It was called George and Martha's and it seemed like the best way to end our day trip.

"Hey, do you think our friend George used to come here when his wife, Martha, was alive?"

"Probably," I said, "although he seems a little sensitive about the George and Martha jokes."

"You're right," T-Bone agreed. "I can't wait to tell him about it."

We sat near a fireplace with a big star hanging above it. While Timmy ordered sliders, T-Bone and I ordered George's Meatloaf, and my grandfather went for the Pilgrim's Feast. It smelled just like Thanksgiving and we all enjoyed every bite. On the ride home, with the help of Timmy and my grandfather, T-Bone and I took notes about everything we saw. There were so many things; we didn't want to leave any out.

"Hey, Nick," whispered T-Bone, "look over there." He was pointing at Timmy who had fallen asleep with a brochure opened on his chest. "We got another one."

"Another what?" I asked.

"*Another buff,*" he laughed, "*another buff.*"

# Chapter Eleven
## Greetings From The Jersey Shore

The next morning I had trouble waking up for school. Our day trips were exciting, but exhausting. My grandfather said that's how you know you've had a great time. T-Bone and I decided to take a few days off from being ambassadors and do some odd jobs. Saturday morning we stopped by George's to help him pack up some things in his garage.

"You sure have a lot of stuff in here," remarked T-Bone as George turned on the lights.

"You'd be surprised how much you can accumulate in a lifetime," George laughed.

"Where are you bringing all of this stuff?" I asked. "It doesn't look like junk."

"Oh, I'm not throwing it out. I'm donating most of it to charity."

"Everything?" asked T-Bone.

"Oh, no," said George. "If that was the case,

I'd just have them come take it all and be done with it. I want to go through some of these boxes and shelves and take out anything sentimental."

"Good idea," I nodded. "I remember when we moved, my mom got so frustrated with packing that she started throwing everything out. She even threw out my baseball cards. You gotta be careful."

"I know what you mean," he laughed. "One time I almost gave away a box that contained our wedding album and my kids' pictures. That was the last time Martha let me organize anything."

"So, if we see wedding or kid pictures, save them?" asked T-Bone.

"Yes," said George. "Definitely save them."

By lunch time we had helped him pack eight appliances that were never taken out of the box, old camping supplies, gardening equipment, and some tools. We came across a box of pictures and laughed at how goofy George and his kids looked.

"Nice hair and mustache," T-Bone laughed. "And nice plaid pants and striped shirts. Were you all on the PGA Tour?"

"Just wait," George smiled, "one day your grandkids will look at how you're dressed and they'll have themselves a good laugh, too."

"No way," T-Bone insisted. "We're not dressed old-fashioned."

"Well, something tells me that fifty years from now, your grandkids may disagree."

There was a photo album behind the boxes on a shelf. I opened it up and looked at the pictures of George when he was young. Except for the clothes and sideburns, he looked like he could have been the father of one of my friends. His hair was so dark and, oddly, he looked taller.

"Where were these pictures taken?" I asked.

"Let's have a look," he said as he pulled his glasses out of his pocket. "Oh, that was when we took the kids to Storybook Land, an amusement park Martha had heard about in Egg Harbor Township. The kids had a great time."

"It looks pretty cool," I observed. "I guess it closed a long time ago?"

"Believe it or not, it's still there," he said. "I drive by there when I visit friends at the shore."

"I've never heard of it," I said.

"That's not surprising," T-Bone laughed. "When you first moved here you asked me if the weather in New Jersey was different than Philly.

"Good point," I nodded. "Hey, George, do

you think it would be a good place for a day trip?"

"I don't know, Nick," T-Bone interrupted. "It's *Storybook Land*. It's sounds kind of babyish."

Before I could agree with T-Bone, George told us his older kids had the same reaction.

"I haven't been there in some time, but I remember my older kids really enjoying themselves," he said. "You know, if you go there for a day trip, you should visit Lucy the Elephant, too."

"Lucy the Elephant?" I laughed. "You want us to go visit one elephant when the zoo and the Six Flags Safari have herds of them?"

George laughed as he started paging through the album. T-Bone and I looked at each other and rolled our eyes. While George's Morristown information was right on the money, Storybook Land and one elephant didn't seem like a great trip.

"There she is," he said, triumphantly holding up a picture of a giant elephant.

"Whoa," T-Bone gasped. "That's some elephant. It's bigger than the buildings behind it."

"It should be, it's about six-stories high," George explained. "And Lucy the Elephant *is a building*."

"No, way," I said. "That elephant is a building?"

"She sure is," he replied. "I don't remember all of the history; it's been a while. But she's pretty impressive and she's the only one left."

"And she's in New Jersey?" I asked.

"In Margate, which is just about 10 minutes from Storybook Land and a few minutes from the famous Atlantic City Boardwalk."

T-Bone and I looked at each other and I knew what he was thinking. We weren't sure if the trip would be a success, but we could end it with a boardwalk and that was always good. We asked George if he minded us taking his ideas and he told us he wouldn't tell, if we didn't tell.

When we got back home I told my parents all about Storybook Land and Lucy the Elephant. They told us that they had heard of them but had never been there. My dad googled it and said they would take us. He even suggested we finish the day at the boardwalk. He must have forgotten about the last boardwalk trip when lucky T-Bone won everything except the actual boardwalk itself. I decided not to remind him.

We spent the week going to school and doing odd jobs. George gave us so many customers that I was starting to feel rich. I decided Mr. Perilli and Mr. Inverso had a point: we should spend a little and save most of it. I asked my dad if I could open a savings account at the Town Center Roma Bank.

"That's a little far, isn't it?" he asked.

"It's not that far," I replied.

"No, it's not that far; it's just that there are a lot of banks between our house and Roma," he said.

"I know," I explained, "but Roma is helping that little boy, Ryan."

"You know," my mom interrupted, "they say you should do three things with your money: spend a little, save a lot, and share some. I think it's nice that you're picking a bank that helps the community. Maybe you could donate a little, too."

"And I guess it doesn't hurt that this particular branch is two blocks from DeLorenzo's?" asked my dad, sensing I had an ulterior motive.

"I think they call that a bonus," I laughed.

I called T-Bone to tell him what I was doing and he wanted to do the same thing. We figured the next time we stopped by the State House we could open our accounts. I was going to make sure we went on a Friday so we might be able to meet Ryan.

The next Saturday we set out for Storybook Land. T-Bone wasn't real excited because he thought we were too old for storybooks. Now, I was the optimist, convincing him to have an open mind.

We arrived and saw a huge castle out front.

"Free parking," said my dad, "I'm already a fan."

"And I have coupons," my mom said, pulling them out of her wallet.

We paid our admission and walked inside. My sisters looked around and froze. I think seeing everything at once was too much for them and they didn't know which way to walk first. There was a huge statue of Mother Goose in the middle, so my mom started assembling everyone for the first group picture. T-Bone wasn't smiling.

"Let's go to the right and work our way around," my dad suggested.

"We want to go on the strawberry ferris wheel," Maggie yelled.

"Strawberries," Emma pointed. "Go on strawberries."

"Okay, okay," my mom laughed and brought them over to the ride.

The first thing I noticed was that while the parking lot was pretty full, there were no long lines. I also noticed lots of trees. Even though it was a warm fall day, the trees kept the whole place really cool. We all walked over to the Whirly Bug ferris wheel and

Emma, Maggie, and Timmy went up to the gate. The operator put them in a berry, let it go half way up and then looked at T-Bone and me.

"No, thanks," said T-Bone.

"Go ahead," my mom nudged us, "it's like carnival rides, but better and without the line."

"Plus, we don't have to spend a million dollars on ride tickets," my dad smiled.

"I'll go," I said.

"Good," my mom smiled. "Tommy, why don't you go on with him?"

"No, thanks," he said, determined not to have a good time.

"Listen," I whispered, "we can't write a report if we don't try everything."

He thought about it for a second and decided I was right. We hopped in a strawberry and the ride began. It was funny seeing Maggie, Emma, and Timmy in their own berry, without any adults. They really thought they were a big deal. When the ride stopped, T-Bone looked like he enjoyed it. The next ride was the Rock-Spin-Roll spinning cups and T-Bone started to perk up. I never knew how much spinning he could take without turning green.

It was great being able to go from ride to ride

without waiting in line. Before I knew it, we were all in the line for the Merry-Go-Round, even my mom and dad. For the rest of the day we all went on every ride they had; even T-Bone enjoyed himself. In fact, he wasn't just enjoying himself a little; he was holding the park map and directing everyone from ride to ride. He played it off like he was just doing it for my sisters, but I knew the truth. He was having fun in spite of himself.

"Okay, let's hit the Happy Dragons, the Balloons and then the Old Tymer cars," he said without looking up.

"I think Tommy is coming around," my mom winked.

Before I could answer, T-Bone saw the Bubbles roller coaster. He kept his hands up the whole time and by the time we went down the first hill, my whole family had their hands up, too. The best part was everyone could go on every ride in the park. And we did. They also had displays inside things like a crooked house, a pumpkin, and the shoe where the old lady with too many kids lived. They were big enough for everyone to walk through and inside some of them, behind glass, was a display that was animated when a button was pushed.

"Boys, this place is fantastic," said my mom. "I've never been to a cleaner amusement park."

"And they don't hit you up for more money once you're inside," my practical father agreed. "I love the word *unlimited*!"

"We wanna to go on the Candy Cane Express," Maggie said, pointing to the Christmas tram car that brought guests through the park.

We hopped on the tram and got a chance to see everything they had. It was much bigger than we realized. They had the Flying Jumbo ride, the J & J Railroad train, Monster Trucks and a Tug Boat ride. As we worked our way around the park, T-Bone led us to the Turtle Twirl. I wasn't sure about going on another spinning ride with him, so I told him I'd better go with the girls. My mom and dad took the turtle behind us and Timmy and T-Bone took the one behind them. While I kept the girls from spinning out of control, T-Bone and my brother spun so fast, they were a blur. Even the turtle looked dizzy.

When the ride finished, I turned around to see them wobbling into each other. A moment later, they both landed face first on the silver metal floor, laughing uncontrollably. My mom ran over to help them; my dad just rolled his eyes.

At one o'clock, we were ready for lunch. My mom knew that we could bring in a picnic lunch so my dad and I ran to the car and grabbed the lunches from the cooler. T-Bone offered to stay behind and take *the kids* on the Tea Time tea cup ride. There was a giant birthday cake and underneath were picnic tables. My mom spread our lunch on two tables and my dad went inside to buy some drinks. When we finished our sandwiches, my dad went back into the Dining Depot and came out with popcorn and cotton candy. As we sat there eating our snacks, I didn't know which was more shocking: that T-Bone was having more fun than anyone or that my dad sprung for snacks.

"I wanna see the animals," Maggie begged. "Please, can we see the animals?"

"Aminals, aminals," Emma repeated, with her usual mixed-up pronunciations.

Three peacocks were chasing each other in an enormous caged area and then spreading their feathers. T-Bone, map in hand, pointed out another animal area where they had deer and sheep. They also had gumball machines filled with animal feed and tubes to slide it down. It was funny how the deer just stood by the bottom of the tube waiting for their feed. We circled the park one more time, hitting every ride and visiting every display. Just like Wild West City, they had a Chapel and a Little Red Schoolhouse. My sisters were so excited to sit at *real desks,* they didn't want to leave. By 4:00, my dad brought us to the Caboose Café and he treated everyone to ice cream.

"Is he feeling okay?" T-Bone asked, noticing my dad was suddenly free and loose with the cash.

"That's when you know he's having a great time," my mom whispered.

When we had been on every ride three times, my mom brought the girls into the restroom. When she came out, she couldn't wait to tell us how clean it was. I never noticed these things myself, but I guess when you're trying to keep two little kids from touching everything, it's something you notice.

"You should see the men's room," T-Bone agreed. "It looks like no one's been in there all day."

We took one last train ride, several more pictures, and walked by the animals. Of course, my mom had every intention of stopping by the gift shop and, surprisingly, my dad didn't stop her. While my mom picked out souvenirs, we stood by a glass case. A woman smiled and asked if we enjoyed our visit.

"I have to be honest," T-Bone admitted, "I really wasn't looking forward to coming here, but now I'm a fan."

"Really?" she smiled. "How did you find out about us?"

"Well," he began with the usual story, "my friend, Nicky, and I are Unofficial Junior Ambassadors working for the Governor. Our job is to find places in New Jersey and give him reports."

"That's very impressive," she said.

"A friend of ours told us he used to take his kids here and we decided to do a report about it."

"Well, my name is JoAnne Fricano," she said, "and we're happy you could join us. My family has owned Storybook Land since 1955 and we're always happy to see new faces."

"That's a long time," I nodded. "Did your parents start it?"

"Yes," she replied. "My mom selected this location because she thought they would get people to stop by on their way to and from the Jersey shore."

"Did it work?" asked T-Bone.

"Of course, it worked," I interrupted. "They're still here, aren't they?"

"Actually," she said, motioning to a man and

a girl near the other counter, "I'd like you meet my brother, John, and my niece, Jessica. This is still a family owned business and I'm sure they'd like to meet you."

She told them what we were doing and they told us how their parents started out small and just kept working hard and adding to the park. We wondered if Jessica would run it when they retired.

"Absolutely," she smiled, "my brother, John, and I love being a part of a place where families can come and have fun."

My mom walked over and we introduced her to the Fricano family. She told them that she was so impressed and would tell everyone in her school about Storybook Land. They told us that many schools come for field trips and my mom thought it was a great way to bring the stories she reads to her kindergarten class alive. I figured she'd schedule a trip during the year. If he wasn't in school himself, *T-Bone would have volunteered to be a chaperone.*

JoAnne then told us they were open from March through December 31st and there were events all year long, including Christmas in July, Halloween hayrides, and a Holiday Light display throughout the park. They even had Mr. and Mrs. Claus at the

Christmas house in the North Pole section from November until they closed.

"Well, we'll be back," my mom smiled. "We'll definitely be back."

As we piled into the van, I was really happy about George's suggestion. I couldn't wait to tell him, but more importantly, I couldn't wait to show him the picture of T-Bone in the strawberry. We headed to Margate which was about ten minutes away. There was no getting lost as there were signs for Lucy the Elephant everywhere. I doubt we could have missed her since she's the biggest elephant in the world. My dad parked outside and smiled when he realized the parking was free. We went into the gift shop and asked if we could go inside.

"Absolutely," smiled a girl named Samantha. "Have you ever been in a six-story elephant?"

"Not lately," T-Bone laughed.

"Well, then you are in for a treat."

While my dad paid for our tickets, a man in a uniform walked over and greeted us. T-Bone immediately told him about being ambassadors.

"Well, it's a pleasure to meet you," he said. "My name is Antonio. Samantha and I would be happy to answer any questions you may have."

"Can we go to the top?" asked Timmy.

"You sure can," he said. "In fact, you can even look out and see what Lucy sees everyday."

"What do you mean?" asked T-Bone.

"Well, Lucy's eyes are made of glass and you can look through them and see what she sees."

"Cool," said Timmy, "when can we go?"

"Since you're official ambassadors, we can take you through now," he winked.

"Actually," T-Bone confessed, "we're *unofficial* ambassadors."

"Oh," he nodded, "they don't pay you, do they?"

"Not a penny," I laughed.

We entered a door in Lucy's hind foot and walked up a narrow, winding staircase. I didn't think it would be finished inside, but the walls were cherry wood and when we reached the top of the stairs it was really nice. Samantha told us that the walls were painted *gastric pink*, the same color as an elephant's stomach.

"Lucy was built in 1881," she said, "and for one year, in 1902, a family actually lived in here."

"Wow," T-Bone joked. "If you lived here you'd never have to memorize your address; you could just tell people you live in the elephant!"

"The original owner, James Lafferty, planned to use Lucy as a real estate office to help him sell land in the area. He even received a United States patent for her. After his business declined, he sold Lucy in 1887 to Anthony and Caroline Gertzen from Philadelphia. Eventually, one of their sons, John, and his wife, Sophia, bought her and they charged ten cents for tours. They hired a child nurse, Hattie, for their daughter and she became the first tour guide."

"Hattie was pretty lucky," said Timmy.

"I agree," Samantha smiled.

"Is she the only elephant like this in the world?" I asked.

"She is now, but there were two others, both designed by Mr. Lafferty. One was in Cape May, the Light of Asia, but it fell into disrepair and was torn down. The other was Elephantine Colossus in Coney Island, New York. It was 122 feet high and contained seven floors of exhibits and rooms."

"That's pretty colossus," I said.

"That's for sure," Antonio agreed, joining our group. "It had thirty-one rooms and sixty-five windows for ventilation. With 263 men, it took 129 full work days to build."

"Is that one still open?" asked my dad.

"No, sir," said Antonio, "it was the victim of a fire that destroyed the elephant and many of the surrounding buildings."

"That's a shame," my mom sighed. "Now, you mentioned someone actually lived in here?"

"In 1902, an English doctor and his family leased the Elephant as a summer home," Samantha explained. "They moved into Lucy's interior and converted the main hall into four bedrooms, a dining room, kitchen and parlor. A bathroom was outfitted in one of the small front shoulder closets using a miniature bathtub."

"That must have been something, living in an elephant," I said.

"I imagine it was," Antonio smiled, "although, it must have been pretty hot living up here without air conditioning."

"So, Lucy is the last elephant standing," T-Bone remarked. "I know elephants are supposed to be lucky, but I guess she's the *really lucky elephant*."

"She wasn't always lucky," said Samantha. "Lucy was heavily damaged in the storm of 1903 and was standing knee deep in the sand before volunteers dug her out and moved her farther back from the sea."

"How do you move a sixty-five foot elephant?" I asked.

"Very carefully," my dad joked.

"Then, according to newspaper accounts, Lucy was converted into a tavern. Rowdy customers kept knocking over the oil lanterns used for lighting and, in 1904, Lucy was nearly burned to the ground as a result of their carelessness. This ended her days as a tavern, although she has had some pretty impressive visitors. A guest register shows that, in 1916, such notables as President and Mrs. Woodrow Wilson, Vincent and John Jacob Astor, the DuPonts of Delaware, and Henry Ford all visited Lucy and climbed her 130 steps to the howdah on her back."

"What's a howdah?" asked Timmy.

"That's the riding carriage on her back. Would you like to peek through her eyes and then stand in the howdah?" asked Samantha.

As we climbed the steps and reached her eyes, we really could see what Lucy looks at; an amazing view of the Atlantic Ocean and the beach. When we reached the top, other than my mom being nervous about Maggie and Emma getting too close to the sides, we were all impressed. It felt like you could see forever and Antonio told us Lucy could be seen from eight miles away without binoculars.

"So who owns her now?" asked my mom.

"The Save Lucy Committee," he answered. "Sophia died in 1963 and her children continued to use Lucy as part of their business on the beach, as a tourist attraction. In 1969, a developer was ready to purchase the land and knock Lucy down, so the family donated her to the city of Margate. The Margate Civic Association was formed to save her."

"Was it hard?" asked T-Bone.

"Extremely," said Samantha. "They had to have a concrete foundation prepared and also raise money to move her to a new location. Preparing her new, concrete feet and prepping her for the move would cost $24,000 and they only had thirty days to raise the money and have her moved."

"How did they raise the money that fast?" I wondered. "Especially, without the internet."

"There were fundraising events, volunteers went door-to-door to every house in Margate, and school children sold cakes and crafts. Unfortunately, they still came up $10,000 short."

"Then what happened?" I asked on the edge of my seat, yet knowing it had to have a happy ending.

"Chairladies Josephine Harron and Sylvia

Carpenter signed a personal note with the help of an anonymous co-signer providing the money needed to proceed."

"That's a relief," I said.

"Not so fast," Antonio continued, "Three days before the moving date the committee was served with legal papers to stop the relocation of the Elephant! The Atlantic Beach Corporation claimed that Lucy would lower the values of property they owned next to the new site. A hearing was scheduled for exactly one day after the deadline for moving. The committee made a desperate appeal to Atlantic County Judge Benjamin Rimm, who agreed to hold a rare Saturday morning hearing in the County Courtroom. Luckily, after listening to arguments from both sides, Judge Rimm ruled in favor of the Save Lucy Committee. If you visit our website, www.lucytheelephant.org, you can see the actual pictures of her being towed down the streets."

"It's amazing she's even here," my mom gasped. "And what a tragedy it would have been if they'd have torn her down. She's like a landmark."

Samantha smiled, "By 1976, Lucy's metal skin and new ornate howdah were in place and freshly painted. The U.S. Department of the Interior recognized Lucy as a National Historic Landmark, taking her place alongside Independence Hall, the Alamo, and other famous sites that possess national significance in commemorating the history of the United States of America."

We finished looking around and headed back to the gift shop, confident that we had found another unique New Jersey destination. Knowing our purchases helped preserve Lucy; my mom, great citizen that she is, did her part. She bought Lucy shirts, Lucy slippers, and wind-up elephants. Samantha and Antonio asked if we could send them a copy of our report and offered to post it on Lucy's website. We happily agreed and made our way to our last stop of the day, the boardwalk.

It was always great being by the ocean. Between the salt air, hearing the birds, and smelling all of the great foods, I couldn't imagine anyone ever having a bad day here. Knowing we had passed *feed-T-Bone-time* again, my dad pulled into the parking lot of the Atlantic City Bar and Grill.

"Who's hungry?" he asked.

"It's past five o'clock isn't it?" said T-Bone.

"A little," my mom lied.

"I'm starving," T-Bone patted his stomach.

"Then you're in luck," said my dad. "Last time Erin and I came here, the lobster tails just melted in our mouths. Everything is always great here."

"It was really good," my mom nodded.

We went inside and my dad walked up to a man named Anthony. They spoke for a minute and he brought us to a table and sent over some bread.

"Dad, how do you know him?" I asked.

"My friend, Rob, is a firefighter here and he and his wife bring us here whenever we visit."

That made sense. I had noticed metal fire decorations on the fence in the parking lot and some firemen sitting at the next table. My mom and dad didn't go out without us too much, less now that we didn't live next to my grandparents. But I knew they did come to A.C., as they called it, once in a while.

We ordered our drinks and looked at the menu. My mom said my sisters would share an order of chicken tenders and a side of fries. My parents and Timmy decided on cheeseburgers and I planned on getting a meatball sandwich.

Unfortunately, no one checked with T-Bone before the waitress arrived. When it was time for him to order, he was ready to go.

"And for you, sir?" the waitress asked him.

"I'd like to start with the creamy lobster bisque, some pick and peel shrimp and then, the twin lobster tails," he said.

"Excuse me, Tommy," my mom said before my dad could holler, "that's an awful lot of food, don't you think?"

"Yeah, but this way I can have some for lunch tomorrow. See, I'm always thinking ahead."

"I know, dear," my mom smiled, "but lobster is a little, you know..."

"Well, I picked the twin tails because it's not the whole lobster, it's just the tails and they're smaller. Plus, Mr. A. said they were great."

"Tommy," my dad turned red and spoke very slowly, "we ordered lobster tails when we were celebrating our anniversary."

"Well, Happy Anniversary," T-Bone smiled.

"Look, Tommy, they have a lot of great choices on the menu," my dad glared. "Why not give it another glance? Maybe a burger or pizza?"

"I don't know," he mumbled, "I'm really not feeling a burger. I guess it's the salt air, but I'm really in the mood for seafood. Yeah, definitely seafood."

"Great," my dad said, turning to the waitress. "Change his whole order to the fish and chips."

"Got it," she said and returned to the kitchen.

Poor T-Bone, it all happened so fast. His enormous seafood dinner was gone as fast as he ordered it and my dad was sitting there with a big grin. I was curious what T-Bone had been thinking, though. He's been out with us enough to know my dad frowns upon kids ordering appetizers, desserts, and extra soda, unless it's included. I figured the salt air must have *really* gotten to him.

The food was great and it was just loud enough that people couldn't hear my sisters singing. When the waitress asked about dessert, my dad explained that we'd have ice cream on the board-walk. After watching my dad revise T-Bone's order, I'm sure she knew what the answer would be before she even asked. We said goodnight to Anthony and headed to the boards for ice cream. We stopped when we saw the huge statue of a soldier holding several dog-tags at the Korean War Memorial. It was really impressive and reminded me of the memorial in Trenton. I was happy to see a big memorial for those soldiers, too.

"Pretty good day, huh?" I asked T-Bone.

"Definitely," he said. "*I don't know what you were so worried about.*"

# Chapter Twelve
## Meetings and Eatings

We spent the following week finishing more odd jobs and schoolwork. By the time Thursday night arrived, T-Bone and I sat down at the kitchen table to count our money. We were shocked at how much we had earned and counted it four times.

"Wow," said T-Bone , "it pays to be odd."

"If that was the case, you'd be a multi-multi-millionaire," my dad laughed as he walked by.

"Seriously, Dad," I said, "I had lost count, but in the last few weeks, we each earned $118.00."

"Really?" he asked, more shocked than we were. "What are you doing with all of that money?"

"We're going to put $75.00 in the bank, give $25.00 to Ryan's Quest, and keep the rest," I announced.

"Very impressive," my mom said as she walked in. "I thought you'd want to spend more."

"We thought about it," I admitted, "but we

have more jobs lined up and we don't have much time to spend it, anyway. Plus, Mr. Perilli and Mr. Inverso said to keep a little and save the rest."

"I agree," said my dad. "When do you want to open up your accounts?"

"We were hoping we could go tomorrow," I suggested.

"I guess we could go after school," my dad agreed. "Any chance you're trying to work DeLorenzo's into the equation?"

"Well, since you brought it up," T-Bone laughed.

Fortunately, it wasn't hard to twist my dad's arm into bringing us to DeLorenzo's. The next day we each separated our money into 3 different envelopes. I put my spending money envelope in the blue sock that I hide in my drawer.

Our first stop was the State House, where we left our reports with the guard. We attached a note telling Billy we couldn't visit because we were opening up bank accounts. Our next stop was the bank. We told the receptionist that we were there to open up new accounts and asked if Mr. Perilli and Mr. Inverso were in. While my dad helped us fill out the forms, my mom tried to keep Timmy and my sisters away from the refreshment table filled with cookies.

Before we finished, Nancy, Mr. Perilli, and Mr. Inverso were heading our way. I introduced them to my mom and everyone shook hands. Nancy had a camera and asked if she could take our picture. T-Bone thought it was because we were New Jersey ambassadors, but Nancy said it was because we were young savers. Mr. Perilli commended us on having initiative and said we reminded him of himself when he was our age, *twenty years ago*. We did the mental math, looked at Nancy, and realized they almost got us again. Mr. Inverso asked how business was and smiled when we told him about the odd job demand.

We waited a few moments and a woman returned with our official bank books, each inside a plastic sleeve and each with a balance of $75.00. It felt good to have money in the bank. While it definitely crossed our minds to head to the mall, we knew that one day we'd be really happy that we saved it. They asked about our latest trips and we told them about all of the great places we found. Before they returned to their offices they thanked us and told us to keep up the good work.

Feeling pretty proud of ourselves, we drove down the street for some tomato pies. We went right to one of the big booths near the ovens and Sam saw us right away.

"Hey, how's Jersey's famous ambassadors?" he asked.

"Starving and rich," T-Bone announced.

"Perfect," Sam laughed, "that's exactly how we like our customers."

We placed our order and Sam introduced us to his wife, Teresa. She bent down and whispered, "I think there's someone you may want to meet."

We looked at the booth behind us and I knew who it was right away. It was little Ryan and his family. She introduced us to Ryan, his brothers David and Mason, and his parents, Maria and Dave. They were so friendly and it was hard to believe that Ryan was so sick.

"Hey, Ryan," said T-Bone, throwing his hand in the air, "I'm T-Bone."

"Hey, T-Bone," Ryan said, giving him a huge high-five.

At first I was nervous and I didn't know what to say. I decided to follow T-Bone's lead and introduce myself. Ryan gave me a bigger high-five. I held out my hand and David gave me a big high-five, too.

Ryan started talking to us and showed us his

police car, fire truck, and airplane. When he held up the airplane, he yelled, "Zoom," and everyone laughed. He was so happy and reminded me of Emma; I figured it was the age. Sam told Ryan's parents about our being both ambassadors and entrepreneurs. Dave asked if we'd be putting Hamilton Township in any of our reports. We told him we had read about the Kuser Mansion, the Grounds for Sculpture, and a Civil War museum. He said he'd be happy to give us some tips when we were ready.

Ryan was a cute kid and he was wearing a Yankees visor and pointed to his blue shirt. He told us it was his sunny day shirt and his mom explained that blue was his favorite color and sunny day is what he calls daytime. He then pulled his leg out from under the table to show us his white sunny day socks. By this time, my mom and dad were also standing and my mom was clapping for Ryan and playing with Mason. When she realized Maria was a teacher, as usual, she started talking shop.

"We should let them get back to their dinner," said my dad.

"It's fine," Dave smiled, "as you can see, Ryan loves the attention."

I walked up to the end of the booth where

Dave was sitting and whispered how we learned about Ryan when we went into Roma Bank with my dad. I explained how we opened up our first savings account there because they were helping Ryan. Then I told him that we put $75.00 in the bank, saved $18.00 to spend, and each had $25.00 for Ryan's Quest. As we reached into our pockets and took out our *Ryan* envelopes, Dave put his head down. Oh man, I thought, we just upset Ryan's dad. He looked up with teary eyes, but a big smile.

"You know, I am constantly shocked at how generous and thoughtful people are and you boys have probably been the biggest surprise," he said. "Most kids your age would have been at the mall, not thinking about saving for the future and helping a little boy you hadn't met. This means the world to us."

Just catching what was happening; Maria looked over and mouthed the words: "Thank you so much." Dave stood up, shook our hands, and then shook my dad's hand. He told him it was an honor to meet us and my dad explained how he had read about Ryan's Quest and now his grocery store was raising money, too.

"Wow," said Dave. "I'm just overwhelmed."

"That's not all," said T-Bone, "We're gonna

see if our school can raise money, too. We want to be on your team and I have to tell you, I usually have pretty good luck."

"I don't know what to say," Maria smiled. "We need as many people and as much luck as we can get on our team."

"I know what to say," said Sam, a little choked up himself. "Tomato pies on the house for my two favorite tables."

We finished eating and said good-bye to Sam, Teresa, and our new friends. When we reached the van my mom looked sad.

"What's wrong?" I asked.

"I just wish we could do more to help Ryan. There's still time to find a cure," she said.

"I know," my dad shook his head. "They're an incredible family. And I'm really proud of you boys, too. I'll raise money at the store and you boys think of ideas for at school. You can even tell your customers about Ryan."

"I'll talk to my principal, also," my mom added with real tears running down her cheeks.

"Hey, mom," I asked. "Do you think we can really make a difference for Ryan?"

"Absolutely," she smiled. "He's counting on

all of us to make a difference."

Three days later, a very official letter arrived from the Governor's Office and it was from the Governor himself. He thanked us for our service to the state, said our reports exceeded his expectations and that he was confident we would help him to improve tourism. He then suggested visiting his official residence in Princeton for our next report.

"Hey, we'll be like the Ford kids in Morristown," T-Bone laughed.

"What do you mean?" I asked.

"Hanging with heads of state," he replied.

"He isn't inviting us to move in," I said.

"Hey, you don't think he's asking us to come because he wants to hire us to rake leaves, do you?"

"No, I'm sure he has people who take care of those things." I laughed.

"Well, that's good news," T-Bone sighed. "Because if the Governor lives there, I'm sure Gumsmacket is big and probably has a lot of trees."

*"Drumthwacket," I sighed. "Drumthwacket."*

The End
*Until the next adventure...*

# Welcome to the
# Franklin Mason Press
# Guest Young Author Section

Turn this page for stories from our three newest Guest Young Authors, ages 9-12 years old. From thousands of submissions, these stories were selected by a committee for their creativity, originality, and quality.

We believe that children should have an active role in literature, including publishing and sharing their stories with the world. We hope you enjoy reading them as much as we did.

If you are 9-12 years old and would like to be a Franklin Mason Press Guest Young Author, read the directions, write your story, and send it in! The first, second, and third place winners receive $50.00, $40.00, and $30.00, respectively, a book, an award, and a party to autograph books. Send us a 150-350 word story about something strange, funny or unusual. Your story may be fiction or non-fiction. For additional details visit:

**www.franklinmasonpress.com**

# 1st Place Guest Young Author

**Samantha Patrick**
**Northside Elementary School**
**Annville, Pennsylvania**

## The Journey of a Snowflake

One day, in the Forest of Heat, a bear named Winter roared and said, "When is there going to be snow? I haven't hibernated in ten years." So he did a snow dance. The winter fairies saw that the animals were very upset from the heat. So they worked their magic. They made one little snowflake and she was beautiful. Her name was Emily and she would change the forest.

While she was on her journey, a cloud came up to her and said, "I will make it so misty, you will not find your way to the Forest of Heat."

*The Psychology of Learning*

# CHAPTER I

# Introduction

The news of the week provides graphic testimony to the range of man's activities—a discovery of the process of electrochemical change regulating thought is reported; an athlete establishes a new world's high jump record; a political leader is murdered; a space probe to an adjacent planet is launched; a conference on nuclear disarmament is under way; a trusted bank employee is discovered to have embezzled a fortune. Although we read of the events with interest, we rarely pause to reflect on the range of human behavior portrayed in any day's news, any more than we reflect on the range of skill involved in our individual actions during the day. Housekeeping, perhaps the most mundane of occupations, requires extensive skill—food preparation, operation of mechanical equipment, purchasing, child care, sewing, and so on. The development of those skills depends upon extended training involving motor skill, memory, computation, comprehension, problem solving, and many other aspects of learning. Few give the process of acquiring and retaining these skills much thought, for learning is a process that goes on with little or no awareness. We are aware of progress in learning, of stages or levels reached, of having mastered a task, but hardly of what occurred to produce the accomplishment. Having learned, we accept its manifestations as a matter of fact in much the same way we take the variety of events in the newspaper for granted.

Each of the events selected demonstrates the ubiquity of learning. The biochemist studying electrochemical changes in the brain had to develop and control exquisitely delicate techniques of exploration and measurement as well as conceive a procedure for catching thought in flight, namely spinning animals in a centrifuge knowing it would yield a predetermined cerebral change. The high jumper not only needed a physical structure suited to the task, but years of training to develop the motor control and coordination that catapulted his body to new height. The murder and the embezzlement, unfortunate activities though they are, nonetheless required knowledge and skill. The murder required planning, systematic preparation and execution, and coordinated group action; the embezzlement, a solitary performance, demanded sustained careful management of bookkeeping procedures over several years. The space probe required the combined talents and training of a diversified corps of scientists and engineers, each of whom underwent long and arduous training, backed by the maximum in technology that our society can muster. These events alone are sufficient to justify designating man the learner.

For a thousand centuries, man has changed little, his behavior much. Where other species survive by engendering new species through selection and mutation, man has survived by modifying his behavior. There is a vastly greater difference between the behavior of the Eskimo living on the arctic icecap and the Lacadone Indian living in the tropical rain-forest than there is between the Arctic hare and the jackrabbit, or between other members of a given genus. Though brothers under the skin, the tools, techniques, and behavior of the two men are completely different. Such modifications occur primarily through learning, the process by which behavior is initiated or changed as a result of experience or, more specifically, through training and practice. Certain contrasts can give the definition some significance.

## Learning and Maturation

At first consideration, there would appear to be no human behavior which escapes the influence and effects of learning. This is largely true, for even physiological processes can be shown to be affected, function and event being interlocked. But many changes occur or are made possible as a result of physiological maturation. No amount of training will induce a mastery of walking in a child of six months or of algebra in one of six years because the capacity to acquire those skills is simply lacking at those ages. Many changes are dependent upon the presence of appropriate neuromuscular development. The most easily observable skills are in the motor area —those requiring hand-eye coordination, such as catching a ball, body control as in diving, or strength—but many aspects of intellectual development are dependent upon maturation such as concepts of time and space.

## Learning and Performance

Learning and performance are intricately interlocked. The former is the process by which behavior is changed; the latter, the gauge of results. The one cannot be taken for the other. Learning produces changes in performance. At the simplest level, this may consist of developing a new response to a stimulus or shifting an existing response to a new stimulus. The change in performance may be at the symbolic level, occurring vicariously, as in language learning. Learning is not the only process that mediates change in performance. Forgetting produces changes whereby performance is impaired; fatigue interferes with the proficiency of performance; maturation and motivation affect performance. Changes in performance are dependent on short term processes, such as fatigue and motivation, and long term processes, such as maturation and forgetting, as well as on learning. Performance is thus an imperfect measure of learning. Usually we attempt to manipulate performance in some tangible manner, particularly in school situations, to produce specific changes. But several aspects of learning are not easily managed. Attitudes, ideals, fears, and symbolic learning are quite intangible, both in acquisition and manifestation, making it difficult to bring the learning process under control, whether by use of performance to influence the process of change, or as a measure of amount of change.

In spite of our most carefully arranged efforts, the results of learning are not always for the better. There is no guarantee of improved performance. A case in point is the painful experience of a young woman who recently set about learning to ski. Inexperienced but highly motivated to learn, she made rapid progress under daily professional instruction. One afternoon a well-meaning friend proceeded to "help" her, teaching her an outmoded style entirely different from that of the professional instructor. Willing to accept help from anyone having experience, the young woman faithfully attempted to carry out the friend's instructions, but found her control steadily deteriorating. The harder she worked, the more she fell.

physical forces such as air masses at different temperature, moisture content, and the like could we understand such phenomena.

The complexity of motivational patterns in humans makes attaining a full understanding difficult. A variety of goals may satisfy a single motive. One's desire for status may be satisfied with a Cadillac, with money, with a professorship, or any other of a number of possibilities. Being a teacher may satisfy one person's security needs; in another it may satisfy a fear of adults, status needs, or desires to please parents. Yet, understanding of motivation is vital to successful teaching.

In looking at motives and attitudes, we are concerned with energy and the direction of it, and with the internal and external stimulus conditions which affect it. By the time children first enter school they have a basic motivational system resulting from the socializing experiences which they have had.

Maslow [15] has described a theory of motivation and its development which is useful to this discussion. He views motives as organized in a hierarchy which evolves from the basic physiological needs. We are born with physiological needs which must be satisfied if we are to survive. Deprivation of nourishment and fluid, extremes in temperature, body chemical changes, and other conditions cause activity. In the young infant the intial activity is a general arousal brought about by the experience of discomfort, but very rapidly such general activity is modified on the basis of experiences. The time schedule on which he is fed affects the rhythm with which he gets hungry or thirsty. The time allowed for feeding affects the speed with which he eats. The type of feeding—breast, bottle, or cup—affects the strength of the sucking response made. At first, an activity doesn't subside until food is received. But the child comes to respond to cues or signals in lieu of food—he will become quiet at the sight of the bottle in anticipation of the food; later, he will become quiet on hearing the sound of his mother's footsteps, knowing they signal food or care. Much later he will respond to verbal cues: *e.g.,* "We'll eat as soon as Daddy gets home." Not only will he learn to respond to signal and symbol as representative of satisfaction of his needs, at least temporarily, but he will also develop food preferences

---

[15] A. H. Maslow, "A Theory of Human Motivation." *Psychological Review,* 50 (1943), pp. 370-96.

(affective reactions to certain classes and kinds of foods). He will learn ways of acting to get food and to eat it once he has obtained it, and he will begin to evolve a hierarchy of social motives as a result of the associational processes in effect. Behavior that successfully leads to satisfaction of a drive is reinforced by a satisfactory outcome; *i.e.,* need or drive reduction. Events which occur contiguous with the satisfaction of a primary drive acquire a reinforcement value of their own. The chain of events associated with feeding—being held, played with, talked to, smiled at, and associated with—acquire a positive valence, and ultimately, functional autonomy. They become ends in themselves and have the capacity to reinforce behavior. There is ample evidence from animal experiments that desires, appetites, and fears can develop through learning, and it is plausible that man's social motives evolve similarly.

Maslow sees a pattern of motives developing, starting with the basic physiological needs and the associated psychological needs of safety which lead children to prefer the known to the unknown, the familiar to the strange, and to avoid perceived danger. Next to develop are the affectional needs, in effect the desire for a person as a token or symbol of the satisfaction of basic needs. The needs for affection, love, companionship, and friendship fall in this group. In addition to acceptance, children wish to have the approval and recognition of the persons who play such a powerful role in regulating their lives. To have this approval enhances their sense of security, not to have it is threatening.

Such approval gotten, it is a short step to the identification of those qualities and actions which gain approval and those which do not. Self-appraisal reflects the appraisal we obtain from others. One develops a concept of himself as being to some extent a worthwhile person, and with it a degree of self-esteem. The concept of what we are good for and the desires we have to be like someone else, the models for identification, represent our self-concept and our ideal self. These are the kinds of motives that are in the process of major development by the time the child enters school. In addition, the procedures followed in the socialization of the child, the kinds of rewards and punishment, the severity of punishment, the affectional relationships and dominance-submission relationships within the family affect the degree of independence shown, the amount and responses or produces negative transfer. A good illustration is the common practice of requiring children to write every spelling word five times. In copying words from the blackboard, a child is likely first to copy the word on the board, thereafter copy the word he has written. An intelligent fourth-grade boy carrying out such an assignment produced the following:

November     Noveber     Novebr     Nvebr

His spellings resulted in part from a difficulty in reading his own handwriting, partly from the drill of error responses. Instead of looking back to the board each time for the correct stimulus, he looked to his reproductions and the errors they incorporated. Clearly it is essential that mastery precede drill or overlearning.

Kreuger [7] compared the effect upon retention of 50 per cent overlearning and 100 per cent overlearning, after a series of learning trials in which 12 nonsense syllables were learned to the end of one perfect performance during a single presentation. Whatever the number of trials taken to learn the syllables, 50 per cent more trials were given in one treatment, and an amount of drill equal to the learning trials in the 100 per cent treatment. Retention was tested at intervals of 1, 2, 4, 7, 14, and 28 days. Retention was superior at all time intervals for both degrees of overlearning, but only slight differences were observed in advantage of the 100 per cent overlearning compared to the 50 per cent method. The study indicates that overlearning, at least to the 50 per cent degree, increases retention and that the longer the interval, the higher the value. Certainly these findings are significant for memory drills and for other cases where long retention is desired.

To be effective however, overlearning requires the same degree of attention as during learning, which is often not the case in the classroom situation. Furthermore, it indicates that the amount of drill should be varied according to the length of time it takes a student to learn. The more the conditions under which practice and drill are similar to the conditions under which the skill will be used, the more effective practice and drill will be. Typing nonsense syllables will not be as useful as typing words. Practice in pronunciation

7 W. C. F. Kreuger, "The Effect of Overlearning on Retention," *Journal of Experimental Psychology*, 12 (1929), pp. 71-78.

of single words of a foreign language will not contribute greatly to skill in speaking the language. There are undoubtedly many places in the teaching of arithmetic and spelling where drill procedures can be markedly improved, if by no more than variations in amount of drill. When Brownell and Chazal [8] checked on the procedures being used by third grade children in making arithmetic computations after two years of training by drill methods in grades 1 and 2, they found that only half the children based their answers on immediate recall. The other half were counting, guessing, or using indirect methods. After a month of daily drill in the third grade, one-third of the class were still not using rote memory, indicating the inadequacy of straight drill as a teaching method.

Recall that in retroactive inhibition, differential amounts of practice on two tasks reduced the amount of interference. Similarly, as materials are overlearned, the interference decreases, and positive transfer increases.

## Guidance of Learning

There is a real art in knowing when to step in and give instruction and guidance and when to let the learner practice on his own. Errors are unavoidable in the course of learning; they can be helpful as long as they contribute to a knowledge of the appropriate actions. An unfortunate effect of instructional practice and the feeling children get that errors per se are bad is their consequent reluctance to try for fear of making errors. Careful analysis of any given skill is needed in order to contrive learning exercises which yield the development of the desired skill with minimal efforts. Several steps can be followed in guiding learning activities:

1. Analyze the skill.
2. Demonstrate the skill by part or whole.
3. Guide initial responses.
4. Provide appropriate exercises.
5. Provide knowledge of results, preferably intrinsically.
6. Help the learner evaluate performance.

---

[8] W. A. Brownell, and Charlotte Chazal, "The Effects of Premature Drill in Third Grade Arithmetic," *Journal of Educational Research,* 29 (1935), p. 17.

*Analyze the skill.* This is the responsibility of the instructor and is for the purpose of clarifying the instructor's understanding of the task so that he can teach the component parts in the simplest fashion possible. Confusion results when an amateur dance instructor begins with, "You start off with your weight on your right foot; step forward with your right foot; no, that isn't right, your weight is on both feet." The results of such analysis are conveyed to the learner in the form of the exercises chosen and the demonstrations given. A few years back, it was common practice in skiing to teach the novice the various weight and balance shifts involved in a given turn: "As you are traversing the slope, your skis are parallel, slightly more weight on the downhill ski. As you approach the turn, put your weight on your downhill ski; counterrotate your shoulders and hips; stem one ski; release the edges of your skis by leaning down the fall-line. As your skis come into the fall-line, rotate hips and shoulders and shift weight to the downhill ski as you complete the turn." The novice had difficulty recalling the sequence of events, to say nothing of executing them—his perception of movements was sufficiently delayed that the action got away from him. Today, instruction would begin by dividing the sequence into a series of components, each of which is an integrated unit, not a meaningless fraction, and devising for each an exercise which demonstrates the action, *e.g.,* having the novice raise his uphill ski as he traverses a gentle slope.

*Demonstrate the skill.* Although little attention is paid to imitation in formal discussion of learning, imitation serves many purposes which go unrecognized, particularly in motor learning. A skill has to be demonstrated in the manner the student will be expected to perform it. An instructor who has his students facing him is providing them with reversed demonstration. The mere presence of the model isn't sufficient—he must be a model who demonstrates clearly what to do. For instance, training in the assembly of a piece of equipment or the operation of a machine is more effective if the learners are behind the instructor rather than surrounding him. The effectiveness of filmed demonstrations and closed circuit television in medical schools is ample testimony to the value of demonstration. Ample research evidence exists to support the empirical demonstrations of such techniques as surgical operations to demonstrate the value of the enlarged visual image provided by film, not only for demonstrations of technique but also for general principles.

Imitation is a major means by which children learn motor skills, acquire language patterns, gestures, attitudes, and a wide variety of social behaviors. A strong argument can be advanced for equating imitation and identification. However defined, there is no question regarding the roles that imitation, reciprocity, and demonstration play in learning. In fact, the educational value of the so-called educational toys which are replicas of household equipment is found in the real equipment that provides repeated demonstrations. Nash [9] has reported how the complex skill of operating a cotton textile machine is taught entirely by demonstration in Guatamala. The apprentice stands by the machine and observes the operator perform the series of responses required to operate the machine. The training proceeds entirely by demonstration and observation, without any instructions, questions, or opportunities to practice. When the apprentice thinks she has mastered the procedure, the machine is turned over to her, and usually with successful results.

*Guide initial responses.* Many skills have two component parts, a motor part and a perceptual part. Dancing, skiing, and running have high motor components but low perceptual. The cues to performance are mainly kinesthetic and have to be sensed internally. Learning follows a course of gradual approximation and refinement toward perfection of the correct response. Verbal instruction is easily overdone and confusing because it fails to call attention to the correct cues for judging and correcting performance. The child learning to row a boat and keep it going in a straight line will become quickly confused and discouraged by a series of verbal commands attempting to correct the veering: "You're going in a curve; pull harder on the right oar; you pulled too hard, now pull on the left oar; don't put your left oar so deep into the water. . . ." Manual guidance can be of assistance where the pattern of movement is not clear, but the fact that learning a motor skill requires voluntary control of movements regulated by the central nervous system places definite limits on its value. Reading, speaking, and map reading are skills with high perceptual, low motor components. Verbal guidance

---

[9] M. Nash, "Machine-age Maya: The Industrialization of a Guatemalan Community," *American Anthropological Association,* No. 2 (1958), p. 60.

can be valuable, but it should be positive and focus on appropriate cues. The learner should be told what to do rather than what *not* to do, by concentrating on the goal to be achieved.

*Provide appropriate exercises.* Pupil skill analyses made by the teacher should lead to the development of exercises that will improve skills. The author vividly remembers an example of superb teaching. A French phonetician instructed a group of men for an hour at a driving pace on the distinctive pronunciations of two phonemes, the vowel sounds in *je* and *j'ai*. The task is superficially such a simple discrimination that it would seem impossible, and unnecessary, to hold a group of adults, even novices, at the task for that length of time. The group was composed of fifteen men from a dozen different countries in Asia, Africa, and the Americas. The instructor proceeded through a series of simple repetition exercises of single sounds, which she corrected man by man, then of combinations of the vowel sounds with the same consonant, then through a series of progressively longer and more intricate combinations of consonant and vowel sounds requiring finer discriminations, both in listening and speaking, in order to accurately distinguish the intended meaning. With an ear as acute as a symphony conductor's for a false note, she detected faults in pronunciation, located the erring member, and then worked with him quickly on a particular combination. Her talent was such that she was able to provide special drills for particular errors associated with a particular mother tongue. For example, those who speak English, Spanish, and Japanese each have unique difficulties learning to pronounce the French "r," because in each of their languages the closest native sound is only an approximation and is created differently. Such special drills are a result of careful analyses of many languages. Such careful analysis and development of special exercises is needed in many subject areas.

*Provide knowledge of results.* An effective guide to improved performance is knowledge of the results of any response. In perceptual-motor learning, automatic feedback of results is an inherent part of most situations. The pilot landing a plane is aware that an angle of approach is too steep, even before the jar of the wheels on the ground. The overstroked tennis drive on its way out-of-bounds is sensed immediately. But in other forms of learning performance is not as readily judged. The pronunciation of sounds in a foreign language depends not only upon vocal mechanisms but upon auditory discrimination. A faultily produced sound or word may sound correct for lack of fine auditory discrimination. In cognitive learning errors are even more difficult to perceive. Improvement in any skill proceeds faster with knowledge of results. The merit of rewards and punishment in many situations rests more upon the information they yield than upon the affective reactions of the learner. Bernard and Gilbert [10] comment on the fact that wrong responses (errors in maze learning by college students) which resulted in an electric shock were eliminated more readily than error responses which went unshocked:

> From the evidence available it seems reasonable to postulate that any well-defined stimulus introduced consistently in connection with either right or wrong responses will tend to favor their repetition if they are right or their elimination if they are wrong, provided that the stimulus is not of such a type or strength as to introduce a distracting effect. In other words, any stimulus which is not highly distracting may act either as a "punishment" or a "reward" depending upon whether it accompanies responses which are arbitrarily designated as right or wrong. . . .
>
> In human subjects, knowledge of a "punishment" stimulus appears to mean much more than direct affective reactions to the stimulus. In the present investigation most of the subjects reported that they tried to avoid the shock mainly because it signified error rather than because it was disagreeable. . . . Shock which was given in the "shock" alleys announced the errors in a definite and cleancut manner and enabled the subject to make the location more accurately.

Criticism of performance has the essential purpose of pointing out error in order to permit correction. It serves this purpose if it is specific, constructive, and encouraging. There is little purpose in advising a student that his sentence construction or grammatical usage is faulty. This may designate the general kind of difficulty, but lacking specific information on kind of error, the necessary steps to improvement remain unknown to the writer. In the same manner, vague admonitions to "try to do better" aren't helpful unless the learner is aware of what steps be can take.

[10] J. Bernard, and R. Gilbert, "The Specificity of The Effect of Shock for Error in Maze Learning with Human Subjects," *Journal of Experimental Psychology,* 28 (1941), pp. 184-85.

In experimental studies, where learners have been informed systematically of wrong responses and compared with another group systematically informed of correct responses, the learning rate of the latter group surpassed that of the former. There is greater advantage in knowing what *to* do than in knowing what *not* to do in any situation affording a choice between more than two alternatives.

Positive criticism has the additional advantage of minimizing such affective reactions as discouragement and frustration. Self-evaluation has the added advantage of avoiding the interpersonal resentments that external criticism can create, as well as aiding the development of individual standards of appraisal and initiative and encouraging their application.

A simple step toward that end available to all teachers is reduction of the emphasis on measurement incorporated in quiz and test sessions, and prompt return of results. Various procedures for having individuals or groups correct their own papers and evaluate their own errors are available. Through self-correction of examinations and group tabulation of the frequency of errors to each question, points needing further instruction can be identified. For example, workbooks are commonly used in many learning situations, from elementary school through college. Too often they serve as busywork, timefillers to occupy one group of children while the teacher is busy with another. The group could be provided answer keys. Tabulation and correction of their errors provides them prompt knowledge of both individual and group weaknesses, suggesting points at which additional work or review is necessary. The same procedure applies to tests. Students could correct their own tests from answers provided by the instructor, thus avoiding the time lag which commonly occurs between taking the test and learning the results and permitting immediate correction of error. Knowledge of results is as valuable as reward and goal setting in its contribution to performance. Helmstadter and Ellis [11] compared three different goal-setting procedures—a self-set goal, an externally established goal, and a goal of improvement with immediate knowledge of results—each procedure being followed in one group on a

---

[11] G. C. Helmstadter, and D. S. Ellis, "Rate of Manipulative Learning as a Function of Goal Setting Techniques," *Journal of Experimental Psychology*, 43 (1952), pp. 43, 125-128.

manual dexterity task. They found that all groups showed similar performance curves.

Inevitably certain students will alter incorrect responses to correct ones, especially where they anticipate the score will be part of a grade. This practice disappears as they become accustomed to the use of the test purely for analysis, and where they understand its contribution to self-improvement.

*Recitation.* In spite of open criticism of it as the unimaginative teacher's procedure, the practice of assign-study-recite-test is still very evident. Many classes at the secondary level are little more than a recitation of assignments given in the last five minutes of the preceding session punctuated at intervals by quizzes and examinations. Research fails to support this procedure as an effective method of teaching for even so limited an objective as the learning of factual information. Such an arrangement fails on several counts: little or no provision for individual differences in capacity, independent work, and motivation; inadequate directions on how to proceed; no provision for checking progress during the course of carrying out the assignment; inadequate review of the teacher. In the usual form of recitation in which students take turns responding to questions placed by the teacher, the students quickly identify the way in which teachers call upon students—alphabetically, seating plan, whatever her scheme—and adapt to it by studying those parts of a given assignment on which they are likely to have to recite. A random order for calling on pupils may foil them, but it still fails to give each pupil more than a fraction of the recitation needed, and fails to identify the points of difficulty being experienced by each pupil.

The criticisms directed against recitation are not that it lacks value but that it is misused. Recitation is a form of review, hence it is best preceded by learning. There is ample evidence to show that recitation fosters or reinforces learning when:

    1. It provides progressive knowledge of results.

    2. It permits better distribution of practice by pointing out parts on which additional practice is needed.

    3. It promotes recall in a way in which the material will characteristically be used.

    4. It contributes to meaningfulness of material.

5. It serves as an incentive by providing confirmation of progress in improvement.

Basically, recitation is valuable to the degree to which it is individualized and makes the materials learned functional. A number of plans have been developed and tried during the last three decades in the attempt to attain these ends. The Winnetka and Dalton Plans, project and activity methods, and teacher-pupil planning and cooperative group activities were developed and used in efforts to provide more pupil-centered, individualized instruction. Two current designs in the effort to provide for differentiated instruction and individual rates of progress are team-learning and team-teaching. Both depend on adequately developed and diversified materials, appropriate grouping of children, and periodic check-tests that permit children to work, learn, recite, review, and check one another on their progress, all done under the supervision of the teaching staff. Team learning is particularly adapted to the one teacher-one class organization, and is especially useful with such subjects as arithmetic and spelling. Small groups of pupils are provided graded assignments on which each works, then compares results with his fellows for agreement. Where disagreement occurs, the pupils check on their errors; if help is needed they turn to the teacher. Periodic quizzes provide a check on knowledge and understanding prior to the introduction of new materials. It can be seen that the teacher's role is here quite different from the traditional assign-review role. She is engaged in the development of materials, introduction of concepts, provision of guidance at points of difficulty, review of progress, and analysis of error. She hears very little formal recitation. Yet the procedure provides more opportunity for pupil recitation through mutual instruction and correction as an integral part of the learning.

Team-teaching is a more complex organizational arrangement whereby a group of teachers pool their resources in order to instruct a group of classes. In its simplest form in the elementary school it is similar to departmentalized teaching in the secondary school, except that teachers move to pupils rather than vice versa, and only one teacher has primary responsibility for a given class. The Detroit Plan is a system-wide variant of this in which specialists in music, art, physical education, and so forth and teachers are alternated between groups on a scheduled basis. In a more highly developed form, team-teaching utilizes a range of graded materials, a variety of learning and recitation devices such as audio-visual devices, teaching machines, projects, and review tests. A highly organized division of labor between teachers permits scheduled contact with individual pupils, small groups, and large groups. The basic attempt is to adapt materials and teaching skills to individual pupil needs and rates of learning.

Both procedures use review tests for regular checks of progress. The emphasis is on degree of mastery of given material rather than on measurement of comparative standing for purposes of grading. Tiedeman [12] advocates the use of review tests immediately after learning and at periodic intervals subsequently. He found more forgetting in one day when retention was not aided by review than was forgotten in 63 days when two intervening review tests were used as aids to retention. By incorporating such review procedures in team-learning situations, a form of recitation is provided all students on all materials. This can be especially beneficial to pupils of below-average ability in whom forgetting is rapid.

*Incentive conditions.* "Motives" are defined as existing within the individual and directing his energies toward certain goals. Though events shape them and conditions may be created which utilize them, they are part of the internal environment of the individual. Those parts of the external environment, those objects or situations which are capable of satisfying a motive are designated "incentives." In any learning situation multiple incentives are usually involved. The student preparing a project for a science fair is usually working on a project which he finds satisfying in its own right, yet he nonetheless hopes that he will win one of the awards. He finds himself under pressure from the science teacher, who wants his students to reflect a good image of him to his colleagues and the community. The student is reluctant to not engage in an activity in which most or all of his fellow classmates are engaged; yet he has some fears about being left behind in the competition. He enjoys the sense of accomplishment he feels when he completes the project and has

---

[12] H. R. Tiedeman, "A Study of Retention of Classroom Learning," *Journal of Educational Research,* 41 (1947), pp. 516-30.

it ready for the fair. Certain of these conditions provide an *intrinsic* satisfaction in that they are a functional part or consequence of the activity. Certain others have no basic relationship. A large portion of our lives is spent in study and work—it would be ideal if we could enjoy these activities for their own sake. Hopefully, the student's main satisfaction in preparation for the science fair would be the enjoyment from a successful project rather than the award or prize to be won. Studying, working, learning, producing should be satisfying in and of themselves. There should be no need for prizes, rewards, winning a competition, honor rolls, and *magna cum laude* degrees, artificial incentives that too often have the unfortunate effect of developing a "what's it worth" or "what's in it for me" attitude. Individual motivation being what it is, the world of work and the inept matching of men and jobs being what they are, nonfunctional incentives will exist for some time, if not forever. Yet our use of incentives can be subordinated to the intrinsic satisfactions to be found in achievement, so well characterized in Mallory's explanation of why he tried to climb Mt. Everest: "Because it's there." This is much the same motivation that prompts the exploration of space.

The decision to be made is not whether or not to use incentives, but how and when to use them and to what educational purpose. Incentives have their value and their place. They encourage effort, particularly in early stages of learning when intrinsic satisfactions are low, and they provide knowledge of results. But, unhappily, they become ends in themselves as a result of overdependence on them.

We overlook more basic motivational conditions in any learning situation and we neglect the effects of our incentive conditions on the developing motives of children in our desires to spur short-term pupil effort for immediate learning. We are so habituated to marking and grading, rewarding and punishing, testing and measuring that we think the entire learning enterprise would end abruptly were we to dispense with them. To not use them is to fail as educators. The intrenchment of this concept in educational thinking was observed recently in conjunction with a project of the Massachusetts Council for Public Schools for providing foreign language instruction via television—"Parlons Français"—to the 150 school systems participating in The 21″ Classroom's in-school television broadcasts. Two fifteen-minute programs per week are provided children in the intermediate grades, to which are added two correlative fifteen-minute practice sessions by the classroom teacher. Where administrative support and teacher enthusiasm is high, the children show considerable progress in learning to speak French. The learning that occurs is self-evident and is further corroborated by end-of-year tests. The teachers were encouraged not to concern themselves with grading or evaluation, in the knowledge that the direct satisfaction of learning to speak a foreign language would be satisfying and motivating to the children.

One need not administer tests to determine if an instructional program in foreign language is going well. If the only time the children make use of the second language is during the practice sessions, if they make no spontaneous use of it, if they cannot respond to simple questions or directions, they are not learning the language. If the teacher does most of the talking during practice sessions, the children speak haltingly or not at all, and the practice consists mainly of games, songs, and mimicking, the instructional program is inadequate. Yet such observational evidence did not satisfy many administrators and teachers. They believed that if they didn't test and didn't grade, the instructional program wasn't educationally respectable. They gauged their effectiveness by the procedures being used rather than by the performance of the children and the satisfactions found in learning and mastering a second language.

Incentive conditions are only one of many factors affecting the motivational climate of a classroom. When young children enter school their needs for the approval of adults, and for the maintenance and development of their self-esteem are quite strong. Their approach to school is a mixture of obedience, curiosity, fear, anticipation, and uncertainty. Gradually, if conditions are favorable, they develop desires to master the tasks which confront them and acquire confidence that they can do so. They also develop an awareness of the emerging peer group and a desire for a place in it and approval from it. Research increasingly supports the principle that the learning that occurs in any classroom is functionally related to the kind of personal relationship existing between a teacher and her pupils and between pupils. One's basic needs for self-esteem, recognition, and acceptance find their satisfaction in this matrix of interpersonal relationships. Compared with the forces of self-acceptance, teacher-acceptance, and group acceptance, the specific incentive conditions created by the teacher are of secondary importance. In part their effectiveness depends on what they signify about the teacher-pupil relationship. If the incentive conditions are low-pressure, work-centered, and related to information about progress they are useful, but if they are high-pressure, personal, and competitive, they are partially self-defeating—they will be effective only with those few children who can and will respond to such conditions. In this context, incentives become part of a total setting affecting motivation, and the research on the specifics of incentive conditions is more meaningful.

## Rewards and Punishment

Reward is one of the foundation-stones of learning. Hedonistic explanations of learning have a long history culminating in Thorndike's law of effect and Hull's theory of primary and secondary reinforcement which, in substance, say that satisfying outcomes reinforce the behavior which leads to the reward because of the reduction in drive which the reward provides. Whether the explanation lies in the reduction of drive, in a change in the stimulus conditions associated with the termination of behavior, or in an increment to the probability of a repetition of the behavior as the more sophisticated applications of modern statistical learning theory suggests (Estes [13]), reward and reinforcement have both a theoretical and practical role in learning. Regardless of theoretical explanation, it is essential that reward be linked with the kind of behavior desired. If quality of work is important, then that is what has to be rewarded—not punctuality, attitude, or some other characteristic. The specificity indicated regarding the effect of rewards lends support to our discussion of the general motivational conditions (pp. 31f). This is illustrated in the manner in which students vary their preparation for an examination in terms of the type of examination being given. Here the student adopts the study technique most likely to yield the favorable mark contingent upon high examination score. The variety of ways

---

[13] W. K. Estes, "The Statistical Approach to Learning Theory," in *Psychology, A Study of Science,* ed. S. Koch (New York: McGraw-Hill Book Company, 1959), pp. 380-491.

*Bibliography*

# Bibliography

*Annual Reviews of Psychology: Learning,* Stanford, Calif.: Annual Reviews Inc., 1950–63.

Blake, R. R. and G. V. Ramsey, eds., *Perception, An Approach to Personality.* New York: The Ronald Press Co., 1951.

Bloom, B. S., ed., *Taxonomy of Educational Objectives.* New York: Longmans, Green & Co. Inc., 1956.

Brunswik, E., "Probability as a Determiner of Rat Behavior," *Journal of Experimental Psychology,* 25 (1939), pp. 175–97.

Bugelski, B. R., *Psychology of Learning.* New York: Holt, Rinehart & Winston, Inc., 1956.

Bush, R. R., and F. Mosteller, "A Model for Stimulus Generalization and Discrimination," *Psychological Review,* 58 (1951), pp. 413–23.

Cartwright, D., and A. Zander, *Group Dynamics, Research and Theory.* New York: Harper & Row, Publishers, 1956.

Coladarci, A. P., ed., *Educational Psychology: A Book of Readings.* New York: Holt, Rinehart & Winston, Inc., 1955.

Cronbach, L. J., *Essentials of Psychological Testing.* New York: Harper & Row, Publishers, 1960.

Estes, W. K., *et al., Modern Learning Theory.* New York: Appleton-Century-Crofts, 1954.

Farber, I. E., "The Role of Motivation in Verbal Learning and Performance," *Psychological Bulletin,* 52 (1955), pp. 311–327.

Ferguson, G. A., "On Transfer and the Abilities of Man," *Canadian Journal of Psychology,* 10 (1956), pp. 121–31.

Festinger, L., *A Theory of Cognitive Dissonance.* New York: Harper & Row, Publishers, 1957.

French, Elizabeth, "Effects of the Interaction of Motivation and Feedback on Task Performance," in Atkinson, J. W., ed., *Motives in Fantasy, Action, and Society.* New York: Van Nostrand Press, 1958, pp. 400–408.

Galanter, E., ed., *Automatic Teaching, The State of the Art.* New York: John Wiley & Sons, 1959.

Guthrie, E. R., *Psychology of Learning,* Rev. Ed. New York: Harper & Row, Publishers, 1952.

Harlow, H. F., "The Formation of Learning Sets," *Psychological Review,* 56 (1949), pp. 56, 51–65.

Harris, C. W., ed., *Encyclopedia of Educational Research*. New York: The Macmillan Co., 1960.

Harris, T. L., and W. A. Schwahn, eds., *Selected Readings on the Learning Process*. New York: Oxford University Press, 1961.

Hebb, D. O., *The Organization of Behavior*. New York: John Wiley & Sons, 1949.

Hilgard, E. R., *Theories of Learning*, 2nd Ed. New York: Appleton-Century-Crofts, 1956.

————, and D. G. Marquis, *Conditioning and Learning*, 2nd ed., rev. by G. A. Kimble. New York: Appleton-Century-Crofts, 1961.

Hull, C. L., *Principles of Behavior*. New York: Appleton-Century-Crofts, 1943.

Humphrey, L. G., "The Effect of Random Alternation of Reinforcement on the Acquisition and Extinction of Conditioned Eyelid Reaction," *Journal of Experimental Psychology*, 25 (1939), pp. 141–56.

Keller, F. S., *Learning (Reinforcement Theory)*. New York: Doubleday and Co., 1954.

Kingsley, H. L., and R. Garry, *The Nature and Conditions of Learning*. Englewood Cliffs, N.J.: Prentice-Hall, Inc., 1957.

Koch, S., ed., *Psychology, A Study of Science*, Vol. 2, New York: McGraw-Hill Book Co., 1959.

Koffka, K., *Principles of Gestalt Psychology*. New York: Harcourt, Brace & World, 1935.

Kohler, W., *Gestalt Psychology*. London: Liveright, 1947.

Krechevsky, I., "Hypotheses in Rats," *Psychological Review*, 45 (1938), pp. 107–34.

Lawrence, D. H., "The Evaluation of Training and Transfer Programs in Terms of Efficiency Measures." *Journal of Psychology*, 38 (1954), pp. 367–82.

*Learning and Instruction, 49th Yearbook, Part 1*. Chicago: NSSE, 1960.

Lindzey, G., ed., *Handbook of Social Psychology, Vols. 1, 2*. Cambridge, Mass.: Addison-Wesley Publishing Co., 1954.

Lumsdaine, A. A., and R. Glaser, eds., *Teaching Machines and Programmed Learning, A Source Book*. Washington, D.C.: National Education Association, 1960.

Mandler, G., and S. B. Sarason, "A Study of Anxiety and Learning," *Journal of Abnormal and Social Psychology*, 47 (1952), pp. 166–73.

McGeoch, J. A., and A. L. Irion, *Psychology of Human Learning*, Rev. Ed. New York: Longmans, Green & Co., Inc., 1952.

McNemar, Q., *Psychological Statistics*. New York: John Wiley & Sons, 1955.

Melton, A. W., and W. J. von Lackum, "Retroactive and Proactive Inhibition, Evidence for a Two-Factor Theory of Retroactive Inhibition," *American Journal of Psychology* 54 (1941), pp. 157–73.

Miller, N. E., and J. Dollard, *Social Learning and Imitation*. New Haven: Yale University Press, 1941.

Mowrer, O. H., *Learning Theory and Personality Dynamics*. New York: The Ronald Press Co., 1950.

———, *Learning Theory and Behavior*. New York: John Wiley & Sons, 1960.

———, *Learning Theory and Symbolic Processes*. New York: John Wiley & Sons, 1960.

Osgood, C. E., *Method and Theory in Experimental Psychology*. New York: Oxford University Press, 1953.

Schramm, W., *et al., New Teaching Aids for the American Classroom*. Stanford, Calif.: Institute for Communications Research, 1960.

Skinner, B. F., *The Behavior of Organisms*. New York: Appleton-Century-Crofts, 1938.

Spence, K. W., "An Experimental Test of the Continuity-Discontinuity Theories of Discrimination Learning," *Journal of Experimental Psychology*, 35 (1945), pp. 253–66.

———, "Behavior Theory and Conditioning." New Haven: Yale University Press, 1956.

Stephens, J. M., *Educational Psychology*, Rev. Ed. New York: Holt, Rinehart & Winston, Inc., 1956.

Stevens, S. S., ed., *Handbook of Experimental Psychology*. New York: John Wiley & Sons, 1951.

*The Dynamics of Instructional Groups, 59th Yearbook, Part 2*. Chicago: NSSE, 1960.

Thorndike, E. L., *Fundamentals of Learning*. New York: Columbia University, Teachers College, 1932.

Tolman, E. C., *Purposive Behavior in Animals and Men*. New York: Appleton-Century-Crofts, 1956.

Tyler, Leona, *Psychology of Human Differences*. New York: Appleton-Century-Crofts, 1956.

Underwood, B. J., *Psychological Research*. New York: Appleton-Century-Crofts, 1957.

Woodworth, R. S., and H. Schlosberg, *Experimental Psychology*. New York: Holt, Rinehart & Winston, Inc., 1954.

*Index*

with "regular" Americans. Who would want to have a beer with Hillary Clinton? She was fake. She was school-marmy. She was too strident. She was too prepared in the debates. She had too much baggage. No one wants a Clinton Dynasty. She should have picked Bernie as her running mate. Heck, if the DNC didn't rig the process, Bernie Sanders would have been the nominee, and Bernie would have won.

And her emails! Her emails!

HER FUCKING EMAILS!

Those reasons are all, at best, lazy. Hillary won more votes than any previous white candidate in American history—hers was the second-highest total of all time, behind only Obama's showing in 2008; how does that make her a bad candidate? Bill Clinton hurt her more than he helped her, without question, but two exceptional individuals who happen to be married does not a dynasty make. Even without the superdelegates, she would have soundly defeated Bernie—who is not a Democrat, by the way, and whose refusal to go quietly once it became clear he could not win the nomination certainly damaged Hillary's campaign. There is no telling if Bernie would have won, because he was never properly vetted, his past is not exactly pristine, and his poor performance among black women suggests that victory would hardly be assured. And her emails were only an issue because the press made them into one.

In actuality, there were three primary reasons for Trump's David-and-Goliath-level upset:

First, the so-called Comey letter, which re-focused the media's attention on Hillary's emails a week before Election Day—for no good reason, as it turned out.

This reinforced the narrative of Hillary as crooked, secretive, untrustworthy, up to no good.

Second, the historically terrible article that ran in the *New York Times* on 31 October 2016: "Investigating Donald Trump, FBI Sees No Clear Link to Russia." Here was the purported paper of record, just nine days before Election Day, proclaiming that Trump/Russia was bunk. Most major media outlets dropped the Russia story like a proverbial hot potato and did not pick it up again for months. *Saturday Night Live* gave more airtime to the red-flag Putin/Trump bromance than the news shows did.

Finally, but most importantly: Trump had help from Moscow.

All three of these reasons—the Comey letter, the *Times* article, and the covert Russian aid—are related to each other, and to Trump's shady business dealings, and to the machinations of his deplorable associates, especially Paul Manafort, Mike Flynn, and Jared Kushner. And the result could not have been more ominous: the nuclear launch codes were in the hands of the wrong person…in every sense of the word.

Donald Trump is nothing less than a threat to the American way of life. His term in office comprises an existential threat to the republic, the gravest since the Civil War. Not since 1860 has the future of the *Union itself* been in such doubt. Other presidents might have lacked good judgment, but we never questioned where their true loyalties lay. George W. Bush loved America, Richard Nixon loved America, Herbert Hoover and Warren G. Harding loved America. Trump loves only himself, cares only about himself, is loyal only to himself. And Vladimir Putin has exploited this weakness, to the detriment of not just every American, but every freedom-loving human being on earth.

The threat posed by Trump transcends politics. Although I am a liberal and was an avid supporter of Hillary Clinton, my politics are irrelevant. It is my belief that Trump's policies, such as they are, are odious and will cause real harm to millions of people, but policies can be defeated politically. As Adam Gopnik wrote in the *New Yorker* just before inauguration: "In such a moment of continued emergency, the most important task may be to distinguish as rigorously as possible between new policies and programs that, however awful, are a reflection of the moral oscillation of power, natural in a mature democracy, and those that are not." Once a democracy falls, once a dictator is installed, the damage is irreversible. This is not a donkey vs. elephant issue. Many of the most prominent and stalwart anti-Trump leaders are conservatives, current or former members of the GOP: David Frum, Rick Wilson, Steve Schmidt, Jennifer Rubin, Max Boot, Evan McMullin, Cheri Jacobus, Bill Kristol. I stand with them.

As I write this, a third of the country rightly recognizes Trump as a clear and present danger. A third will defend him no matter what he does, as a matter of blind faith. Whether the middle third is able to call out the naked emperor standing before us may well determine whether the United States survives this unprecedented crisis.

There are powerful forces working to silence these cries of "The Emperor has no clothes." The talking heads at Fox News and InfoWars, the editorial writers at Breitbart and the *Wall Street Journal*, and an army of bots on Facebook and Twitter are adamant that Trump is wearing only the finest threads. Mainstream media outlets insist on giving equal time to the "Trump's new clothes are fabulous" crowd, despite his indisputable nakedness. To too many evangelicals, to denounce Trump as a naked emperor is to renounce Jesus Christ Himself.

Furthermore, the story, the real story, strains credulity. Are we really to believe that a Russian dictator helped install his compromised asset in the White House, and is now exerting influence over said asset's key decisions? That is the stuff of bad spy movies, surely; not the AP wire!

And yet here we are.

Beginning with my first essay on 1 November 2016, I've written hundreds of thousands of words on Trump/Russia, consuming as many news articles and threaded tweets as I could find, in the service of calling attention to the most consequential story of my lifetime. To be clear: I am a novelist, not a journalist. I have no sources of my own. My role, as I see it, is to take all of the stray pieces of information, separating the good reporting from the disinformation, and give them shape and structure, to make the narrative easier for my growing readership to understand. My experience writing novels is the ideal background for this self-imposed assignment, because novelists must be able to tell long, complicated stories in a way that readers can easily process. It's no coincidence that Louise Mensch (*née* Bagshawe), one of the first Trump/Russia reporters and certainly the most controversial, is the author of several novels. A novelist is trained to connect disparate storylines and weave them together into a coherent narrative. I know Mensch is derided in certain circles as a conspiracy theorist, of which more later; but on 6 November 2016, she published an exclusive on the existence of FISA warrants that was only confirmed by the mainstream media four months later, and the working theory she laid out in "Dear Mr. Putin, Let's Play Chess," written on 17 January 2017, has proved remarkably prescient. Another journalist may have gotten the FISA scoop, but it took a *novelist* to write the "Chess" piece.

For, like a Tolstoy novel, the unabridged story of Trump/Russia is long and complicated. The *dramatis personae* alone runs to half a dozen pages. There are a lot of moving parts, a lot of threads that seem at first blush not to be related, a lot of different players with different agendas, involved for different reasons, and many of them have unpronounceable Slavic surnames. This makes it hard to wrap your head around, and harder still to explain.

Trump once boasted that he could shoot someone on Fifth Avenue and not lose the support of his voters. I beg to differ. If he did that, there would be irrefutable evidence of a terrible crime, a literal smoking gun, and that would (I like to think) sway the minds of even the most obdurate #MAGA apologists.

Trump/Russia, however, is not bang-bang. There is no single smoking gun. Instead, there are thousands of them, firing simultaneously, and the result is a noxious fog that hangs over everything, clouding our view.

This book is an attempt to see through the fog.

# II
## THE RUSSIA LIE: "You're the Puppet!"

LET'S BEGIN WITH THE LIES—or, rather, with one lie, the same lie that was repeated time and time again. The Big Lie, the *große Lüge*. The Russia lie.

Throughout the campaign, during the transition period, and after inauguration, Donald Trump and his surrogates vehemently denied meeting with Russians of any stripe, for any purpose. Every time they were asked about a connection between the campaign and the Kremlin, they shot it down. And they were *indignant* about it. The response was always something along the lines of, "Russia? Us? How dare you accuse us of such a thing!"

Here are some examples:

### 24 July 2016, Paul Manafort, Trump campaign chair:

"...pure obfuscation......That's absurd. And, you know, there's no basis to it."

### 24 July 2016, Donald Trump, Jr:

"I can't think of bigger lies. But that exactly goes to show you what the DNC [Democratic National Committee] and what the Clinton camp will do. They will lie and do anything to win......These lies and the perpetuating of that kind of nonsense to gain some political capital is just outrageous."

### 27 July 2016, Donald Trump:

"I can tell you, I think if I came up with that, they'd say, 'Oh, it's a conspiracy theory, it's ridiculous.' I mean I have nothing to do with Russia. I don't have any jobs in Russia. I'm all over the world, but we're not involved in Russia."

### 25 September 2016, Kellyanne Conway, campaign manager:

"If [Carter Page is] doing that [meeting with Russians], he's certainly not doing it with the permission or knowledge of the campaign, the activities that you described. He is certainly not authorized to do that."

### 24 October 2016, Trump:

"I have nothing to do with Russia, folks, I'll give you a written statement."

**11 November 2016, Hope Hicks, campaign communications director:**
"It never happened. There was no communication between the campaign and any foreign entity during the campaign."

**18 December 2017, Conway:**
"Those conversations never happened. I hear people saying it like it's a fact on television. That is just not only inaccurate and false, but it's dangerous."

**11 January 2017, Trump (tweet):**
"Russia has never tried to use leverage over me. I HAVE NOTHING TO DO WITH RUSSIA - NO DEALS, NO LOANS, NO NOTHING!"

**15 January 2017, Mike Pence, Vice President-elect:**
"Well of course not. I think to suggest that is to give credence to some of these bizarre rumors that have swirled around the candidacy."

**7 February 2017, Trump (tweet):**
"I don't know Putin, have no deals in Russia, and the haters are going crazy…"

**16 February 2017, Trump:**
"I have nothing to do with Russia. To the best of my knowledge no person that I deal with does."

**19 February 2017, Reince Priebus, White House chief of staff:**
"I can assure you and I have been approved to say this: that the top levels of the intelligence community

have assured me that that is not only inaccurate, but it's grossly overstated and it was wrong. And there's nothing to it."

### 20 February 2017, Sarah Huckabee Sanders, deputy White House press secretary:

Trump/Russia is "a non-story because to the best of our knowledge, no contacts took place, so it's hard to make a comment on something that never happened."

### 24 February 2017, Sean Spicer, White House press secretary:

"Well, again, there are no connections to find out about. That's the problem. I think, a), he [Trump] has answered it forcefully. You can't disprove something that doesn't exist. He's talked about the fact how many times he's talked to Putin. He has no interests in Russia....There's only so many times he can deny something that doesn't exist."

### 26 February 2017, Trump (tweet):

"Russia talk is FAKE NEWS put out by the Dems, and played up by the media, in order to mask the big election defeat and the illegal leaks!"

### 11 May 2017, Trump:

"I have had dealings over the years where I sold a house to a very wealthy Russian many years ago. I had the Miss Universe pageant—which I owned for quite a while—I had it in Moscow a long time ago. But other than that, I have nothing to do with Russia."

**18 May 2017, Trump:**
"…the entire thing has been a witch hunt. There is no collusion—certainly myself and my campaign—but I can always speak for myself and the Russians—zero."

These were all lies—the same big lie, repeated over and over. This repetition of the "Big Lie," it should be noted, is a propaganda technique developed by the Nazis. Hitler wrote about it in *Mein Kompf*, one of very few books Trump is believed to have read. Either way, Trump has employed the Big Lie technique for years—lying regularly about his wealth (he lied his way onto the *Forbes* wealthiest Americans list), his fitness (he coerced his physician to lie about how healthy he was), his sexual prowess (a tabloid headline allegedly from ex-wife Marla Maples, saying Trump was the best sex she'd ever had), and so forth.

But this was different. This wasn't about the size of his bank account, his good cholesterol levels, or his penis. This was about national security, about cozying up to an enemy. And yet still, Trump and his minions went on TV, took to Twitter, stood behind the podium in the White House Press Room, and lied egregiously to the American people, over and over and over and over.

In July of 2017, when the press got wind of the Trump Tower meeting between Donald Trump, Jr. and a Russian attorney that took place the previous June, the Big Lie became impossible for any thinking person to believe. Yet even with this bombshell, the denials continued. Junior put out a statement on 8 July 2017—one his father the president helped him craft, with help from his communications director Hope Hicks and others: At the Trump Tower meeting, Junior explained, "[w]e primarily discussed a program about the adoption of Russian children that was active and popular with American families years ago and was since ended by the Russian government, but it was not a campaign issue at the time and there was no follow up."

Three days after Trump's namesake son issued that statement, the *New York Times* was set to publish the emails proving that Junior had in fact met with Russians, and damned well knew what was going to be on the agenda. How could he not have known? The subject line of the emails was this: "RE: RUSSIA - CLINTON - PRIVATE AND CONFIDENTIAL."

That's not a joke. That's not me being cute. That was the *actual email subject line*. And it appeared in the inbox of Junior, and also of Jared Kushner and Paul Manafort. (Trump, a Luddite, famously does not use email). Astute readers will observe that the word "adoption" is nowhere to be found in the subject line. Nor was it in the email exchange itself, which Junior published himself on Twitter, to "get ahead of the story" and scoop the *Times*.

Again, this happened in July of 2017—more than a year after that Trump Tower meeting. Until then, for months and months, it was a string of denials, the Big Lie repeated *ad infinitum*. It took a major newspaper threatening to publish emails *proving* Russian contact to finally get the Trumps to cop to the truth.

Maybe this could be forgiven if the Trump Tower meeting were unique—if that rendezvous had been the only time Donald & Co. powwowed with the

Russians. But this was not the case. Contrary to their vehement denials—their reiterations of the Big Lie—there were many meetings between associates of Donald Trump and agents of Vladimir Putin. Not two or three. Not a few. *Many.*

This is an accounting of the most significant of those meetings, listed here in chronological order:

**Mayflower Hotel**
*27 April 2016: Mayflower Hotel, Washington*
At a VIP-only foreign policy speech attended by most of his inner circle, Donald Trump promised a "good deal" for Russia. Russian Ambassador Sergei Kislyak attended, in breach of protocol. Also present: Paul Manafort and Jared Kushner, who arranged the event at the last minute; then-Senator Jeff Sessions; foreign policy advisers JD Gordon and Walid Phares; adviser Stephen Miller; the oil lobbyists Bud McFarlane and Richard Burt, who helped craft the speech; Donald Trump, Jr.; Corey Lewandowski and Hope Hicks; the ambassadors to Singapore, Italy, and the Philippines; Dimitri K. Simes, president of the Center for the National Interest, the event's host, and Jacob Heilbrunn, also of CNI, who planned the event. Implicit in Trump's speech was a promise to play ball with Putin if elected. Notably, the venue for this event was changed at the last minute to allow Kislyak to come.

**Trump Tower**
*9 June 2016: Trump Tower, New York*
Donald Trump, Jr. met with the Russian attorney Natalia Veselnitskya, who'd promised "dirt" on Hillary

Clinton. Also in attendance were Manafort and Kushner, representing the Trump campaign, and on the Russian side, Russian-American businessman Rinat Akhmetshin, money laundering enthusiast Ike Kaveladze, the KGB-approved translator Anatoly Samochornov,[1] and "useful idiot" publicist Rob Goldstone, who helped arrange the meeting. Candidate Trump was also at Trump Tower that day, but claimed not to have attended—or to have been told about it afterward. Yet that very afternoon, within an hour of the Russians leaving, Trump began tweeting about Hillary's "missing" emails for the first time.

**Moscow School**
*1–5 July 2016: New Economic School, Moscow, Russia*
Trump foreign policy adviser Carter Page[2] traveled to Moscow, with his expenses paid for by Russians. While there, he met with top Russian government officials, including Deputy Prime Minister Arcadiy

---

[1] The KGB is now called the FSB, and has been for years. However, I'm going to use KGB because it's more familiar to American readers…and also because it sounds cooler.

[2] Page is one of the more inscrutable characters in Trump/ Russia. He was one of Trump's foreign policy advisers until he suddenly wasn't, and after the election was said to be in the running for ambassador to Russia (by the *Moscow Times*, no less!). He's also a key figure in the Steele dossier; his sudden ouster from Trump's inner circle is thought to be because of his questionable ties to Rosneft, the oil company. But Page was in the know enough to announce, at a December lecture in Moscow, that Rex Tillerson would be named Secretary of State…before Trump had informed the American people. The contents of that lecture made it very clear where his sympathies lie (hint: with Moscow).

Dvorkovich and Igor Sechin, CEO of the oil company Rosneft (of which more shortly). Page had requested permission to take the trip from his presumed boss, JD Gordon, who told him no; he then went to Corey Lewandowski and Hope Hicks, who gave him the green light. When Page returned, he explained that he got "some incredible insights" from his Moscow meetings. No doubt.

## RNC

*18–21 July 2016: Republican National Convention, Cleveland*

Russian Ambassador Kislyak was again in attendance, meeting with Jeff Sessions after a 18 July Heritage Foundation soirée, and with Trump advisers JD Gordon and Carter Page after a convention-related Global Partners in Diplomacy event at Case Western Reserve University on 20 July. As for the convention itself, exactly one change was made to the long Republican platform, aligning the GOP's official position on Ukraine/Crimea with Vladimir Putin's. Gordon later revealed that this was in accordance with Trump's direct personal wishes.

### Prague

*Late August 2016: [undisclosed], Prague, Czech Republic (?)*

Trump personal attorney and self-proclaimed Russian mobster Michael Cohen met in the Czech Republic with Russian officials, Russian crime figures, or both. He denied traveling to Prague, and this meeting, outlined in the Steele dossier, of which more later, remains unconfirmed as of this writing. Tellingly,

Cohen vehemently denied having been to Prague that August; his denials of meeting with Russians in Europe were markedly less vehement.

## Capitol Hill
*8 September 2016: Capitol Hill, Washington*
Jeff Sessions and two undisclosed aides met in the Alabama Senator's offices with Ambassador Kislyak. Testifying before Congress months later, Sessions lied under oath about this meeting, omitting its mention. This was particularly unusual, because Sessions would have had little reason to meet with the Russian ambassador in his role as Senator.

## Backchannel
*1–2 December 2016: Trump Tower, New York*
Jared Kushner and Mike Flynn met with Ambassador Kislyak, who was "snuck" into Trump Tower, suggesting a secret entrance, perhaps through the offices of Carter Page, which are next door. At the meeting, Kushner proposed a Russian embassy backchannel to avoid having to disclose communication between the camps going forward. Whatever went on at this sit-down, Kushner and Flynn went to great lengths to avoid discovery.

## Rosneft
*8 December 2016: Rosneft offices, Moscow, Russia*
Carter Page met with Rosneft senior executives in Moscow. Some background: In 2012, Rosneft, one of the world's largest publicly-traded oil companies, entered into a $500 billion joint venture with ExxonMobil, which at the time was run by Rex

Tillerson, Trump's first Secretary of State; it was this mammoth joint venture, apparently, that inspired Putin to award Tillerson the Medal of Friendship in 2013. The oil reserves in the Arctic, the reason for the venture, are estimated to contain 85 billion barrels. At a conservative price of $50 a barrel, that amounts to a staggering $4.25 *trillion* in potential gross revenue. These are dizzying numbers—but Putin will not see a kopek as long as the US continues to impose sanctions on Russia. In his intelligence report of 18 October 2016, Christopher Steele wrote that there was a plan in place to sell a 19% ownership stake in Rosneft; Trump was reportedly offered the commission on the sale, which by my calculations would be about $270 million, for his part in Trump/Russia. (This detail is often misreported, with Trump said to have been promised the *entirety* of the 19% stake—a preposterous figure). The sale did in fact take place in January of 2017, with 19.5% of ownership share purchased by string of shell companies, one of them a Qatari concern whose chief financier met with Trump, Mike Flynn, and Michael Cohen at Trump Tower on 12 December 2016. Whether or not Trump received any of the commission, perhaps in the form of debt forgiveness, is not yet known. Page continues to insist that he is innocent, and refers to Steele's intelligence reports as "the dodgy dossier."

### Newark Airport
*13–14 December 2016: [undisclosed], Newark Airport(?) ("VEB")*
Kushner ventured out to Newark Airport to meet Sergei Gorkov, one-time KGB agent and president

of Vnesheconombank (VEB), the Russian state bank that was, and remains, on the US sanctions list for its close ties to Putin. VEB later claimed that the meeting "was conducted with Kushner in his role as the head of his family's real estate business," according to the *Washington Post*. The White House, meanwhile, will describe it as a "diplomatic meeting," whatever that means. Immediately after the rendezvous, Gorkov flew directly to see Putin, halfway around the world, ostensibly to report back in person. Wherefore the urgency, if all they had discussed was real estate?

## Seychelles
*11 January 2017: Four Seasons (?), Seychelles*
Trump surrogates Erik Prince (head of the mercenary outfit Blackwater) and Elliott Broidy (a big GOP donor) voyaged to this remote tropical island resort to meet with Kirill Dmitriev, the head of a Russian government-controlled wealth fund, at a clandestine "backchannel" meeting arranged by the government of the United Arab Emirates, where Prince lived. Prince is a Trump supporter suspected of being a shadow adviser, and was involved with the events that produced the Comey memo just before the election (more on this later). He is the founder of Blackwater, literally a company of mercenaries; he had ties to the Trump campaign via the adviser Steve Bannon, and is the brother of Betsy DeVos, Trump's education secretary. Later, he lied under oath to Congress about the nature and purpose of the Seychelles meeting.

*2017: [undisclosed hotel, maybe Loews
York*

_ ᴖᴇn and former Trump business partner Felix Sater met with Andrii V. Artemenko, a Putin-aligned Ukrainian politician, to negotiate sanctions—or, perhaps, to receive sanction orders from Moscow. Both Cohen and Sater, who are childhood friends, have extensive ties to the Russian mob. An enigmatic figure, Felix Sater served time in prison for a bar fight in which he attacked someone with the broken stem of a martini glass. His father was allegedly a *capo* in the Russian mob, as was the Kazakh real estate developer Tevfik Arif, founder of the Blackrock Group, for which Sater served as managing director. Trump has tried to walk back his relationship with Sater, once storming out of a BBC interview when the subject was pressed. He testified under oath that he would not recognize him if he was sitting next to him, and yet Trump Org issued business cards to Sater, naming him a "senior adviser to Donald Trump." At the meeting, Sater gave Cohen a written proposal in a sealed envelope that Cohen delivered to then-National Security Advisor Mike Flynn in early February. Notably, Cohen changed his story of what happened that day four times.

**Oval Office**
*9 May 2017: The White House, Washington*
One day after firing FBI Director James Comey, Trump held a closed-door meeting with Kislyak and Russian Foreign Minister Sergei Lavrov in the Oval Office. To the corpulent Russians, Trump expressed

relief that Comey's Russia investigation wouldn't be bothering him anymore. Details were not released. Also at this meeting, Trump gave the Russians a piece of highly classified intelligence provided to us by an ally, reportedly Israel. US photographers were not allowed in, so the images released of the meeting are the work of Russian photographers. In fact, we only know about this meeting because it was covered in the Russian press.

AGAIN: THESE ARE JUST THE MAJOR MEETINGS, and just the ones we know about. Even so, that's a lot of meetings, especially given the vehement denials of Trump and his surrogates.

In case you were wondering if it's standard operating procedure for presidential candidates to meet with Russians: it isn't.

Hillary Clinton did not meet with the Russians during the campaign.

Barack Obama did not meet with the Russians during the campaign.

Obama's foreign policy adviser and eventual ambassador to Russia, Michael McFaul, did not meet with the Russians during the campaign.

Why did Trump? And why did he lie about it? Why is he *still* lying about it?

Colloquially, the word for the covert coordination between the Trump campaign and the Kremlin is *collusion*. In the court of law, however, there is a different and more poetical term: Conspiracy Against the United States.

# III

## CONSPIRACY AGAINST THE UNITED STATES: A Plot Summary

CONSPIRACY AGAINST THE UNITED STATES sounds dramatic, like something from a Tom Clancy novel, or a spec script of *Scandal*. But it is real—one of the actual charges on which former Trump campaign chairman Paul Manafort was indicted. And Manafort is almost certainly guilty.

Read the last paragraph again, because it's important to keep that in mind: Paul Manafort, who ran the Trump campaign from May through August 2016—an interval that included the hiring of Cambridge Analytica, the changing of the party platform at the Republican National Convention to soften its stance on Russian incursion in Ukraine, and Junior's notorious Trump Tower meeting; peak treason season—stands accused of *conspiring against his country*.

This is not Pizzagate-style conspiracy theory. This is not uninformed speculation. This is not something posted anonymously on Reddit. This is an actual charge, filed by the Special Counsel of the US Department of Justice investigating Trump/Russia. And the individual accused of this heinous crime was the *chairman* of the Trump campaign. Not an intern. Not a coffee boy. The guy in charge.

Manafort's "Conspiracy Against the United States" is multi-pronged. In subsequent chapters, we will go into more detail, but for now, let's confine ourselves with a plot summary:

## Big Picture

Donald Trump and associates inside and outside his campaign conspired with Vladimir Putin and other Russian oligarchs, Russian intelligence, and Russian organized crime to steal the election.

For his efforts, Putin was to receive a blind eye toward his conquest of Crimea, a weakened NATO, veto power over key appointments, and, crucially, the lifting of sanctions against his oligarchs.

Trump and his family would receive the aid of Russian hackers in turning the election, as well as other to-be-determined financial considerations, probably debt forgiveness. In addition, *kompromat* gathered on him during his ill-fated trip to Russia for the Miss Universe Pageant in 2013 and earlier—and the hacked RNC emails that the Kremlin possessed but declined to release—would not be deployed.

## Negotiations

The quid pro quo between Trump and Putin did not emerge out of thin air. A number of intermediaries was utilized during the period of negotiations that began in earnest when Manafort joined the campaign in the spring of 2016, and remain ongoing as of this writing.

The Trump negotiation team consisted of: Manafort and his deputy Rick Gates; Donald Trump, Jr. and Jared Kushner, the president's son and son-in-law; Trump's personal attorney Michael Cohen and his former business partner Felix Sater,[3] childhood friends who both have deep ties to the Russian mob; then-Senator Jeff Sessions; Mike Flynn and his son and aide Mike Flynn, Jr.; foreign policy advisers George Papadopoulos, Carter Page, JD Gordon, Sam Clovis, and KT McFarland; Blackwater founder Erik Prince; RNC bagman and GOP donor Elliott Broidy; and Indiana governor and transition chair Mike Pence.

Anyone who met with, and failed to disclose, meetings with the multi-chinned Russian ambassador Sergei Kislyak—who was both Moscow's diplomat and spy-runner—was part of the "negotiation" team.

---

[3]    Sater, it should be noted, may well turn out to be an FBI plant and a white hat.

## Technology

Russian cyber operatives 1) hacked the DNC and RNC servers; 2) weaponized American social media in critical swing states especially, using illicitly-acquired data gathered by Facebook and other companies; 3) released hacked information at key moments during campaign. They did this in coordination with Trump's people.

The Trumpist tech team included: Kushner, who helmed the Trump campaign's social media operation; Steve Bannon, Peter Thiel, and Robert & Rebekkah Mercer, each with ties to the Orwellian data company Cambridge Analytica; web guy and Trump's 2020 campaign manager Brad Parscale; dirty trickster Roger Stone, an old partner of Manafort's, who coordinated with the Russian hacker Guccifer 2.0; Julian Assange of WikiLeaks, who has been a Russian asset since at least the Edward Snowden affair; and various Kremlin-affiliated hackers (e.g., the "13 Russians" indicted by Robert Mueller).

Also involved was Peter W. Smith, a longtime GOP operative, who on 12 May 2017 committed suicide two weeks after admitting in an interview with the *Wall Street Journal* that he had actively pursued acquiring Hillary Clinton's emails from Russian hackers.

## Fat Cats

Trump was not the only beneficiary of the deal with Putin. His Cabinet is honeycombed with wealthy men and women who gained from dealings with Putin and the oligarchs, or who stood to profit from the lifting of sanctions and/or Trump's tax policies. Wilbur Ross and Rex Tillerson are the most obvious names here. Both have long ties to Putin and the Russian oligarchs. One-percenters Steven Mnuchin and Betsy DeVos have also personally benefited from their positions.

## Obstruction

This group includes those who became aware of Trump/Russia and actively sought to cover it up, whether by making knowingly false media statements, failing to report illicit activity to the FBI, or otherwise abetting the initial crimes.

In Trump's circle, this includes: former White House communications director Hope Hicks, former bodyguard Keith Schiller, White House counsel Donald McGahn, Ivanka Trump; advisers Stephen Miller, Sam Nunberg, and Seb Gorka; former RNC chair and White House chief of staff Reince Priebus; the press secretaries Sean Spicer, Anthony Scaramucci, and Sarah Huckabee Sanders; former New York mayor Rudy Giuliani, and Kellyanne Conway.

Members of Congress and other politicians who obstructed justice by attempting to derail the various Russia investigations despite knowledge of the truth include: Devin Nunes, Jason Chaffetz, Dana Rohrabacher, Trey Gowdy, Paul Ryan, Mitch McConnell, Tom Cotton, Chuck Grassley, Lindsey

Graham, Matt Gaetz, Ron DeSantis, Steve King, and current Secretary of State Mike Pompeo.

Media personalities who actively disseminate(d) false or misleading stories include: Sean Hannity, Bill O'Reilly, Jeanine Pirro, Gregg Jarrett, Alan Dershowitz, Assange, Lara Trump, Mike Cernovich, the *Fox & Friends* crew, the editorial page of the *Wall Street Journal*; Breitbart; Newt Gingrich, Mike Huckabee, and Alex Jones.

## Useful Idiots

Prominent Americans who, wittingly or not, parrot Putinist talking points: Bernie Sanders and Jill Stein; Glenn Greenwald and the other Russia skeptics at The Intercept; ideological Leftist purists like Susan Sarandon and Cornel West; Maggie Haberman and other slipshod reporters at the *New York Times* and elsewhere (hi, Chris Cillizza!); and—it should be noted—plenty of well-intentioned people.

Let's be clear about something: I was a useful idiot at one point. Most of us were, to some degree.

All of us made mistakes and erred in our judgment regarding Trump/Russia.

All of us were played.

ONE OF THE COMMON ERRORS OF LOGIC in tinfoil-hat conspiracy theories is the assumption that members of a conspiracy share the same motive, move in perfect tandem, and seek to achieve the same goals. The truth is never so simple. Every individual who threw in with Donald Trump had his or her own individual reason for doing so. Ivanka Trump's decision to #MAGA is very different from, say, Stephen Miller's.

Another way to organize the various characters in Trump/Russia, then, is by *motive*. Trumpists can be organized into several categories:

## Grifters
*Flat-out thieves*
Jared Kushner, Ivanka Trump, Donald Trump, Jr., Steven Mnuchin, Wilbur Ross, Betsy DeVos, Elaine Chao, Scott Pruitt, Ryan Zinke.

## Opportunists
*Careers advancers, here to ride Trump's ample coattails*
Kellyanne Conway, Hope Hicks, Sean Spicer, Anthony Scaramucci, Donald McGahn, George Papadopoulos, JD Gordon, Corey Lewandowski, Sarah Sanders, Rudy Giuliani, all three of Trump's wives.

## Ideologues
*Advocates of far-right policies*
Mike Pence, Jeff Sessions, the Mercers, the Kochs, Peter Thiel, Mitch McConnell, Paul Ryan, the NRA and its spokespersons, Stephen Miller, Steve Bannon, Reince Priebus, Erik Prince.

## Russian Assets
*Putin puppets*
Paul Manafort, Mike Flynn, Devin Nunes, Carter Page, Dana Rohrabacher, Seb Gorka, Rex Tillerson, Michael Cohen.

**Nutjobs**
*God knows what these people were thinking*
Mike Flynn, Ben Carson, Carter Page, Roger Stone, and most of Trump's celebrity following.

There is some overlap, of course, in this venal Venn diagram, but if we start to look at the motivations of Trump's circle, the picture becomes less of a jumbled mess.

OTHER THAN DONALD TRUMP HIMSELF, the three most important characters in the collusion narrative, in my mind, are Paul Manafort, Mike Flynn, and Jared Kushner. They are the Father, Son, and Holy Ghost of Trump/Russia.

**Paul Manafort** is Bond-villain-level bad. He's spent most of his adult life as a Washington-based lobbyist for unsavory foreign leaders like Mobutu Sese Seko, Jonas Savimbi, Ferdinand Marcos, and Viktor Yanukovych, as well as various Russian oligarchs and Pakistan's ISI.[4] He raked in a boatload of money from his recent misadventures in Ukraine. It was after he became chairman of the Trump campaign that the Russian meetings took place, so it stands to reason that he was the man who initiated the collusion, probably at the behest of his Kremlin whoremasters.

A former general and head of the Defense Intelligence Agency, **Mike Flynn** was a lobbyist for both Turkey *and* Russia throughout the campaign,

---

[4]    If you have some free time, Google these people. They are all scum of the earth.

which he failed to disclose. A Qatari financier bragged about having bribed him, and there is reason to believe that this boast is true. Trump hired him despite ample warnings from the likes of President Obama and Acting Attorney General Sally Yates that he was bad news, and named him national security adviser—granting him access to eyes-only secrets, the choicest cuts of US intelligence. Trump defends him to this day, despite the fact that Flynn has already pleaded guilty to lying to the FBI.

As for **Jared Kushner**, I read it this way: when he joined the Trump campaign in the fall of 2015, he was neither straight-up evil like Manafort or touched like Flynn. Rather, the president's son-in-law was arrogant, opportunistic, creative…and end-of-his-rope desperate.

This made Mr. Ivanka the perfect mark for Vladimir Putin.

# IV

## BOY WONDER MEETS THE COUNT:
### The Turning of Jared Kushner

THE BEST WAY TO EXPLAIN TRUMP/RUSSIA, it seems to me, is to focus on one key player (Jared Kushner) and one key time period (March-July, 2016). That was when the Faustian bargain was made between the Trump campaign and Russia—when it was decided that Donald Trump would accept help (and dirty rubles) from Vladimir Putin in order to win the White House.

To be fair, Jared Kushner did not set out to betray his country. He didn't grow up in Livingston, New Jersey, a ten-minute drive from my own suburban hometown, with big dreams of becoming a KGB asset. I will give him the benefit of the doubt on that. But that's what he did, and that's what he became.

Kushner is notoriously private. Secretive, even. He's had a Twitter account for nine years and has yet to post a single tweet. He rarely gives interviews. I've heard his voice exactly twice. He's basically the J.D. Salinger of the Trump Administration. Most of what we know about him derives from Steven Bertoni's excellent *Forbes* profile of 22 November 2016, a few weeks after the election, which tells the story of how "Boy Wonder" Jared applied *Moneyball* principles to the flailing, disorganized Trump campaign, and won his father-in-law the White House. That profile offers insight into Kushner's critical role with both the campaign and its dealings with Russia, and demands a second (and third and fourth) reading in light of what we've discovered in the interim.

What follows in the rest of this chapter is a dramatization of events, based on the *Forbes* piece and lots and lots of other reporting. I am taking a few liberties with how I tell the story, for dramatic effect. But this is basically what went down:

IN THE SUMMER OF 2015, Jared Kushner was living large. He was young and fabulously wealthy. His wife was gorgeous and well known. He was a Millennial one-percenter, a rich Manhattan Democrat, enjoying his privileged lot in life. He was not interested in politics, much less politics involving Vladimir Putin's Russia.

Then, in November of 2015, he formally joined his father-in-law's seat-of-the-pants campaign—and all of that changed.

Fast-forward to the following March. Jared Kushner had been an active member of the Trump campaign for almost five months. His work with social media had been a smashing success, impressing his easily-bewildered father-in-law. After Kushner took over, "the Trump campaign went from selling $8,000 worth of hats and other items a day to $80,000," according to the profile at *Forbes*, "generating revenue, expanding the number of human billboards–and proving a concept."

Moreover, by March 2016, Trump had sewn up enough delegates that the Republican nomination looked like a sure thing. Maybe it wasn't 50/50 that he'd win the White House that November, but a victory was still in the realm of possibility.

But then reports trickled out about unhappy delegates, a disgruntled GOP establishment, and the unthinkable prospect of a contested convention that July. Could Ted Cruz or John Kasich somehow pull the chair right out from under Trump's prodigious derrière?

So Kushner did a little research on contested conventions. He learned that the last time that had happened to the GOP was back in 1976, when President Ford managed to stave off a challenge by California governor Ronald Reagan. (This was ancient history to him; Kushner was not even born until 1981.) The man in charge of Ford's effort back in '76 was a young Republican strategist and lawyer named Paul Manafort, who would later broker conventions for George H.W. Bush in '88 and Bob Dole in '96.

Not only did Manafort have truck with the GOP establishment, but given his experience with brokering conventions, he seemed uniquely qualified to lead Trump to the nomination. Too, he owned an apartment in Trump Tower, and in fact had known Trump for decades. When Tom Barrack, a billionaire real estate investor and friend of both men, suggested that Trump hire Manafort, Kushner was delighted. On 28 March 2016, with the enthusiastic blessing of the Boy Wonder, Paul Manafort joined the Trump campaign.

Although Manafort had not worked on a US race in 20 years, the consensus in the media was that this was a smart hire. Here was a seasoned pro who would bring establishment bona fides to the upstart campaign. Kushner was certainly charmed by the guy. Nicknamed "The Count" during his days as a convention broker, the 67-year-old Manafort was well-educated, worldly, independently wealthy, and smart—in stark contrast to the provincial mouth-breathers comprising most of Trump's team, especially loutish then-campaign manager Corey Lewandowski, whom Kushner disliked.

What Kushner did not realize is that during those two decades spent away from convention-brokering, Paul Manafort had been spending most of his time with a host of unsavory characters: despots, mostly, from foreign dictatorships—and, more recently, a pair of shady Russian oligarchs, Oleg Deripaska and Dmytro Firtash. His most recent client, Viktor Yanukovych, the former president of Ukraine, was a particularly noxious fellow. All three men were thick as thieves with Vladimir Putin.

Kushner did not know that Manafort had been paid many millions of dollars by Yanukovych, illegally. He did not know that Manafort was in dire financial straits, and that Russian intelligence has made a cottage industry of "turning" powerful Americans with money problems. He had never heard the word *kompromat*. He did not know that Manafort was, in effect, an agent of the Kremlin.

So when the charming, debonair, non-mouthbreather Paul Manafort suggested that he, Kushner, take a call with Sergei Kislyak, the Russian ambassador to the United States, Kushner did so. And he was glad he did! Kislyak, like Manafort, was smart and charming and funny, and seemed to have really good ideas on how they could work together.

And when Manafort suggested that they move the big foreign policy speech scheduled for 28 April 2016 from the National Press Club to the Mayflower Hotel, so that Kislyak and some of his cronies could attend, Kushner not only agreed—he helped organize the event. That spring evening, after a cocktail party at which Kislyak hobnobbed with virtually every key campaign figure, Trump in his speech promised a "good deal" for Russia, while dutifully refraining from any criticism of Putin.

This all seemed on the up-and-up to Kushner. He was following the lead of Manafort, after all, whom the Republican establishment still respected—and not some brash idiot like Lewandowski.

What Kushner also may not have realized is that Kislyak was a KGB spymaster in addition to being an ambassador…and that already, he was being recruited.

RUSSIA IS AN AUTOCRACY. Its elections are a sham, its government riddled with corruption, its human rights record deplorable. The purpose of its lousy economy, almost exclusively based on petroleum, is to enrich the despotic Vladimir Putin and his profligate cronies, who are collectively called oligarchs.

A vast segment of Russia's total wealth is in the hands of these oligarchs, most of it gained through corrupt and/or criminal means, much of it secreted away overseas, in quasi-Western places like Cyprus. The sanctions imposed on Russia by Barack Obama targeted the oligarchs personally, which was why they were so brutally effective—and why Putin wanted them lifted at all costs. Furthermore, for Putin to continue to stay in power, he needed a stronger economy. He also required propaganda so he could paint the West as just as weak, corrupt, and authoritarian as Russia. The sanctions hurt him badly on both fronts.

A Donald Trump presidency, as unlikely as it seemed in early 2016, would be a godsend to Putin. Trump was a megalomaniac with the heart of an autocrat, an easily-flattered weakling who would screw up America's standing in the world, who would bring chaos to the West, and who would, crucially, lift the sanctions. Here was a man who already openly admired Putin, who was actively trying to start a massive real estate project in Moscow...and whom Putin could easily blackmail. *Kompromat* had already been collected on Trump during his visit to Moscow in 2013, in the form of strange sex tapes; the campaign was sure to produce more lurid dirt.[5]

---

[5]    The "pee-pee tape" is largely thought to be apocryphal, but the BBC reports that the consensus among the IC is that there are tapes, plural, of Donald Trump engaged in activities much more heinous.

To achieve his aims, Putin routinely enlisted his friends at the KGB to compromise key Americans and turn them into pawns in his own geopolitical chess game. Usually this involved money: one of his oligarchs would do a shady business deal, or help finance a campaign illegally, and boom, an American was in his thrall. One of his turned Americans, the general Mike Flynn, had already penetrated Trump's inner circle. Another, Carter Page, had ingratiated himself into Trump's foreign policy team.

But on 28 March 2016, Putin could not believe his luck. The Trump campaign, more or less on its own, had taken the Yanukovych consultant Paul Manafort, one of his most compromised American assets—a man who was almost comically in Russia's back pocket—and *inserted him directly into the campaign*! *Spasibo*, guys!

Putin already had dirt on Trump. He already had Flynn in his pocket. He already had Page listed as a foreign affairs adviser for the campaign. He had the Green Party's Jill Stein, whom he'd personally dined in Moscow in 2015, poised to siphon votes from Hillary Clinton on the left. He'd already hacked into both the DNC and RNC servers, and had emails of both to release through WikiLeaks, which Russia was actively supporting, at the moment of his choosing. He knew he could unleash his army of social media "bots" to manipulate the election in Trump's favor... but he needed some help on the inside. Manafort would provide that inside help.

All that remained, as Putin saw it, was to turn Jared Kushner. If he had Trump's son-in-law, the presumed brains of the operation and the director

of Trump's social media operation, he was in like...
well, like Flynn.

JARED KUSHNER WAS IMPRESSED. The phone call with
Sergei Kislyak had gone well, and meeting him in
person at the Mayflower had been even better. The
ambassador was funny, charming, insightful, and
eager to help. Kislyak also seemed to know about the
Kushner company's financial pickle. See, Kushner
needed another $1 billion in loans—that's billion,
with a "b"—in order to retain ownership of 666 Fifth
Avenue, a white elephant of a Manhattan skyscraper,
and stave off possible bankruptcy. American banks
had not exactly been lining up to help, but the ambassador hinted that financial institutions in Europe
might be more sympathetic to his predicament.[6]

Meanwhile, Manafort was giving him excellent
advice on the social media front, steering him and his
tech guy Brad Parscale to a British firm, Cambridge
Analytica, which in less than a week was already
making massive inroads. Per *Forbes*:

> Kushner's crew was able to tap into the
> Republican National Committee's data machine,
> and it hired targeting partners like Cambridge
> Analytica to map voter universes and identify
> which parts of the Trump platform mattered
> most....Kushner built a custom geo-location

---

[6]   After an initial loan in October from Deutsche Bank,
Kushner would eventually receive this ginormous loan. As
of this writing, we don't know the identity of the creditor.
Crucially, it is not American.

tool that plotted the location density of about 20 voter types over a live Google Maps interface.

Before Manafort came aboard, Kushner never really thought Trump could pull it off. But now that he was in such capable hands? The idea of President Trump was not so far-fetched. He'd come this far, staked his own reputation. Unlike most of his associates on the campaign, he liked Hillary Clinton well enough. But he had his own reasons for wanting to win this thing. The survival of his business may well hinge on it.

So when his brother-in-law, the doltish Donald J. Trump, Jr., sent him an email about a meeting with a Russian attorney who promised incriminating information on Hillary Clinton, Kushner's interest was piqued. If this attorney could deliver what she promised, it might be a game-changer.

One thing made Jared Kushner nervous: the people Trump favored tended to be Chatty Cathys. Corey Lewandowski, for example. Junior. Steve Bannon. And of course Trump himself. If Kushner were to coordinate with the Russians, he needed to be able to trust that his comrades would keep their mouths shut. Loose lips, dot dot dot. He also had to make sure not to leave a paper trail, if these meetings were to continue. Sending an email, he decided, was an unwise thing for Junior to have done.

He took these concerns to Manafort, who agreed, but assured him that the meeting would be okay to attend. How could they know what the attorney would say? What *was* important, however, was to keep Trump *himself* away from the gathering. It was bad enough that he knew about it at all. Given that the meeting was to take place at Trump Tower, and that Trump would be in the building, keeping him away was a tall order.

"He can call in if need be," Manafort said, "but he cannot be in the room." Kushner agreed. Manafort further suggested that they bring Reince Priebus, the chair of the RNC, to Trump Tower to babysit the candidate while the meeting took place—to mitigate the temptation for Trump to crash the meeting. Kushner thought this was legit genius.

The fateful meeting took place on the afternoon of 9 June 2016. In attendance were Rob Goldstone, a flamboyant British music publicist who used to write for the tabloids; Natalia Veselnitskaya, a Russian attorney; two Russian representatives of Trump's Azeri-Russian oligarch chum Aras Agalarov; and a Putin-picked translator. After some pleasantries, Veselnitskaya went on a long tirade about adoptions, which irritated Kushner: apparently some piece of legislation, the Magnitsky Act, was preventing Americans from adopting Russian children. Her arguments were passionate. Then one of the men piped up, mentioning some amazing way a Russian tech company could "weaponize" Facebook and other social media against Hillary Clinton. All they needed was more information about exactly where and how to do so—information Kushner was intimately acquainted with, thanks to his association with Cambridge Analytica.

Were the Russians proposing some sort of quid pro quo without explicitly saying so? Kushner glanced at Manafort, who was fiddling with his phone; The

Count seemed to already know what was going to be discussed. Junior was saying something with much bluster and no meaning, as he was wont to do. Kushner decided that the Russians did indeed have something worthwhile to offer, but if word of this ever leaked out, he would personally hang for it. The rest of his crew were blithe about the legal risks, because they did not really understand the stakes. But Kushner's father Charles had gone to prison; Kushner would not make the same mistake as his old man. So he quickly excused himself.

After the Russians left, Manafort didn't give Donald Trump the full details. He only told him what to say next: "Hit Hillary about the missing emails. Hit her hard. Don't stop. People don't like her, people don't trust her, and the email thing confirms their suspicions. That private email server of hers is going to give you the White House."[7]

Trump took to Twitter that same afternoon and tweeted a reply to an earlier Clinton tweet: "How long did it take your staff of 823 people to think that up—and where are your 33,000 emails that you deleted?"

This was Trump's first mention of Hilary's 33,000 "missing" emails.

It would not be the last.

Kushner, meanwhile, knew that such an operation would have to be done in secret. He set about dreaming up ways to keep the dialogue with the

---

[7]    To be clear: this is my conservative version of the events. We may well learn that Trump knew all about the meeting, and even listened in by phone.

Russians open without the press—or, worse, the Democrats—finding out.

The capabilities of the Russian cyber agents were astonishing. Given the proper data, they could use social media to hammer home whatever narrative they wanted to promote, and make sure that the only ones who saw were the micro-targeted audience. And thanks to its shady relationship with Facebook, Cambridge Analytica *had* all the data. The crazy shit that people could be made to believe, if it turned up in their Facebook feed!

It was like a turbo boost on what Kushner's people were already doing.

It was like fixing the 1919 World Series.

After the meeting, Kushner was convinced he'd need the Russians to win the election. Every subsequent move he made aimed to achieve that result. On 21 June 2016, the mouthbreather Lewandowski was fired as campaign chairman—he'd manhandled a female reporter, not that Trump gave a shit, but it was a good excuse to get rid of him—and replaced by Manafort. Manafort immediately arranged a VIP meeting on the eve of the Republican National Convention, the primary purpose of which was to soften the party's platform on Russian involvement in Ukraine—a symbolic gesture, perhaps, but the symbolism was clear: Republicans heart Russia. That this was the *only* substantive change made to the 60-page platform is telling. Manafort also convinced Trump to select beleaguered Indian governor Mike Pence, an evangelical darling, as his running mate; Pence had email issues of his own, but he kept his mouth shut, was as sycophantic as it was possible to be, and his loyalty was absolute.

Kushner considered the options. Was it worth lifting some pesky sanctions in exchange for all that help with the election? Of course it was. And the beauty part was, because of the clandestine nature of the internet, it would be impossible to say for sure whether Russian hackers were involved. Oh, the intelligence agencies may say so, but this was complicated stuff. Who would the American people believe, the Washington spooks who screwed up our entrée into Iraq, or "straight shooter" Trump?

So Boy Wonder gave his consent.

Two months later, Manafort was gone. His ties to Ukraine, and through Ukraine to Russia, had made him a political liability. Kushner let it be known to some reporters that he was uneasy about these connections, so that the press would paint him as unaware of whatever Russia stuff might come out, but it didn't matter. The media was not much interested in Moscow ties, Manafort's or anyone else's. After The Count's departure in August, there were still debates to cover, and the horse-race of the most consequential presidential tilt in a generation. Kushner couldn't believe how much the press flat-out missed. For one thing: the $285 million loan he was able to procure from Deutsche Bank on 8 October. It was almost like the bank somehow knew Trump was going to win the election, because without the imprimatur of the White House, how could Kushner ever hope to repay such a vast sum?

And then, later that month, something happened that overshadowed the rest of the news…

# V

## SEXTS, LIES & VIDEOTAPE:
### October Surprises

On 7 October 2016, trouble came for the Trump campaign. The *Washington Post* posted a video of Donald Trump and Billy Bush, the host of *Access Hollywood*, in which the former could be heard saying some horrible things:

> I moved on her, and I failed. I'll admit it. I did try and fuck her. She was married.
>
> And I moved on her very heavily....I moved on her like a bitch. But I couldn't get there. And she was married. Then all of a sudden I see her, she's now got the big phony tits and everything. She's totally changed her look...You know I'm automatically attracted to beautiful—I just start

kissing them. It's like a magnet. Just kiss. I don't even wait. And when you're a star, they let you do it. You can do anything. Grab 'em by the pussy. You can do anything.

Trump was already loathed by the social justice warriors, the feminists, the cuck libtard snowflakes; he'd already been accused of sexual assault by more than a dozen women. There was even a statutory rape case against him, brought by a then-13-year-old victim, which his fixers had somehow managed to quash. But that was allegation, many years old, easily refuted. Now there was audio. There was video. There were witnesses. How could Trump recover from *this*?

The Trump/Russia defense team had a plan. Through seasoned dirty trickster Roger Stone—a lobbyist partner of Paul Manafort once upon a time, and the youngest of Nixon's notorious "ratfuckers"— the Trump organization coordinated with WikiLeaks, the self-styled journalist organization that is actually an organ of Russian intelligence, about the release of the hacked emails in its possession. Julian Assange, the head of WikiLeaks—who had been holed up in the Ecuadorian embassy in London since 2006 to avoid sexual assault charges of his own—was forever extolling the virtues of full transparency. But to indiscriminately publish a tranche of stolen emails is not transparency, it is invasion of privacy—and it is dangerous.[8] Donald Trump, Jr. was in contact with

---

[8]    It's also Stalinist. Indeed, one of the first moves made by the Bolsheviks after the Russian Revolution was to publish diplomatic correspondence of the Romanov government.

WikiLeaks during the campaign, and Candidate Trump lauded the organization many times on the campaign trail. "I love WikiLeaks!" he proudly proclaimed.

Within hours of the *Access Hollywood* tape, WikiLeaks began publishing emails stolen from John Podesta, the chair of the Hillary Clinton campaign, by Russian hackers. That there wound up being little of interest in the emails was irrelevant—the press felt compelled to stop covering Trump's *Access Hollywood* gaffe and read through the dumped documents. That journalists had no right to publish the illegally-obtained emails did not stop most outlets from doing so. Few seemed to call this what it was: an act of political sabotage.

But the WikiLeaks operation, while effective, paled in comparison to what Trump's dirty tricksters pulled off next.

In coordination with rogue agents at the FBI's New York field office—a division so devoted to the Republican candidate that it was nicknamed "Trumplandia"—Trump's people coerced James Comey, the director of the FBI, to not only re-open the investigation into the missing Hillary Clinton emails…but *to publicly confirm that he did so.*

From the outside, it looked like this:

On 26 October, former New York City mayor and Trump surrogate Rudy Giuliani boasted on TV about an October surprise coming that would mortally wound Hillary Clinton's campaign. She was way up in the polls at the time, so most people wrote this off as the ranting of a deranged, hateful old man. But Rudy was right.

Two days later, Comey sent his infamous letter to Congress, explaining that more Hillary Clinton emails had been found on a laptop recovered from the home of disgraced former New York Congressman Anthony Weiner, and that the Bureau was investigating the matter.[9] The letter was promptly leaked by Utah's Jason Chaffetz, a big Trump cheerleader and Benghazi enthusiast.

OMG! The missing emails had been found! And they were scandalous!

Republicans had a field day with this bombshell, which seemed to confirm all their worst suspicions about "Crooked Hillary"—and, it must be said, to fit in pretty nicely with the fake news that the Russian bots were promulgating on social media. The press fed on the email story like pigs in at the proverbial trough...or, if you prefer, like vampires on a virgin. Anonymous sources at the FBI (read: the "Trumplandia" New York field office) told Brett Baier of Fox News that the case against Hillary was "likely an indictment." Baier reported this on the air on 2 November 2016—just six days before the election.

*Hillary Clinton. Missing emails. Indictment.*

By the time Comey announced that the emails were duplicates, that nothing new or incriminating had been found—and by the time Baier apologized for his mistake—the damage had been done.

---

[9]    Weiner's estranged wife was Huma Abedin, Hillary Clinton's most trusted aide; this is how Clinton's emails may have appeared on a laptop in that household.

No less an authority than Nate Silver believes that absent the Comey letter, Hillary's victory would have been "almost certain."

THE *ACCESS HOLLYWOOD* TAPE should have been the end of Donald Trump's candidacy. And then the Comey letter snatched victory from the proverbial jaws of defeat. How had this sudden and unexpected turn of events happen?

On 9 June 2016 a new "news" website appeared: True Pundit. At first, True Pundit presented as yet another rightwing aggregator, with links to conservative concerns like Breitbart, The Daily Caller, Fox News, and InfoWars curated by a pseudonymous figure calling himself Thomas Paine, after the famed Revolutionary pamphleteer.

After the Pulse Nightclub massacre of 12 June 2016, True Pundit revealed itself to have actual sources at the FBI—specifically, in "Trumplandia." The site reported stuff only well-placed New York FBI would know. And its aim was as blatantly political as it was crystal clear: Hillary Clinton must be defeated at all costs.

Early adopters of True Pundit included Donald Trump, Jr., Mike Flynn and his namesake son, Julian Assange's WikiLeaks—and Russian "bots," who disseminated far and wide a slew of the site's egregiously false stories about Hillary Clinton: that she tried to have Assange murdered, that she was colluding with Facebook to swing the election, that she was not being straight with the American people about her failing health, and so forth.

On 2 October 2016, agents of the FBI's New York field office seized a laptop belonging to Anthony Weiner, which had previously been confiscated by the NYPD in connection with his sexting-with-minors case.[10] Comey wanted the laptop to be searched immediately for the alleged "missing" Hillary Clinton emails. But his order was ignored. Instead, Trumplandia agents sat on the laptop for weeks and did nothing with it. The closer it was to the election, they knew, the more explosive the laptop's contents would be…whatever they were.

Then, in the waning days of October, rogue elements of the Bureau's New York field office, through their mouthpiece at True Pundit, threatened to leak the "missing" emails supposedly found on the laptop. On 24 October 2016, FBI deputy director Andrew McCabe informed Comey that in his assessment, the True Pundit sources were "heavyweight"—whether the missing emails existed, he could not say; but there really *were* rogue FBI agents in the know leaking to True Pundit, so it was a possibility.

This was a bluff. In fact, the Trumplandia operators had no more idea of what was on the laptop than James Comey did. But the Director didn't know that. Comey didn't want to take the risk, and have legit missing emails leak. That would make it look like he was hiding something about Hillary Clinton that the

---

[10]    How the NYPD came to find out about this is a bit of a mystery. Louise Mensch has long believed it is the work of Russian hackers, specifically one named Yvegeny Nikulin, who was arrested by INTERPOL in Prague in October 2016. Nikulin was recently extradited to the United States.

American people needed to know. So he decided to get ahead of the story, to cover his ass. He wrote the letter to Congress that turned the election.

True Pundit's response to the Comey letter was a work of fiction masquerading as a news article with this lurid headline: "BREAKING BOMBSHELL: NYPD Blows Whistle on New Hillary Emails: Money Laundering, Sex Crimes with Children, Child Exploitation, Pay to Play, Perjury." With the help of Russian "bots"—as well as the Twitter accounts of Kremlin helpmates like Donald Trump. Jr. and Mike Flynn[11]—the story got major play. Kushner's social media barracudas at Cambridge Analytica made sure the piece popped up in the Facebook feeds of anyone on the fence in key swing states.

On 4 November, Blackwater's Erik Prince was on Breitbart Radio, echoing the story's ridiculous claims. "Because of Weinergate and the sexting scandal, the NYPD started investigating it," Prince told listeners. "Through a subpoena, through a warrant, they searched his laptop, and sure enough, found those 650,000 emails. They found way more stuff than just more information pertaining to the inappropriate sexting the guy was doing. They found State Department emails. They found a lot of other really damning criminal information, including money laundering, including the fact that Hillary went to this sex island with convicted pedophile Jeffrey Epstein," a wealthy financier and pedophile.

---

[11]    True Pundit's beefs about the FBI mirror the thinking of Mike Flynn, and there is speculation that he was somehow involved in this.

The mention of Epstein was particularly brash. It was at one of Jeffrey Epstein's lavish parties that Donald Trump was alleged to have raped his 13-year-old accuser. To summon that particular genie from the bottle took an enormous amount of chutzpah, a quality Prince would again display months later, when he perjured himself before a Congressional committee.

On 4 November, Giuliani boasted on TV that it was his friends at the Bureau who tipped him off that this was in the works. "Did I hear about it?" he said. "You're darn right I heard about it, and I can't even repeat the language that I heard from the FBI agents." The next day, the former mayor amended his story, claiming that his sources were *former* agents.

We still don't know the identity of those agents, or of "Thomas Paine," who runs True Pundit. We do know that Giuliani and Prince, at a minimum, had advance warning of the operation. Donald Trump, Jr. and Mike Flynn, too, seemed to be well aware of what was happening; both retweeted True Pundit almost immediately after the fake story broke, and subsequently deleted the RTs, as if trying to create distance between themselves and the True Pundit Hoax.[12]

A week later, Donald Trump would talk about the strength of his victory, the number of electoral votes he received. He would hang a map in his office, proudly displaying all that red.

---

[12]  "True Pundit Hoax" is the coinage of Trump/Russia researcher Seth Abramson, whose research informed the bulk of this chapter.

But it was Comey's letter that turned the election—and the Russians had helped make that happen.

# VI

## THIEVES-IN-LAW: The Brainy Don & The Not-So-Brainy Don

So what if the Russians helped Trump get elected? Who cares? The libtards are just making a big deal about it because Hillary lost, because they cannot accept that they ran a lousy candidate. Like Trump always says: Isn't it nice that the two former superpower rivals are now getting along?

This reasoning is often used as a defense against the allegations of "collusion" between the Trump campaign and the Russians. Donald Trump himself has made this point many times. On 28 April 2016, he told since-fired Bill O'Reilly: "I'm saying that I'd possibly have a good relationship" with Vladimir Putin. "He's been very nice to me. If we can make a great deal for our country and get along with Russia that would be a tremendous thing. I would love to try it."

No one doubts that Putin has been "nice" to Trump, or that the wannabe and the actual autocrat have a "good relationship." But the Donald/Vladimir bromance is extremely troubling.

Vladimir Putin—murderer, tyrant, crook—is antithetical to American values. He is a mobster thug. We don't *want* to make nice with this guy.

More importantly, it is illegal for American presidential campaigns to coordinate with foreign governments. It is illegal for American political candidates to accept *any* money from foreign sources. It is illegal for American citizens to negotiate US foreign policy with foreign governments. This cuts right to the bone of what it means to be an American—by coordinating with an enemy power, Trump and his associates were doing what the Founding Fathers most despised and feared. Even the *appearance* of financial impropriety by the US president, especially as related to foreign governments, was anathema to the Framers, which is what prompted the inclusion of the Emoluments Clause in the Constitution. As law professor Zephyr Teachout wrote in the *Washington Post*, "The framers knew what a headache [the Emoluments Clause] could become, but they included it anyway because of the lessons of history. They knew that foreign governments would necessarily attempt to influence US policy, and they wanted the Constitution to protect against that."

Why did Trump and his surrogates feel compelled to have so many meetings with Putin's agents? Why, if there was nothing untoward in their intentions, did they lie about it so vehemently? What happened, and what were they trying to conceal?

VLADIMIR PUTIN SUCCEEDED BORIS YELTSIN as acting president of Russia in 1999. He has been in power ever since. Under his reign, Russia has regressed from a burgeoning democracy to a veritable dictatorship. Putin consolidated power, destroying the independent judiciary, clamping down on press freedoms, using false-flag operations to win popular support, and exploiting his power for personal gain. He is more like a tsar than a president—although the Romanovs did not possess nuclear weapons, and their wealth, obscene as it was, paled in comparison to Putin's own.

Bill Browder, the American-born British national who was an early investor in Russia after the collapse of the Soviet Union, and who left the country after the government became too corrupt to continue doing business there, tells a story about Putin: After the rise of the oligarchs in the early 2000s, Putin had the richest, most powerful oligarch—Mikhail Khodorkovsky, head of the energy concern Yukos—arrested. At a humiliating show trial during which the accused oligarch was kept in a cage, Khodorkovsky was found guilty of fraud. He was sent to prison, and his sizable assets seized. After this sobering display, the other oligarchs approached Putin and asked what they needed to give him to avoid the same fate as Khodorkovsky, whose fate none of them wanted to share. Putin replied: "Half." Since then, ill-gotten gains have poured into his coffers. The oligarchs boast fabulous wealth, but by virtue of claiming *half* of their money, Putin bests them all. Browder has suggested that Putin may well be the world's richest individual.

Here is another story that reveals Vladimir Putin's character. When President Obama imposed the sanctions after the annexation of the Crimea, Putin had no proportionate way to respond. Russia has no exports we want. Our wealthy citizens do not go there on vacation. What Putin decided to do was ban American citizens from adopting babies from Russian orphanages.[13] In this way, he punished the neediest and most vulnerable of his own population in retaliation for a punishment imposed on him for his own thuggish misdeeds. Little children are literally dying because of this decision. Putin, piece of shit that he is, doesn't care.

But then, he is not really a politician, as we define the term. He is a Mafioso.

Russia is a mafia state. The line between the government and organized crime is so blurry as to be meaningless. The head of the government is Vladimir Putin. Semion "The Brainy Don" Mogilevich, now in his seventies, is the *capo di tutt'i capi* of the *Vory v Zakone,* or "thieves-in-law"—the Russian mob.[14] Putin and Mogilevich work hand in glove, with the latter's minions performing functions too unseemly for the former's to participate in. They are two foci of

---

[13]   This is why a meeting about "adoptions" was really about sanctions.

[14]   Technically, *Vory v Zakone* has a more specific meaning, but I'm using it here as a synonym for the Russian mob entire.

the small circle of oligarchs who own almost everything of value in Russia.[15]

The Russian mob is not La Cosa Nostra, the quaint Italian mafia of Don Corleone or Tony Soprano, which it more or less usurped in the early 90s after the fall of the Soviet Union. It does not confine itself to racketeering and assassination. It is orders of magnitude more ambitious. Its tentacles are everywhere. Activities in which *Vory v Zakone* are known to have engaged: narcotics and opioids, human trafficking, sex slavery, illegal arms dealing, systematic computer hacking to rig elections, massive bribery, and money laundering on an unprecedented scale. The Russian mob more resembles *SPECTRE* than *GoodFellas*—the best of the best of criminals.

On 22 November 1963 in Dallas, Texas, Lee Harvey Oswald shot and killed John F. Kennedy. It seemed impossible to believe, but it was true. A lone gunman, perched with a sniper's rifle in a third-floor window, had assassinated the President of the United States. The police arrested him hiding out in a movie theatre.

The authorities determined that Oswald acted alone. The Warren Commission arrived at the same conclusion. But doubts persisted. How could a

---

[15]   For more on the Putin/Russian OC relationship, read Karen Dawisha's *Putin's Kleptocracy: Who Owns Russia*, which discusses Putin's involvement with the diversion of municipal funds, illegal arms shipments, the food shortage scandal of 1991, gambling, and money laundering for the Cali drug cartel.

schmuck with so little training be such a good shot? Was there not perhaps a second gunman, hiding behind a grassy knoll? Was Oswald's subsequent murder by nightclub owner Jack Ruby not part of a conspiracy? Why had the Secret Service allowed the president to parade through a hostile state like a sitting duck?

Surely the simplest explanation—that Oswald shot JFK—was inadequate to the occasion. There must be more! The mob had Kennedy killed, because he had slept with a gangster's girlfriend. LBJ had Kennedy killed, so he could seize power for himself. The CIA had Kennedy killed, because he screwed up the Bay of Pigs. Fidel Castro had Kennedy killed, in retaliation for assassination attempts on *his* life. The real killer was a Corsican hit man, a trio of vagrants, Ted Cruz's father. And so on. These were all grand narratives, and they all made a helluva lot more sense than some disgruntled commie pipsqueak morphing into the American Sniper and taking down the Leader of the Free World.

Which is what made this particular KGB operation so successful.

Yes, it's true: JFK conspiracy theories were promulgated by the Soviets. The KGB exploited this American tragedy to spread disinformation, or *deza*, leading to the widespread belief that there was something fishy about the JFK assassination. Anyone who wrote about this was unwittingly helping the Russian effort: Jim Garrison, L. Fletcher Prouty, Oliver Stone, Jerome Corsi, and yes, Yours Truly. The objective of *deza* is to sow doubt, and through doubt, to bring dissention and foster a mistrust of our institutions.

The Russians have been at this a long time, and they are very, very, very good at it.

Another example: Edward Snowden. Here's a guy who presented as a smart, savvy patriot, out to blow the whistle on the nefarious Deep State. He seduced countless well-minded people, among them the left-wing journalist Glenn Greenwald and the documentary filmmaker Laura Poitras (and, for some time, me). In fact, Snowden is a Russian spy and a traitor.

In 2011, Edward Snowden, who'd resigned from the Central Intelligence Agency two years earlier, began working on Dell Computer's CIA account, where he liaised closely with chiefs of the Agency's technical branches. Exactly when Snowden was recruited by one of the Russian moles at the National Security Agency is unclear, but by April of 2012, he was already illegally downloading classified files. In 2013, he took a job with the government contractor Booz Allen, with the explicit goal of obtaining top-secret documents from the NSA's facility in Hawaii. On 20 May 20 2013, he took a leave of absence from Booz Allen, ostensibly to return to the mainland for medical reasons. Instead, he flew to Hong Kong, where a bizarre sequence of events led him to Moscow.

The *Guardian* and the *Washington Post* began publishing the stolen classified documents on 4 June 2013. On 21 June, the United States formally charged Snowden with espionage; the next day, his passport was revoked. Julian Assange was able to provide him with Ecuadorean travel papers.[16] Snowden flew to Moscow, where he was to take an Aeroflot flight to Cuba; from there, he was to proceed to Ecuador, which would grant him asylum. Under pressure from the American government, however, both Cuba and Ecuador decided against granting Snowden's asylum request, and he has been in Russia ever since. Snowden continues to insist that his desire was always to live in Latin America; the US government, he says, has "trapped" him in Russia. Given that his extradition would be much easier in Ecuador or Bolivia, where CIA influence is strong, it's more likely that the government that wants to keep him in Russia is not America's, but Putin's. After all, Putin can point to Snowden's presence in his country as proof of his desire for freedom and transparency. The American asylum-seeker, like Donald Trump, is a useful Russian prop. In the first few months of Trump's presidency, Putin floated the idea of extraditing Snowden, as a favor; but this will never happen, because a trial will prove conclusively that Edward Snowden is not a whistleblower, but a KGB asset.

A more recent Russian op concerns a large-scale military training exercise that took place in the summer of 2015 in Texas. The KGB spread the rumor that Operation Jade Helm 15 was the first step in a plot by President Obama to round up dissidents, who would be interned in Walmart parking lots, and impose martial law. The *deza* was so successful that it

---

[16]    Among other things, Snowden's "Great Escape" establishes, early on, collusion between Julian Assange of Wikileaks and Vladimir Putin of Russia.

fooled Texas governor Greg Abbott, who ordered the National Guard to monitor the Jade Helm operation. Michael Hayden, former director of both the CIA and the NSA, fingered the KGB in this op. "Russian bots and the American alt-right media convinced many Texans [ that Jade Helm] was an Obama plan to round up political dissidents," he said on the *Morning Joe* podcast. Abbott's hysterical response, Hayden said, demonstrated to the Russians that their active measures were working. "At that point, I'm figuring the Russians are saying, 'We can go big time. At that point, I think they made the decision, 'We're going to play in the electoral process.'"

Finally, CALEXIT—the proposed secession of California—was also a Russian active measure, designed to sow division and make the US weaker. In 2016, a group called Yes California sought to secure enough signatures to put secession on the state ballot, and propositions on ballots in California have a way of being unpredictable. As appealing as a nation of California might be—or a "Blue-topia" nation of California, Oregon, Washington, New York, New Jersey, Connecticut, Massachusetts, Vermont, New Hampshire, Maine, Rhode Island, Delaware, and Maryland—a fractured United States is nothing short of Vladimir Putin's wildest dream. An independent California would be akin to the collapse of the Soviet Union: a huge win for Moscow. Indeed, a closer look at the Yes California movement reveals plenty of Russian fingerprints. Both of its founders, Marcus Ruiz Evans and Louis Martinelli, are conservatives and have registered as Republicans. Evans lives in Fresno, the district of Devin Nunes; Martinelli, in *Yekaterinburg, Russia*, of all places—site of the Bolshevik massacre of the Romanov royal family. And while the latter's choice of residence may be perfectly benign, I'm not the first to raise an eyebrow at the coincidence. As Katie Zezima reported in the *Washington Post*:

> But Yes California has had to fend off a torrent of questions about Russian influence. In September, Marinelli represented the group at a Moscow conference hosted by the Anti-Globalization Movement of Russia; 30 percent of conference funding came from the Russian government, but none went to Yes California, according to its organizer. Yes California opened a "cultural center" at the movement's Moscow headquarters in December. Marinelli has compared California independence to the annexation of Crimea, and Yes California has received a flurry of news coverage from the government-funded RT.

Zezima then printed Martinelli's denial of official Russian involvement: "We don't have any communication with or contact with or receive any support of any kind from the Russian government or any Russian government officials." This may have been perfectly true, but it sounds uncannily like the Trump team's denials of Russian influence chronicled previously.

Unable to hit us militarily or economically, Russia uses asymmetric warfare to fuck with us. The KGB has been doing this quite successfully for decades. Putin is a creature of the KGB. Deceit is in his DNA.

Why do we want to be BFFs with him?

THE MOST RATIONAL EXPLANATION for Donald Trump's craven refusal to release his taxes or speak a discouraging word about Putin, his ability to bounce back in real estate after numerous bankruptcies, his out-of-nowhere victory in the election, and, for that matter, his fascination with cheap Eastern European labor, whether it be Polish demolition workers, Romanian Mar-a-Lago waiters, or Slovenian wives, is that he's in debt to the Russians. And not just Vladimir Putin and the Russian government. He owes the *Vory v Zakone*, too.

You see, Trump is no stranger to organized crime. His father, Fred Trump, had to deal with La Cosa Nostra to build his real estate empire; the younger Trump inherited these unseemly arrangements. Introduced to still more mobsters by his mentor Roy Cohn, Trump has benefited mightily from the Mafia in his various real estate ventures. The most egregious incidents involve his use of ready-pour concrete in the construction of Trump Tower and the exploitation of illegal and underpaid Polish immigrants to demolish the Bonwit Teller building, but there is much, much more. The media generally ignored this rather obvious link during the campaign, preferring to focus on the horse-race. This lack of wide reportage does not make the mob ties any less real.

Michael Cohen was long portrayed in the press as Trump's personal attorney. He *is* an attorney, insofar as he holds a law degree from literally the worst law school in the United States, but he's more of a fixer—for Donald Trump, and also for the Russian mob. As Jonathan Chait wrote in *New York* magazine:

> Cohen's uncle…worked closely with La Cosa Nostra and gained the organization's trust. Cohen's first employer was a criminal, his father-in-law was a criminal with ties to the Russian Mafia, and Cohen maintained extensive criminal associations throughout his public life. Sometimes people involved in mostly legitimate business have gangster friends, but if you're surrounded at all stages by gangsters—including operating your business out of a criminal headquarters, as Cohen did—then your real profession is "crook."

It is telling that one of the few non-family-member fixtures in Trump's inner circle is a glorified mobster. It hints at the larger truth.

As discussed, the Russian mob is the most successful criminal organization the world has ever known. They make bank on an unimaginable scale. The enormous amounts of cash generated by the far-reaching enterprises of the *Vory v Zakone* necessitate a vast and byzantine system of money laundering, unprecedented in scope and volume. Trump Org is one of the countless vehicles through which Mogilevich and his ilk make legit their dirty rubles.

Back in 1992, as the *Vory v Zakone* were supplanting La Cosa Nostra in the United States, Mogilevich dispatched Vyacheslav "Little Japanese" Ivankov, who had just completed a prison sentence in Russia, to New York, to oversee his American operation. For the next three years, Little Japanese ran amok, consolidating power, organizing criminals, taking over turf from other mobs; the FBI finally arrested Ivankov on 8 June 1995, charging him with the extortion of $2.7 million from an investment advisory firm.

For those three years, when he was arguably the most powerful mobster in the country, Little Japanese resided in either Trump Tower or the Taj Mahal Casino.

Both were Trump properties.

Ivankov was hardly the only Russian crime figure with a Trump address. As the former NSA spook John Schindler reports, "There are literally dozens of Russian OC scams, some gargantuan, that we know were based at Trump properties." This begs the question: Why did so many *Vory v Zakone* maintain addresses at various Trump properties?

A series of reports in the *Financial Times* delve into the Trump Org/Russian OC relationship dating from his sixth(!) bankruptcy, when Trump's credit at US banks prevented him from accessing more capital. And yet somehow, Trump managed to fund several major real estate deals—and paid for a number of them in cash. How?

The 2016 election was not the first time Donald Trump negotiated a quid pro quo with Russians. After his sixth bankruptcy threatened to shut down his business, he made a deal: in exchange for an influx of capital, he would help launder Mogilevich's dirty rubles. Real estate is well suited for this purpose, as there is a lot of capital, a lot of money changing hands, and, as what we've seen of Trump's taxes indicate, a lot of wiggle room with the IRS. Trump could buy an apartment for $5 million and sell it for $10 million in dirty rubles; the new owner could then sell it, even at a 50% loss, and the money from the sale would be "cleansed" by the transaction, and thus available for deposit in Western banks. Too, the sales could be masked by shell corporations formed in places like the Cayman Islands or Panama. It would be very hard to trace. Risk to Trump would be minimal. This is what happened in 2008, when the oligarch Dmitry Rybolovlev bought Trump's $40 million mansion in Palm Beach, Florida, for $95 million, as Rachel Maddow famously explained.

This clears up the oft-quoted remark by Donald Trump Jr., made at a real estate conference in New York in 2008: "Russians make up a pretty disproportionate cross-section of a lot of our assets." And: "We see a lot of money pouring in from Russia." All Junior meant was that Russian mobsters were snapping up apartments in Trump Tower and other Trump properties—and not for a song, either.

It's not just flipping real estate that provides an opportunity to launder money. Construction costs, too, can be massaged to suit that purpose. And while regulators in New York may be tough to fool, projects in other countries would be far less so. Take the massive Trump Tower building in Baku, Azerbaijan. The *New Yorker*'s Adam Davidson wrote a wonderful exposé on this white elephant of a deal, which looks like a vehicle to launder money for the Iranian National Guard, presumably one of our most dangerous enemies. Baku has been strategically important since the discovery of oil in Azerbaijan a century ago. The Trump Tower Baku, however, is not in a thriving part of the city, but in the middle of nowhere. It would be like deciding to build the Empire State Building in Flushing. Much of the work was paid out in cash, with one local contractor receiving $180,000 in banknotes, which he stuffed in his laptop bag. Furthermore, there was a lot of front-end money, some $100 million, spent on renovation. Stuff was torn out to make way for new stuff. Constant renovation can be expensive even when done on the up-and-up, but if used as a boondoggle to hide cash payments? It's a perfect money-laundering vehicle. If you claim you paid $10 million for white marble tile, and then you remove it, how can anyone prove the money was ever really spent, in this corrupt country halfway around the world from Trump Organization headquarters?[17]

In short, by 2016, Donald Trump's real estate concerns, which had already gone belly-up six times, were being underwritten by the Russian mob...*when Trump was running for president.* What are the chances that a recidivist failure like The Donald would not screw up a seventh time, and be even more in hock to Mogilevich & Co.?

The Brainy Don was holding it over the Not-So-Brainy Don.

Trump's mob ties were not exactly a state secret when he began his run for president, especially in New York. Plenty of journalists had reported on it, most notably Wayne Barrett at the *Village Voice.* Trump's Russian ties were also painfully obvious to any enterprising reporter who chose to look.

Why did the media not take Trump's connections to the criminal underworld seriously?

---

[17]   This idea was suggested to be by Alison Greene in her Twitter thread on the Baku fire.